Re-Educating Racehorses

A Life after Racing

Re-Educating Racehorses

A Life after Racing

Fred Cook and Rowena Jane Simmonds

The Crowood Press

First published in 2012 by
The Crowood Press Ltd
Ramsbury, Marlborough
Wiltshire SN8 2HR

www.crowood.com

British Library Cataloguing-in-Publication Data
A catalogue record for this book is available from the British Library.

ISBN 978 1 84797 253 8

Every effort has been made to trace the copyright holders of the images in this book. The authors and publishers apologise for any inadvertent omissions, which will be rectified at the first opportunity.

Dedication
Without the wonderful inspiration derived from many happy years with Leosaid, we may not have ventured so purposefully along the path of working with the horse out of training. Consequently this book is dedicated to his memory, a memory that will never fade.

Frontispiece: The authors with Charismatic Charli, a racehorse off the flat being retrained for dressage.(Photograph courtesy of Nico Morgan Photography)

Typeset by Jean Cussons Typesetting, Diss, Norfolk
Printed and bound in Singapore by Craft Print International

Contents

Foreword

To most readers, I shall be better known as a dressage judge and Manager to the British Dressage team, but I have also been a racing addict since my childhood, especially following National Hunt Racing. I have always loved the thoroughbred horse with its willingness and desire to please and its active but sensitive mind with such a quick learning capacity. It is what makes them so versatile. The second horse I ever owned, Sha Tin, was a thoroughbred. Although she never actually raced, she was so adaptable that she completed in all spheres from open team chasing through to Intermediare dressage, and was even accepted onto the Hannoverian register due to her successful competition record.

Thereafter a succession of young thoroughbreds recently retired from flat racing came my way – Dealer's Delight, Access Holidays, Access Festivals, Barmarina and Gara Rock, all proving very trainable and competitive especially in the dressage field, up to the present day where our own retired point-to-pointer, Theme Park, retrained to become the RoR/SEIB champion dressage horse for 2010.

In writing *Re-educating Racehorses – a life after racing*, Fred and Rowena have produced the most informative guide possible to help the everyday rider transform a racehorse into a riding or competition horse, trying to eliminate any of the pitfalls that could occur along the way. The book is written with passion and experience and is a must for anybody starting out on a retraining programme. In fact it is a must-read for anyone training any horse, not just an ex-racehorse.

David Trott

Introduction

This book is intended to provide constructive and practical advice for those who are considering giving a home to a horse that has been retired, for whatever reason, from racing. Whilst primarily aimed at the less experienced, we hope that more experienced readers will also find information that proves helpful or enlightening.

The material concerning feeding and management issues, although strictly extraneous to the subject of retraining, is included because these aspects do impact on a horse and its performance.

The information and advice given in this book is not by any means incontrovertible: what works for one horse doesn't necessarily work for another. Training horses requires not only patience but also flexibility, and a trainer must always be prepared to change tactics, adapting to suit the individual. This is important when following a retraining programme with any horse, not just the racehorse, because the already so-called trained horse has an established mindset, which causes it to react and behave in certain ways. This basically means that all a racehorse has been taught previously must be in effect erased and entirely new skills put in place, whilst at the same time addressing any behavioural issues that may creep in – and there may be good reason for these, as horses don't 'misbehave' just to annoy us. How successfully this is done depends upon the handler's experience.

We have always been passionate about thoroughbreds, but it was our own 'Leosaid' (Georgie) who really set us on the path of retraining racehorses. At just four years of age he was retired from racing due to injury, and a

Figs 0.1 and 0.2   The racehorse is very adaptable and with time, patience and correct training, can readily adjust to another equestrian sport. Light the Fuse (right) didn't start re-training until he was twelve years of age.

Fig. 0.3 Leosaid (Georgie) was very challenging to work with at times, but well worth it. proving that patience and perseverance are key factors in racehorse retraining.

promising career came to an abrupt end. Georgie was of very mixed character – extremely sensitive when it suited him, but very tough and single-minded. One of his favourite tricks was to rear up and walk on his hind legs; on long lines he could walk as happily backwards as he could forwards!

In our view you never stop learning from horses, and we learned a huge amount from Georgie because he threw everything at us that a horse possibly could. Hence this book is dedicated to his memory, a 'thank you' for the valuable experience we gained from having such a character to work with, and subsequently the many years of fun we had with him until his passing at the age of twenty-five.

A LIFE AFTER RACING

The 'ex-racehorse' used to be given a bad press as a matter of course, and still does to a certain extent by those who consider him to be bad mannered and too highly strung to be usefully re-employed. This, however, is an extremely prejudiced view propounded by people who are not prepared to be enlightened. It is interesting

to observe that on a race day these fit, highly tuned athletes generally walk quietly round the paddock, whereas at any hunt meet or show you will often see horses leaping about and behaving extremely badly!

The thoroughbred horse is very intelligent and generally a quick learner; he is easily bored, and needs variety and new challenges to keep him mentally occupied. Consequently he is often one step ahead of his owners! It is accepted that when some horses leave the race-training environment they are apprehensive and tense, seemingly 'flighty' and highly strung. Nevertheless, although it may take a while for your relationship to become established, once the trust and understanding is there, you will find you have an affectionate friend who just wants to please – and if that isn't happening, then there is either a breakdown in communication or an aspect of management that needs addressing.

Basically the training of any animal means allowing him plenty of time to learn, having endless patience, and being highly sensitive as to how he is reacting to you. Body language is singularly the most important communication tool, and you should learn to read the signals your horse gives out, just as he will learn to read yours. You should always be clear and consistent in your training. And while training should be varied, your approach should always be logical, systematic and clear. If you aren't speaking to your horse clearly, you can't expect him to understand what is being asked of him. There is no mystique to re-educating the racehorse and it is readily achievable; however, if his trainer lacks feeling, confidence and skill, then understandably difficulties will arise. Furthermore because the thoroughbred is so sensitive, he is easily upset, so don't be afraid to seek help if you doubt your capabilities.

Because the thoroughbred is basically bred to race we have to accept that the majority will never reach the top-class competition circuits of eventing, dressage or show jumping, where the

Figs 0.4 and 0.5   Horses out of flat racing traditionally found themselves on the polo field and chasers in the hunting field or team chasing. (Photo left: courtesy of Hurlingham Polo Association; photo right: courtesy of Tik Saunders)

professional rider needs horses that are specifically bred for the discipline in order to be seriously competitive. Nevertheless the career for the retrained racehorse most definitely need not be confined to hacking, sponsored rides or hunting, and he is more than capable of fulfilling the ambitions of many riders by holding his own in a variety of competitions. In recent years a growing number of ex-racehorses have found their way into a variety of other disciplines: showing, both in hand and ridden (including side-saddle), horseball and polocrosse, Le Trec, even endurance. The ex-racehorse also adapts well to some Western riding – indeed this discipline often suits those horses that don't accept a 'proper' contact with the bit as demanded in most other equestrian disciplines.

It is also a fact that some horses out of training do find their way into top flight competition, though these have usually been produced by professional riders – for example, in British Eventing at the time of writing there is Miner's Frolic (Tina Cook), Poilu (formerly with Clayton Fredericks but now Zara Phillips), Cool Mountain (William Fox-Pitt). British show-jumping riders today tend to favour the warmblood, so in the UK we have to go back

several decades to find ex-racehorses such as Workboy and Philco prominent in the world of showjumping. Nevertheless there are thoroughbreds that are currently working their way up through the BSJA levels, horses such as Roaring Thunder, Charlie Tee and Island Sound.

Dressage has traditionally been a sport where it was generally considered that the thoroughbred could never realistically compete against horses specifically bred for that discipline, because neither its temperament nor its conformation was suitable to attain the level of training and suppleness required. However, horses such as Louis Feraud are proof that the thoroughbred is not only trainable, but has the ability and paces to excel in the dressage arena. In more recent years a growing number of determined riders have proved that a horse that has raced can be trained well beyond unaffiliated levels – for example, until recently Gift Star and Mr Bojangles competed very successfully at Intermediare I and Advanced Medium levels respectively, each having amassed over 300 BD points.

Retraining the racehorse is hard work and a considerable challenge – but that is what makes the achievement all the greater, and so much

Fig. 0.6   *Louis Feraud, owned and ridden by Emma Zwetsloot, is probably the best-known thoroughbred competing in dressage today. He didn't race but clearly illustrates what the breed is capable of. (Photograph courtesy of John Tyrrell Photography)*

more rewarding. To take a horse out of one career and retrain him to do something completely different is a tremendous achievement whatever the discipline, and whatever the level.

MAKING THE TRANSITION

Most of these horses make the transition from their racehorse identity quite happily, given time, patience and understanding on the part of the owner/trainer. However, owning an ex-racehorse is gaining wider appeal, and a growing number of horses are finding homes with people who don't always have enough experience of training horses generally. For many the journey will be relatively straightforward, but unfortunately there are people who do experience difficulties. This is usually only because they lack suitable experience, or are not communicating clearly enough to their horse. This is most definitely not a criticism, just a fact, and the right thing to do is to seek help and advice, or perhaps just reassurance. Owning a horse is supposed to be a pleasure, not an experience you begin to

dread, so we hope that this book provides a guide as to what you might come up against and why, and how to resolve it.

Many of the issues which present are not just the preserve of the horse off the track, yet there is a certain conviction that some problems occur purely because the horse is an ex-racehorse – even though two or three years may have elapsed since he left the training environment. Re-educating the racehorse is akin to starting a youngster in terms of it having to be taught everything, but the one major difference between the two is that the racehorse has already been trained to do a job, and apart from accepting someone on his back, everything else he has been taught must be superseded: he must be completely reschooled.

Reading posts on internet forums show that there is a huge fan base for these horses, although people do readily admit that their journey hasn't always been easy – but then this is true for many owners of any horse. Some will also admit that their ex-racehorse does retain a degree of over-excitability, is less settled in or out of company, becomes more anxious at shows – but then most horses, whatever their

Fig. 0.7 Light the Fuse (Bombie) shows ability in the dressage arena.

breed, reveal a shortcoming of temperament at some point in their career, and all the best horses have a quirk of some sort!

So why does the horse out of training appear to be problematic at times? It is possibly because, from the horse's point of view, when all else fails – he can't trust or understand his trainer or rider or the situation he is in – he will instinctively revert to 'racehorse behaviour', which is what he knows best. Racehorses commence their training at a very early age, when their counterparts are still frolicking in the field; this means they are mentally 'conditioned' in their formative years, and this is the root of much of their adult behaviour.

THE RESPONSIBILITY OF OWNERSHIP

If you wish to rehome a racehorse, be sure to take on ownership in full awareness of the possible problems, and be sure in your own mind that you have the time, the patience and the experience. If you haven't owned a horse before, an ex-racehorse is probably not the most suitable for you to start off with – whilst we all know of someone who has done just this and not come to grief, it must be appreciated that retraining a thoroughbred is no easy task, and that for the purposes of this book, generalizations have had to be made.

We have tried to provide an informative and interesting book that addresses the most commonly experienced situations, and we hope that whatever their level of experience, every reader will glean something of benefit.

The horse 'models' that are used are of differing ages and temperaments, mares and geldings, off the flat and out of National Hunt racing. None has been as successful as the racing 'greats' – Desert Orchid, Denman, Daylami, Dansili Dancer – though some have been winners; the others have left racing because of lack of form, or injury which has precluded what might otherwise have been a successful career. But whatever his origins, within this book we cover all aspects of re-educating the racehorse, in order to give him a life after racing.

1 Considerations when Rehoming a Racehorse

So why do you want a horse that has raced? When electing to rehome a racehorse, there are more things to consider than if you were purchasing an already schooled thoroughbred. However, by weighing up the advantages and disadvantages you will be taking on the new relationship fully aware that the retraining process might not always be straightforward.

So what is the attraction of an ex-racehorse? In its favour the thoroughbred has intellect and presence, and is a truly versatile horse with great ability and usually an excellent temperament. It generally adapts well to a new lifestyle, and being light in frame is quite easy to ride and 'hold together'.

So why an ex-racehorse? If you like a 'project', why not go for a young, newly backed horse instead? And do you want him to be a serious competition horse, or more of a fun horse?

There are several disadvantages to taking on the thoroughbred just out of training: first, he will need double the work to undo the 'in training' mindset and educate him as a riding horse (have you the time?), and the retraining process can be frustrating (have you the patience?). Ideally you should be experienced yourself and you may also need someone to assist you at times; appropriate facilities such as a stable and a safe riding environment are also highly recommended.

Soundness may be an issue: as retraining progresses, old injuries may recur which may need treatment, the worst case scenario being

Fig. 1.1 Do a realistic appraisal of why you want to home a horse that is supposedly a speed machine. (Photograph courtesy of Jon Fullegar, Sandown Racecourse)

Fig. 1.2 You need time and patience to turn horses like these into riding horses. (Photograph courtesy of Clive Cox Racing)

that if the horse does not stay sound, he will effectively only be a field companion.

So would you go for an older horse or a younger one? If you are looking to retrain for competitive purposes, opting for a younger horse ensures that by the time the training work comes together, he is still relatively young and has plenty of life left in him. He has also had less time to become 'institutionalized' – there is a consensus of opinion that the longer a horse is in training, the longer the basic retraining process will take. He will have suffered less wear and tear on limbs and ligaments, and will usually adapt more quickly to his new life.

However, this is not to gainsay the older horse, many of which leave training perfectly sound and readily take up a new career.

Ultimately, the retraining experience may be a considerable learning curve, but it is a hugely satisfying experience. To know you are responsible for the horse's gradual transition from racehorse to riding horse brings an incomparable feeling of achievement.

SOURCING YOUR HORSE

Racehorses out of training can be obtained from various outlets: bloodstock sales, direct from a training yard, from an advertisement in the paper or on the internet, or from a rehoming centre.

Buying from a Sale

Buying from a bloodstock sale is not the best route for the inexperienced or first-time owner, although increasing numbers of people are doing so – and you can always ask a seasoned 'sales' buyer to accompany you.

The main disadvantage of this option is that there is no foolproof way of establishing exactly what you are taking on. Although you can see horses walk and trot in hand, they are not ridden, so it is not possible to fully assess a horse's way of going, as weight on the back makes a big difference to the way it travels.

Remember that the horse is being sold for a good reason: owners don't sell horses that are doing well. Check it for lumps, bumps, swellings, heat and sore spots – and not just the legs, but along the neck, down the shoulders, the withers and along the back, paying particular attention to the lumbar region. Pick its feet up, and if it is unshod, ask why. Also be

Fig. 1.3 The Sale Ring at Doncaster Bloodstock Sales. (Photograph courtesy of Doncaster Bloodstock Sales)

Figs 1.4 and 1.5   This young horse can clearly use his hocks as evidenced by the way he is 'sitting' on them as he prepares for take-off; however, once off the ground he is unable to flex his back properly. The lack of lift from the shoulder may be consequent upon this. However, in this case it is purely due to physical weakness – a large frame at a very young age.

aware that the handler with the horse on the day may not be familiar with its character so may not be able to answer some of your questions.

When purchasing from a sale you can have a free vetting, so on that day at least you know the horse is sound, and that its eyes and heart are fit and healthy.

Study the 'Conditions of Sale' very carefully, as these can vary. When you get the horse home, if a problem comes to light you have a certain amount of recourse to the auctioneers.

There is plenty of information available regarding the purchase of a horse from a bloodstock sale, so do your research and you will be better equipped for the experience.

Direct from a Training Yard

Buying direct from a training yard is again not the best route for the inexperienced, but at least you can see the horse in his usual environment and get an idea as to his general demeanour and attitude. Also most trainers are happy for you to ride the horse and to spend some time with him – though be mindful that while he may be very quiet here, once you have him home he may be transformed into the high-powered racing machine the trainer wished he had been!

Another advantage is that you can talk to stable staff to gain knowledge about a horse's history.

From an Advertisement

Buying from an advertisement also carries a risk as some vendors do attempt to hide certain things. It is advisable to make a list of questions to ask, and to take an experienced person with you.

First, find out why he is for sale. If he has behavioural issues, this doesn't mean that he came out of training with them; they might have been brought about by mismanagement or a lack of understanding. Furthermore people might have tried to reschool him already and failed – so he may already have had more than one home.

This is not the horse's fault. It means the lines of communication have not been open and clear, so there have been misunderstandings that have escalated. This often comes about as a result of inexperience on the part of those trying to effect the reschooling.

Another reason may be an old racing injury that is preventing or limiting his retraining, or which precludes the horse from following the desired activity.

Ask to see the horse's passport; this will verify his age, and that he has raced in the UK, which is a requirement if you want to compete in RoR classes. Many horses are coming over from southern Ireland, so are not eligible.

Check thoroughly for lumps and bumps, questioning any you find. Pick the horse's feet up; if he is not shod, ask why.

Ask to see the horse ridden before you ride him yourself, so you can see how he reacts under saddle – and be wary of the person who makes an excuse for not riding the horse themselves, or says that it '…can't be ridden at the moment': find out why not. Ask to see the horse jump – loose or on the lunge is fine if under saddle is not possible, although this should only be because the horse hasn't progressed to that stage of his retraining.

It is advisable to have the horse vetted.

Rehoming Centres

The best way of sourcing an ex-racehorse is from a rehoming centre. There are several around the country, and you can spend plenty of time with the horse of your choice, and have more than one ride on it. Once home, should it prove not to be suitable, the centre will have it back.

WHY IS THE HORSE COMING OUT OF TRAINING?

If you want to compete with your ex-racehorse, you need to consider carefully the reasons why he needs a home. It may be simply that he is too slow or has not shown any form, perhaps because he is immature, i.e. still physically weak. Given time and the training work the horse will undergo, this is not a problem.

He may have suffered an injury that prevents the continuation of training. Depending on the nature of the injury, he may not be suitable for you if you wish to go eventing, say, but it may not preclude the horse from showing if there is no visible blemish, or from hacking or hunting.

It may be that he is prone to sore shins or

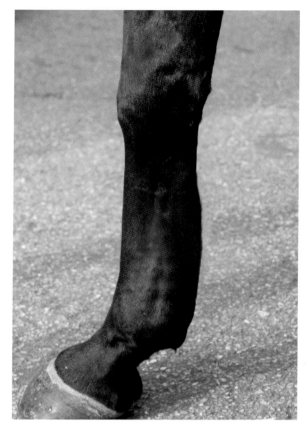

Fig. 1.6   Tendon injuries generally do not cause problems for the significant majority of ex-racehorses provided proper conditioning work is carried out to strengthen the leg.

jarring of the shoulder so doesn't stay sound. Depending on what you are aiming for, this need not be a problem, however these horses are probably better suited to light work or to life as a companion.

In his racing career the horse may have been a bleeder – that is, prone to bursting a small blood vessel in the nose (epitaxsis). It is not always possible to know exactly why this happens, but basically it indicates that his lungs can't cope with the physical stress of racing. However, even non-racing horses have an occasional bleed on exertion, just as some people do, so it may not be anything to worry

A WORD OF WARNING

However 'normal' for your horse, all episodes of epitaxsis should be noted, as any change in what is 'normal' (for your horse) could be a sign of something less simplistic.

about too much if his new career will be less strenuous.

He may have a tricky temperament. A yard will happily tolerate a racehorse with a quirky nature if he shows some degree of talent, but if he doesn't, he will be moved on, as many yards don't have enough time to spend on the individual to find out what makes him tick.

If he has a stable vice he may not hold his condition. Certain 'vices' cause a horse to lose condition (and therefore fitness), and indicate that he is of a more nervous or highly strung disposition and so not really suited to racing.

Mares fall into another category, since a well-bred mare is generally sent to stud – so why not this one? If she is small this won't be a problem if her new career is as a show hack, and if she is too slow as a racehorse that won't affect her dressage or showing jumping ability; however, if she has a conformational defect that prevents her from performing to the best of her ability on the racecourse, this should be looked into because it may impact on your chosen future activity and may be the reason that her connections did not wish to breed from her.

GENERAL CONFORMATION

Conformation is basically the evaluation of a horse's bone structure and body proportions in relation to each other. Musculature is not part of conformation as this can be considerably improved with correct training and work. Whilst poor conformation is not so critical for the horse that isn't ridden, once he is asked to carry a

Fig. 1.7   *This horse is clearly a bit uptight on race-day. (Photograph courtesy of Jon Fullegar, Sandown Racecourse)*

Fig. 1.8   *Captain Gerard is a fine example of a typical 'sprinter'. (Photograph courtesy of Bryan Smart Racing)*

rider it can be very influential, not so much in his actual ability to carry weight, but in terms of how efficiently he does this, i.e. with engaged hind quarters, a poll-high head carriage, etc. It may even affect his soundness if it causes him to injure himself, as in brushing, overreaching or body strain.

Generally good conformation makes it easier for the horse, given the correct training, to perform at his best, whilst poor conformation can put undue stress on certain joints and/or muscles, or result in the under-use (and so wastage) of other muscles. This can readily lead to soreness and even lameness.

Many who have taken on an ex-racehorse may not have paid much attention to his conformation at all; perhaps he needed time to recover from injury, and the fact of giving him a chance at a new life was more important than his physical 'defects'. Besides, when agents attend the sales for their clients they do look for certain physical characteristics that predispose the horse to being a good athlete, so one can assume that a racehorse's conformation won't be that bad to begin with.

Although the horse's bone structure can't be altered, his musculature can change significantly with different management and another training regime. This inevitably has a

Fig. 1.10 *The thoroughbred conformation doesn't preclude it from performing dressage movements. (Photograph courtesy of James Zwetsloot, Zwets Photography)*

Fig. 1.9 *Take a look at horses walking round the paddock on race-day and you could be forgiven for thinking that very few of them would pass the trot up at Badminton! (Photograph courtesy of Jon Fullegar, Sandown Racecourse)*

bearing on how he moves and carries himself; he can become much more athletic and his paces be improved dramatically. This can help to overcome some defects of conformation, which therefore need not be a handicap to the horse, depending on his new career – though obviously if you are intending to compete in showing or dressage classes, a horse with poor conformation is unlikely to become top class.

There are plenty of books on conformation to refer to, and everyone has their own view as to what is acceptable or not – but there are always exceptions to 'the rule', and horses with less than perfect conformation are often still able to perform well.

2 The Physical Stresses of Racing

The purpose of this chapter is to provide an insight as to how certain injuries can impact on a horse and his way of going. Armed with this knowledge it will enable you, the new owner, to better understand the implications, and to make a realistic appraisal of what you can achieve with your horse.

It is important that everyone is aware of what can typically happen within the racing world. This is not a criticism of any individual, but a fact of racing. Unfortunately the racing world isn't always able to give a horse the time it needs to recover because the associated costs are so high; nevertheless with careful rehabilitative work, much can be achieved, especially if the injury is allowed the time it needs: Nature is a great and wonderful healer.

We must also put our trust in veterinary science, and should always work in consultation with our vets; but just as in the medical profession where patients have defied the odds, so too have horses. And just look at the ever-growing number of people who are happily competing ex-racehorses without any problem.

Sadly the horse in training can readily sustain a variety of injuries which can compromise its very complex physical structure. However, horses can, and do, recover from all manner of injuries with proper treatment. Whilst some injuries can impact on retraining, most horses don't need to be written off as they are perfectly capable of performing a wide range of leisure activities (subject to talent), even if they are precluded from higher levels of

Fig. 2.1 Rehoming an ex-racehorse is a risk in terms of an physical injury it may have incurred, which might just possibly have an impact at a later date. (Photograph courtesy of Jon Fullegar, Sandown Racecourse)

competition. For example, Light the Fuse has had bone chips removed from both knees, has broken a bone in his knee, severed a tendon and ruptured his back. Whilst the last injury ended his racing career, with careful rehabilitation and an on-going sympathetic training programme he is still enjoying life to the full at eighteen years of age.

The following section is not necessarily technically correct in terms of veterinary science – we are not vets. As explained above, in discussing the injuries so often incurred in racing we hope to provide an insight as to how they might impact on the horse and his way of going, which will help you, the new owner, decide on the most appropriate course of treatment, and in the light of this, the most suitable career path for the horse.

We also recommend that horses are vetted so that if any issue arises relating to past injuries it can be fully assessed and discussed with your veterinary surgeon.

LEG INJURY: CAUSE, TREATMENT AND PROGNOSIS

The horse's leg is an extremely specialized structure, allowing a huge range of movement beyond simply walking, trotting and cantering. For the ridden horse, his legs are the most important and influential part of his conformation, and any major defect or weakness in his physical make-up will increase the likelihood of lameness problems, possibly cause secondary issues elsewhere (typically in the back region) and may have a negative effect on athletic ability. Furthermore, if there are problems with the fundamental structure of the foot, the horse will spend more time lame than sound. The saying 'no foot, no horse' is very true.

In racing, the horse's forelegs suffer most with sprains and strains; veterinary data confirms that 75 per cent of injuries are tendon-related.

Fig. 2.2 Age need not be a barrier to an active life for the older horse, as illustrated by the eighteen-year-old Light the Fuse.

Because the National Hunt horse has to negotiate hurdles or steeplechase fences, additional stress is put on his forelimbs, over and above that incurred by just running at speed on the flat.

Whilst some injuries are relatively minor and very treatable, others can be more severe as they are part of a more complex injury involving other structures of the leg. Some horses can't return to racing, but following prolonged rest and controlled rehabilitative exercise they can lead an active life in a less strenuous activity.

Tendon Injury

The tendons (which attach muscle to bone) comprise groups of collagen fibres tightly packed together, which, in the lower limbs, are sited in tendon sheaths (sacs lined with synovial membrane) that lubricate the tendon so it can move easily. Most racehorses will have suffered tendon strain at some time, damage to the superficial digital flexor tendon (SDFT) being the most common. The SDFT lies at the back of the cannon bone and is the tendon we readily see. The deep digital flexor tendon lies just under it; under that is the suspensory ligament. The SDFT takes the full loading on the leg before the action of the deep digital flexor

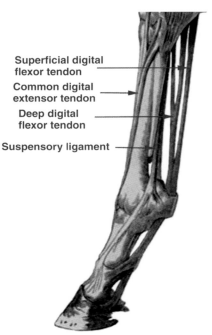

Superficial digital
flexor tendon

Common digital
extensor tendon

Deep digital
flexor tendon

Suspensory ligament

ABOVE: *Fig. 2.3 This photograph shows just how much strain is placed on the tendons and ligaments of the horse in training. (Photograph courtesy of Doncaster Bloodstock Sales/Trevor Jones)*

RIGHT: *Fig. 2.4 The primary structures of the lower fore limb.*

tendon (DDFT) kicks in; thus damage to the DDFT or the check ligament is not seen so routinely.

A horse naturally carries more of his own weight on his front legs (up to 60 per cent), and whilst training for other equestrian disciplines focuses on adjusting his natural centre of balance backwards – so that he takes more weight behind – everything about training racehorses encourages them to be on the forehand. For instance, Jockeys, and often work riders, ride with considerably shortened stirrups, thus taking their weight off the horse's back, but the weight instead is placed over the withers and shoulders, creating additional loading on the forelegs.

When a tendon is strained or stretched beyond its capacity, usually as a result of over-extension of the fetlock joint when the horse's weight is all being carried on one leg, the tendon fibres tear and rupture, and then swell. Anything that causes the loading on the tendons to be unbalanced puts them under strain, for example:

- Poor conformation.
- Deep going/rough/uneven ground.
- Landing after negotiating a jump.
- Lack of fitness.
- Continuing to work (race) a tired horse. As a tendon tires, it loses its elasticity, making it more vulnerable to strain.
- The SDFT is traumatized during fast work.
- Improper shoeing, particularly if the toe is left long; this alters the geometry of the foot, and hence affects the horse's action.

Damage can also be cumulative – stress and fatigue of the tendons over time.

When there is little swelling or heat and no sign of lameness, outside the world of racing such injury is not regarded as being too serious. The following, however, are more serious tendon injuries:

- Direct trauma such as an overreach, resulting in profuse and sudden swelling, combined with a great deal of heat and pain.

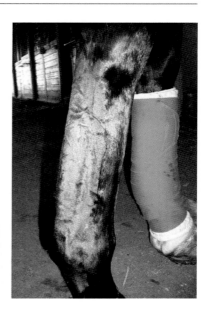

LEFT: *Fig. 2.5   A healthy foreleg.*

RIGHT: *Fig. 2.6   A typical SDFT injury.*

BELOW LEFT: *Fig. 2.7   This image is a scan of the SDFT of a left foreleg. The black area is the lesion where the tendon has torn apart and blood and serum has accumulated.*

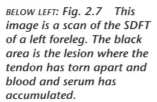

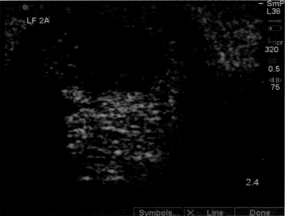

Fig. 2.8   All tendon injuries should be taken seriously, but don't necessarily signal the end of a horse's working life; some horses do return to racing.

- Core lesion, or 'hole' in the tendon, where the tendon fibres have been ruptured and torn apart, the resultant hole filling with blood and debris. A horse may have more than one such lesion.
- Bowed tendons, where the swelling at the back of the leg causes it to take on a convex appearance – hence the term 'bowed tendon'.

Tendon injuries vary considerably; some can be relatively minor, but a more serious injury can result in a complete rupture, the leg losing all its support so that the fetlock joint virtually touches the ground (hence the term 'broken down'). They take a long time to heal – twelve to eighteen months is routine because the tissues of the tendon have a very poor blood supply. However, with the advance in veterinary techniques, the healing process can be positively assisted by preventing the formation of scar tissue (which is nature's way of healing), promoting the removal of necrotic (dead) tissue, and stimulating the formation of the right type of collagen as opposed to scar tissue.

Tendon injuries usually need the requisite time to heal, followed by a carefully structured exercise programme to ensure a strong repair.

Ligament Damage

Ligaments attach two bones together and provide support to the joints; they are much more fibrous and have virtually no elasticity compared to the tendons; also their blood supply is very poor, which makes healing a lengthy process. The suspensory, check and collateral ligaments are generally the ones

involved in a racing injury, and the causes of damage are the same as for the tendons.

Suspensory Ligaments

The suspensory ligament is attached to the cannon bone just below the knee. Further down the cannon bone it divides and continues to run down the leg and attaches to the sesamoid bones. Injury to the upper section of the suspensory PSD (Proximal Suspensory Desmitis) is not commonly seen in the racehorse. However, the central section of the ligament and the lower branches are the areas most likely to be damaged when a horse is in training; this is easily diagnosed because

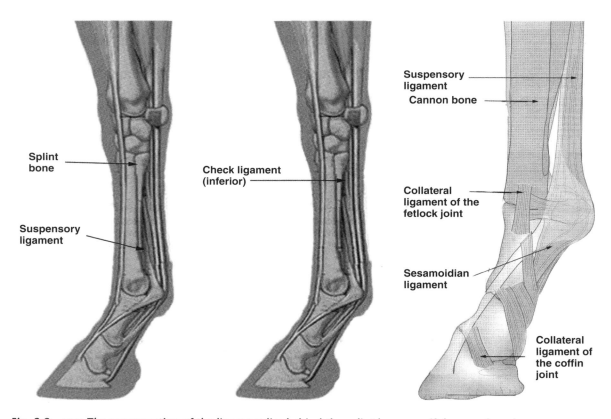

Fig. 2.9 LEFT: *The upper section of the ligament lies behind the splint bones so, if damaged, such damage is very difficult to confirm as you can't even feel it!* CENTRE: *Check ligament injuries are more routinely seen in older horses but the sub-carpal check ligament can easily be damaged during jumping.* RIGHT: *The primary collateral ligaments.*

the related inflammation (termed desmitis) is clearly visible.

The Check Ligament

The check ligament (talked of in the singular but actually comprising three ligaments) protects the deep digital flexor tendon (DDFT) from being overstretched and damaged. Injury to this ligament can take a long time to heal: even the most minor check ligament injuries require at least six months rest, but nine to twelve months is typical. Careful rehabilitation is required once all the swelling has subsided in order to restore full mobility.

Collateral Ligaments

Collateral ligaments are sited on both sides of most of the joints – the stifle, hock, elbow, knee and fetlock. The suspensory and sesamoidean ligaments comprise the stay apparatus which keeps the fetlock joint in place. They are typically damaged when a horse stumbles violently (knuckles over on his joints). Damage can also result from poor foot conformation and/or farriery.

Sesamoiditis

The sesamoid bones are under extreme stress in the horse racing at speed: sited at back of the fetlock joint they can be readily fractured, and are vulnerable to concussion, which can cause inflammation of the proximal sesamoid bones, known as sesamoiditis.

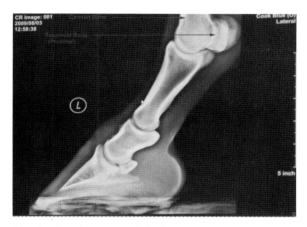

Fig. 2.10   This x-ray of the bones of the lower foreleg shows the position of the (proximal) sesamoid bone – at the back of the fetlock joint so it is vulnerable to injury.

Fig. 2.11   When a horse hits solid part of a fence or hurdle with its knees, bone chips can be incurred. (Photograph courtesy of John Pike, Racing Images)

While some injuries are relatively minor and very treatable, others can be more severe if part of a more complex injury involving other structures of the leg. Some horses can't return to racing, but following prolonged rest and rehabilitative exercise they can lead an active life in a less strenuous activity.

JOINT INJURY: CAUSE, TREATMENT AND PROGNOSIS

A horse's joints are extremely efficient shock absorbers and able to withstand incredible amounts of pressure, but they are subject to wear and tear even when just walking around the field. Younger horses that race on the flat are not so prone to tendon injuries as jumpers, but they suffer a higher proportion of joint-related injuries/problems.

A horse has three types of joint: synovial, cartilaginous and fibrous. Fibrous joints are found in the skull and in some of the long

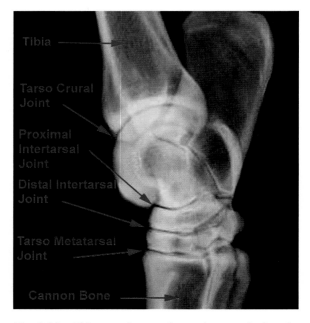

Fig. 2.12   This x-ray image shows the complexity of the hock joint.

Tibia
Tarso Crural Joint
Proximal Intertarsal Joint
Distal Intertarsal Joint
Tarso Metatarsal Joint
Cannon Bone

> **PHYSITIS**
>
> Young thoroughbreds that grow too quickly can have a temporary growth disorder known as physitis, which affects the growth plates of the knees causing swelling; this is relatively short-lived and has no long-lasting effects.

bones of the body and are basically 'fixed', and similarly cartilaginous joints, as in the pelvis, have limited movement, so both are unlikely to suffer any form of joint disease. Synovial joints, however, include the extremely active joints of the knee, hock and fetlock, and are most prone to injury and disease.

The Knee Joint

The knee is a very complex joint and the incidence of knee problems is high, mainly due to the fact that it is small relative to a horse's size and bodyweight, and both the cartilage and bone are subjected to repeated concussion. Bone chips are often a consequence of trauma to the knee, and their removal is a commonly performed operation. However, some horses are then unable to flex the knee joint fully, which can limit their jumping ability over higher fences.

Furthermore arthritis may subsequently set in, depending on the extent of the initial damage; a joint supplement or injection to help reduce inflammation and nourish the joints enables the horse to continue to lead an active life.

The Hock Joint

The hock is an extremely complex structure, but hock damage is more usually associated with the non-racing performance horse due to the

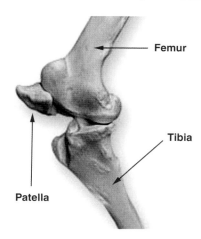

Fig. 2.13 *Stifle injuries actually account for more hindlimb lameness than previously thought.*

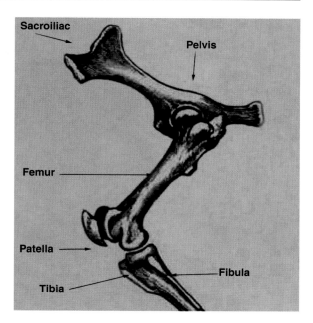

Fig. 2.14 *Damage directly incurred to the pelvis is usually a fracture and more often than not repairs without any difficulty.*

nature of its training, which encourages the displacement of the horse's weight on to the hind limbs. Thus osteoarthritis (DJD) is not so readily associated with racehorses.

This doesn't mean that the hock is a trouble-free joint for the racehorse; it is just that the tendons and ligaments of the forelegs invariably give out first because they take the primary loading.

The Stifle

The stifle is the largest synovial joint in the horse. The collateral and cruciate ligaments of the stifle are easily torn, especially when a horse leaves a leg behind or wrenches the stifle when jumping, so inflammation and swelling is common.

The Pelvis

A correctly working pelvis is crucial for the horse as all the power comes from the rear end: the pelvis is the engine.

Fractures usually go hand in hand with injuries to muscles and ligaments, and these injuries don't repair so readily, adhesions and scar tissue being routine consequences. When viewed from behind there will be evident asymmetry of the pelvic profile, and there may be muscle wastage on the injured side.

Once a fracture has healed, locomotory abnormalities are often noted when exercise under saddle is resumed: the horse may not be sound, or he may just not 'feel right', usually because he tracks up short, almost without exception a symptom of a muscle injury in the pelvic area. He may compensate with other limbs, and have improper placement of the foot, making him more prone to injury. There may be strain (or pull) on the spine, and he may not be able to back up properly, and/or is unable to cross his legs when asked to turn a tight circle.

However, if special attention is paid to establishing his core and pelvic stability by

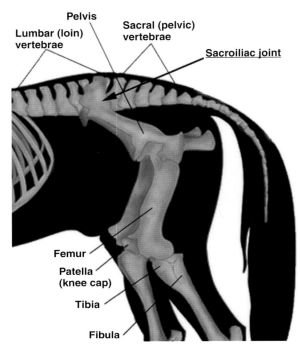

Pelvis
Lumbar (loin) vertebrae
Sacral (pelvic) vertebrae
Sacroiliac joint
Femur
Patella (knee cap)
Tibia
Fibula

Fig. 2.15 The sacroiliac joint firmly fixes the horse's pelvis to the spine.

lungeing/long-reining work combined with exercises over raised poles, he should be perfectly able to cope with Riding Club and lower level competition. Your chiropractor should be able to advise on the type of exercise to be undertaken.

The Sacroiliac Joint

The sacroiliac is another complex joint which is the seat of many ills. Symptoms range from hind limb lameness and lack of impulsion to the horse 'not feeling right' in his movements. The joint is not accessible by way of touch/feel or x-ray as it is covered by such a huge muscle mass; hence it is difficult to confirm a diagnosis, and treatment is usually symptomatic.

Acute damage to the joint is usually the result

of a fall, or of slipping or twisting awkwardly, particularly when jumping. Chronic damage is generally the result of wear and tear, or if the joint has been under continual stress; this may be suspected if a horse has problems in the canter, such as changing the leading leg, bunny hopping/bucking into canter, or cantering disunited. A 'jumper's bump' is actually the result of torn (strained) sacroiliac ligaments at the top of the croup, usually caused by a fall, or in a young horse because he has been asked to exert himself too soon over fences.

Unfortunately when this crucial joint has been damaged it doesn't readily return to normal, but once the pain has gone and the joint stabilized, most horses happily return to an active lifestyle. Successful treatment relies on pain management, and building up the supporting muscles of the area, particularly in chronic cases where controlled exercise is usually required.

The Pastern and Coffin Joints

These joints are susceptible to injury through direct trauma or ligament strain as a consequence of an overreach, a mis-step, or the effects of galloping on firm ground. Exostosis (bone growth) – commonly known as ringbone – within these joints is common, as are fractures and arthritis.

JOINT MEDICATION

The medicating of joints is a common treatment of horses in training. Unfortunately when a horse leaves the training environment this information is not always passed on. This explains why lameness issues can crop up in the first few months of rehoming.

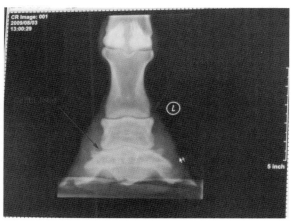

ABOVE: **Fig. 2.16** *This x-ray is taken from behind so as to illustrate the seating of the coffin and pastern joints. The conformation of this particular lower limb is about as perfect as can be.*

LEFT: **Fig. 2.17** *Don't confuse a Jumper's Bump with a horse that lacks muscle on his hindquarters. This horse just lacks muscle.*

'temporomandibular dysfunction', or TMD. The horse's body reacts negatively to any tension or dysfunction of the TMJ.

TMD can be caused by a trauma to the head, such as incurred by a fall over hurdles or fences.

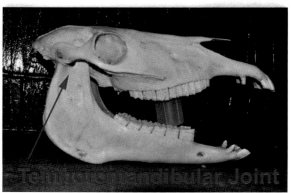

Fig. 2.18 *The TMJ is the part of the cranium where the mandible (jaw) articulates with the temporal bone, this bone being where the ears are sited. (Photograph courtesy of Fellowes Farm Equine Clinic)*

The Temporomandibular Joint (TMJ, the Jaw)

Proper function of the TMJ is vital to a horse's health. If the bones become misaligned and do not articulate as they are designed to, the surrounding tissue of the TMJ is stressed and the joint mechanism becomes out of balance, which not only affects how effectively a horse can chew and digest food, but also his balance and biomechanics. This is termed

The Back

Back injuries range from soreness and inflammation to misalignment of the spinal vertebrae. Typically the racehorse works in a hollow outline, which causes tightness, especially in the region of the withers, and the build-up of more muscle on the underside of the neck than on top. Half-tree saddles are often used in flat racing yards to minimize the weight carried, but these offer little support to the back compared with conventional riding saddles; rubs and pressure points are common, a typical tell-tale sign being white hairs in the region of the withers. Furthermore some jockeys do 'bump' down on the saddle, especially if the horse is not running on very well, and this can cause the formation of calcified lumps along the spine.

Misalignment of the spinal vertebrae is caused by slipping, twisting awkwardly over a fence, stumbling on landing and falls; also in flat racing if a horse bumps his hips as he comes out of the starting stalls this can cause a 'twist' in the pelvis, which in turn causes a build-up of tension within the lumbar vertebrae.

Back injuries therefore vary considerably in severity, and some can continue to affect the horse throughout the rest of its life. However, given time, coupled with sensitive, patient and rehabilitative training, in most instances the affected horse can lead an active life.

FRACTURES: CAUSE, TREATMENT AND PROGNOSIS

The successful treatment of a fracture depends on its type, whether it is simple, comminuted, stress, chip, open or displaced; the site – which bone, or part of a bone has been damaged; whether any other injuries are present, for example to soft tissue structures; and how old the horse is.

The following are common fracture sites:

The pedal bone: The prognosis for pedal bone fracture is excellent, provided the fracture does not affect the coffin joint.

The pastern: Provided a pastern fracture is diagnosed early on, it heals well, and the horse may return to an active life. It is usually the long pastern bone that is damaged.

Fig. 2.19 *Typically the racehorse works in a hollow outline, which actually has a negative effect on the back. (Photograph courtesy of John Pike, Racing Images)*

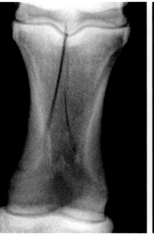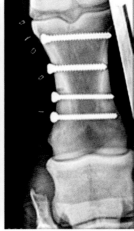

Fig. 2.20 *A fractured pastern that has then been screwed back together.*

The sesamoids: A fractured sesamoid bone is a serious injury, mainly because the high tensile forces continually exerted on it cause the broken bone to pull apart rather than knit together. Natural healing is weak because the blood supply to the area is poor, and the horse will not be able to withstand strenuous exercise in the future.

If there is severe damage to the suspensory ligaments and possibly the distal sesamoidean ligaments, euthanasia is often the chosen route. However, if damage to these ligaments is only minimal, grafts or screws can be used to hold the bone together.

The cannon bone and splint bone: The prognosis is good for a horse returning to a high level of work following a splint bone fracture. However, if the suspensory ligament has also been strained there is an increased likelihood of lameness reoccurring.

The knee: A fracture to the main carpal bone doesn't necessarily signal the end of a horse's racing career as the fractured bone can be screwed together.

The olecrannon (elbow): In the case of a simple, closed fracture the prognosis is good, as screws and a plate are usually inserted to aid nature. However, with an open, multiple fracture the prognosis is less than good, and the horse is unlikely to be able to return to an active life.

Radius (forearm) and tibia (thigh): In the case of an incomplete or stress fracture the horse will probably make a full recovery, provided it is allowed adequate rest and recovery time; complete fractures, on the other hand, have a very poor prognosis due to their site.

The pelvis: Incomplete stress fractures in young horses heal very well if caught early enough, but a complete fracture to the pelvis cannot normally be successfully treated.

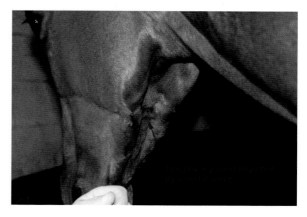

Fig. 2.21 This horse has had his jaw secured back together with a metal insert. (Photograph by kind permission of David Arbuthnot)

The neck: Fractures can occur when a horse falls head first, when it is often killed outright.

In fracture cases the prognosis is not always good. Because the horse is such a large animal, fractures are difficult to treat, especially in the upper limbs; each fracture case must therefore be considered on its own merits, and not all horses can be restored to full pain-free locomotion. In younger horses hairline/stress fractures are common during their training, and can readily develop into a true break.

Furthermore horses that have recovered from a fracture will be prone to arthritis later in life, and degenerative joint disease if a joint has been affected; inevitably athletic ability will therefore be compromised.

MUSCULAR INJURIES: CAUSE AND TREATMENT

A muscle is a group of fibres that controls all bodily movements. For correct and efficient function, a regular supply of blood to provide nutrients and oxygen is required, as are the correct nerve impulses. Injuries that compromise any of these functions result in damage and consequently muscle wastage.

Of the three types of muscle the horse has (cardiac, smooth and skeletal), it is the skeletal that has the responsibility of holding the horse together and enabling it to move. There are two types of muscles fibre.

- Slow twitch (Type I fibres) – aerobic muscles, i.e. they need oxygen to function. These are more dominant in the horse that has strength and endurance (e.g. an event horse) as this type of muscle has the ability to reduce lactic acid (lactic acid production being part of the process of muscle function).
- Fast twitch (Type II fibres) – anaerobic muscles, i.e. they need very little oxygen to function. They are more dominant in the horse that has speed (e.g. a flat racehorse) as they can only perform over shorter

distances due to the fact that they don't have the ability to remove lactic acid.

The horse has two distinct layers of muscle – the superficial layer and the deep layer. It has no muscles below the knee and hock, and this is a primary reason why horses suffer so many lower limb injuries – there is no muscle to act as a shock absorber.

Every bone of the body has a pair of muscles attached to it, and as one contracts to flex a joint, the other muscle lengthens – they work antagonistically, so both muscles are in constant use, as each does its job of mobilizing a joint. The horse has a large muscle mass – more than 60 per cent of his bodyweight is muscle – most of which is sited in the hindquarters; therefore most muscle injuries occur in the pelvic area.

Muscle damage is usually a progressive process caused by wear and tear, unless it is the consequence of a slip or fall when fibres are

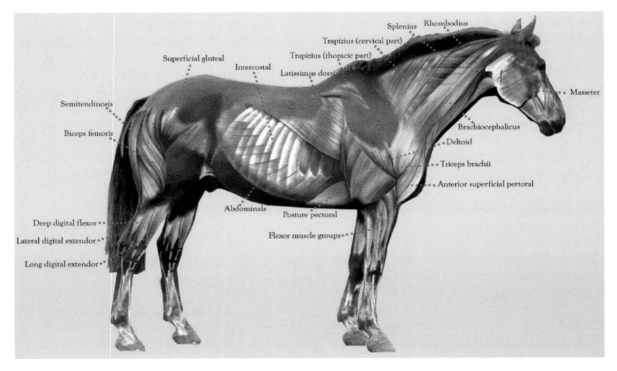

Fig. 2.22   The muscles of the superficial layer.

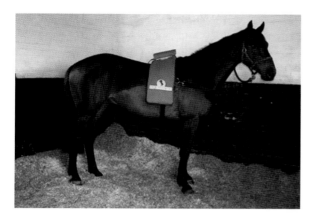

Fig. 2.23   Regular use of Equissage (or similar provides) can assist horses with tight, tense muscles.

usually violently torn. The horse's range of movement is compromised, resulting in reduced performance, usually altered stride length. Muscle damage in the hindquarters is often compensated for by other limbs and muscles, as well as the spine. This compensation leads to further deterioration of movement and performance, which leads to lameness if left untreated.

It is possible that your new horse may be suffering from spasms that usually occur secondary to strains and injuries to a muscle, a spasm being a sudden, involuntary contraction of one or a group of muscles (resulting in a shortening of the muscle so its partner has to compensate by lengthening; this can cause strain to the tendon connected to it).

As a result of muscle injuries and spasms, and the consequent impairment of the blood supply, or if there is pain and/or damage to the nerve supply, muscles can actually waste – known as atrophy. Atrophy can result in an over-development of muscles on the opposite side of the body to the injury site as the horse will compensate for any injury he is carrying. Treatment involves physiotherapy to restore the blood supply and proper muscular contractions (this is vital it order to restore full function) coupled with controlled exercises.

Spasms associated with illnesses such as colic and tetanus should not be confused with spasms that are management/exercise-related e.g. Exertional Rhabdomyolysis. A muscle spasm should not be confused with fasciculations, which are very mild, routinely occurring twitching of muscles. Horses have the panniculus muscle, which covers most of their body (not face or lower legs), which they can twitch at will in response to stimuli such as an insect landing on them.

WIND PROBLEMS: CAUSE AND TREATMENT

Sometimes when galloping a horse makes a noise as he breathes; this is often referred to as 'whistling' or 'roaring'. This happens because the increased air flow into the pharynx and larynx that is required by the horse at the faster pace is restricted, because the muscles of

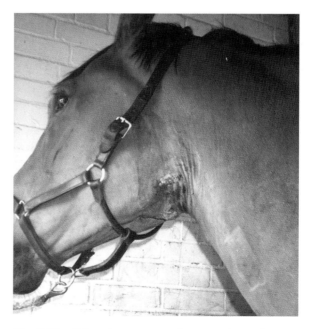

Fig. 2.24   It is not uncommon for a racehorse to have had hob-day or tie back operation – and usually both.

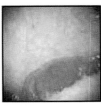

Grade 0 Ulcer
Intact mucosal epithelium (may have reddening and/or hyperkeratosis)

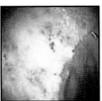

Grade 1 Ulcer
Small single or multiple ulcers

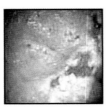

Grade 2 Ulcer
Large single or multiple ulcers

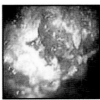

Grade 3 Ulcer
Extensive (often coalescing) ulcers with areas of deep ulceration

Fig. 2.25   Ulcers are graded 1–5 in relation to their severity.

(normally) the left side of the larynx (voice box) are partially or totally paralysed.

This condition is known as laryngeal hemiplegia (one-sided paralysis), and does not resolve on its own, in fact it gradually worsens. Treatment involves surgery, either a hobday or a tie-back operation, and often both. In a hobday a piece of the laryngeal tissue is removed, resulting in a scar which causes the remaining tissue to tighten, thereby opening up the larynx a bit more.

In a tie-back operation (laryngoplasty) – considered necessary when the condition is more serious – sutures are used to pull open

the paralysed side of the larynx. Following surgery there is a risk of infection at the suture site, coupled with aspiration of foodstuffs into the airways.

EQUINE GASTRIC ULCER SYNDROME

The vast majority of racehorses, an increasing number of competition horses, and indeed riding horses generally, are routinely diagnosed with gastric ulcers – the erosion of the stomach lining by acid, which the stomach actually produces. Whilst it was once thought that the high cereal content of the 'racing diet' was effectively the culprit for causing ulcers in the racehorse (because fermentation of cereals in the stomach produces damaging acids), it is now established that there are other contributory factors, which is why non-racing horses are also suffering.

It is now known that ulcers may be caused by an inappropriate feeding regime, intensive exercise, or stress.

An inappropriate feeding regime: Horses are trickle feeders, so there is permanent digestive fluid on hand for the digestive process; hence acid is continually secreted into the stomach, at the rate of 1.5ltr every hour! Saliva helps to neutralize the acid, but as this is only produced when the horse is eating, if he goes for long periods without food (so no salivation) there is nothing to neutralize the acid; this leads to ulceration of the delicate lining of the stomach. Moreover bile can be refluxed back into an empty stomach, and this in itself can cause ulceration. Depriving a horse of food results in a very rapid development of ulcers – in as little as twenty-four to forty-eight hours.

Intense work: It has been proved that there is a link between intensive exercise regimes and ulceration. When a horse is galloping or undergoing strenuous exercise, pressure is exerted on the stomach from the abdomen, causing it to contract. This contraction causes the acid to be pushed from the lower section of the stomach (where it is actually secreted and so is less sensitive to its effects) into the much more sensitive upper section, where the primary damage is done. Also the natural blood flow to the stomach (which helps to remove the acid) decreases with exercise.

Stress: Stress may be caused by a severe injury, surgery, shock or illness, or management factors such as lack of companionship, boredom, travel or confinement.

Medication: Some treatments may trigger ulceration, such as very high doses of NSAIDs.

Signs that ulcers may be present are:

● a dull coat and listless demeanour
● lack of condition
● signs of bad temper, in particular when grooming the abdomen, girthing up
● poor performance
● windsucking
● recurrent colic.

Ulcers can readily be treated by feeding products which reduce the production of stomach acid. However, good management and a more suitable feeding regime are also extremely important in both the treatment and future prevention of ulcers, especially for horses that are easily stressed.

BURSAL INJURIES

A bursa is an isolated sac of synovial membrane filled with fluid situated in locations around the body to prevent friction – for instance, allowing a tendon to smoothly move over bone.

Bursal strains and injuries (known as bursitis)

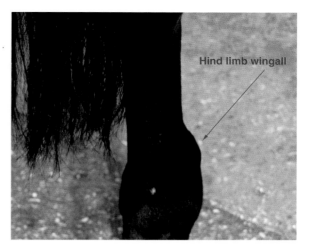

Hind limb wingall

Fig. 2.26   Some bursal injuries are caused by repetitive, low-grade trauma, while windgalls, thoroughpins and bog spavins are the result of a strain.

occur when damage to the bursae (sacs) around bony areas causes an over-production of the lubricating synovial fluid contained within the joints; this shows as soft swelling. Commonly such damage is caused by pressure; capped hocks and elbows are the most routinely seen and are usually acquired when a horse lays down on a hard floor with insufficient bedding. Although there are sometimes more complex reasons behind a bursal injury, particularly if it is a young horse, they are basically superficial and, although unsightly, do not affect the horse's performance.

OTHER INJURIES

Splints

Splints are not unique to the racing world, and once they have settled down they rarely cause any problems other than being a blemish. They occur due to tearing of the interosseus ligament, which attaches the splint bone to the cannon bone. The resultant inflammation leads

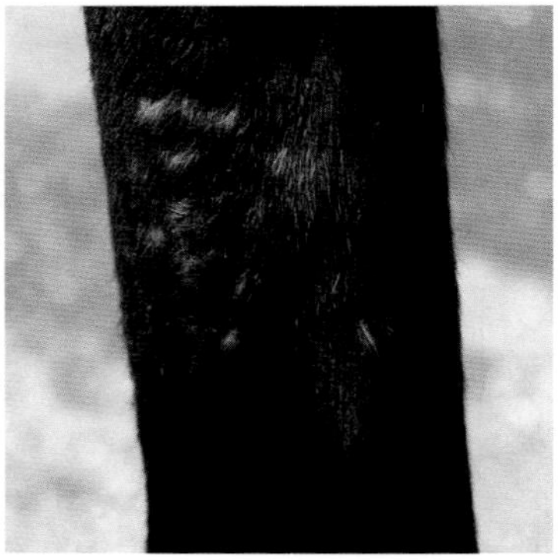

Fig. 2.27 This photograph illustrates where a splint has been removed.

to prolific bone growth, resulting in the formation of a hard lump known as an extosis (in this case called a splint).

If a splint occurs too high up it can interfere with the knee joint and/or suspensory ligament; any lameness will remain until the splint is surgically removed.

A collection of white hairs on the inner aspect of the leg indicates that a splint has been removed, routine practice in racing.

Sore Shins

Some horses are prone to sore shins, and whilst this is a problem for the horse in training, it is not a problem outside racing as it is generally associated with fast work. Unless you are told, you will not know if the horse has ever had sore shins.

Scars

Many horses will come out of racing with a few scars, and although nothing to worry about, it is advisable to ascertain how they were acquired, if possible. Scar/ granulation tissue from old injuries may also be present, and large masses of scar tissue can restrict muscular movement; however, it is now recognized that it is possible to reduce, if not fully eliminate, this

scar tissue long after it formed, with massage and other therapies.

Equine Rhabdomyolysis Syndrome (ERS)

Exertional rhabdomyolysis – also known as tying up/setfast, and azoturia – involves chronic tension in the muscles due to overwork; the severity of an attack varies (azoturia tends to be the accepted terminology in more serious cases). Whilst not an injury, some horses that have tied up in the past are more likely to do so again, and it is useful to know whether a horse is predisposed to this so that your management routine can be suitably structured.

Epistaxis (Nosebleeds)

Horses obviously bleed for a reason, but sometimes the exact cause cannot always be found. Epistaxis is primarily the preserve of racehorses, and once removed from the racing environment the condition often disappears.

CHIROPRACTIC MATTERS

Chiropractic is the diagnosis and treatment of conditions primarily of the spine, but also of joints, ligaments, tendons and nerves. Manipulation is effected to the spine and associated joints in order to realign the (skeletal) frame to improve function and relieve any associated muscle spasms and/or pain. Chiropractic is a holistic treatment that works to eliminate the cause of a problem rather than just treating the symptoms.

When we ride we actually sit on the weakest part of a horse's structure, so it is our responsibility to recognize and then eliminate anything which may be causing discomfort and possibly pain; treating the symptoms is not

Fig. 2.28 The chiropractor checks the length of the spinal column as part of her assessment.

Fig. 2.29 An adjustment is a rapid, high velocity, low force 'thrust' against a specific vertebra in a specific direction.

satisfactory – the cause of any physical problem needs identifying and resolving otherwise much longer term damage can result.

The spine is a very complex structure stretching from head to tail, with more than 170 joints. It also comprises muscles, ligaments and nerves. Each vertebra has an upward projectile known as a dorsal spinous process (DSP). Between each bone is a disc that acts as a shock absorber to soak up concussion. The shorter the horse's back, the closer the DSPs will be to each other. Depending on the conformation of the individual, the DSPs may actually curve forward. The spine has five distinct sections of vertebrae:

- seven cervical (neck) – contrary to popular belief, these do not follow the crest but form a curve within the neck.
- eighteen thoracic (withers region) – the first few of these have longer DSPs, giving the withers their shape; the DSPs are shorter in those of the lumbar and sacral area.
- six lumbar (back), commonly termed the 'loins' – there is very little movement between these bones as they create stability for the hind-leg attachment.
- five sacral (croup), more popularly known as the 'sacrum' – these are fused together so there is no movement. The sacroiliac joint lies here, connecting the sacrum to the pelvis.

- fifteen to twenty-one coccygeal (tail) vertebrae (the 'dock'), which decrease in size – the number varies from horse to horse.

The spine is subjected to forces from tension, compression and vertical and horizontal sheer. Although quite rigid in terms of its construction, the spine has axial rotation, lateral flexion and the ability to extend to a certain degree. This means that it has enough flexibility to allow the horse to bend left and right, arch his back and raise and lower his head and, with training, perform athletic manoeuvres such as half pass and piaffe. It can't bend, so when a horse executes a circle it is an illusion that the spine bends, simply because of the degree of movement of the neck vertebrae and rib cage and the fact the horse can move its legs nearer to or further away from its body. Within the spine lays the spinal cord from which a network of nerves branch out from in between the various vertebral joints. These nerves spread throughout the body, carrying out orders from the brain.

If anything occurs that compromises the relationship between adjoining vertebrae, this causes a misalignment, correctly termed a subluxation. There is an extensive list of causes of a misalignments, so if your horse suffers any loss or change of performance, has difficulty with his schooling (stiffness, resistance, etc.), there is an alteration in his behaviour, he slips or bumps himself or his proprioception (the body's co-ordination mechanism which tells him where his body is in relation to his environment) appears compromised, then call your chiropractor.

A subluxation involving any part of the skeleton leads to changes in posture and gait (and even lameness) as well as resulting in a knock-on effect of abnormal stress being imparted somewhere else in the body. This is because horses will do their best to compensate for discomfort by adjusting their way of going. Thus a lame horse will often develop a bad back and a horse with pelvic problems can develop tendon troubles.

A subluxation can also cause alterations to muscle due to the effect on the nervous system network; this may be manifested in a muscle sweating, and increased sensitivity to touch, heat and cold.

In a spinal subluxation, nerves are actually nipped and remain so until the subluxation is corrected. Thus a trapped nerve, say in the hindquarters, is most likely due to a subluxation to the lumbar or sacral vertebrae. Whilst pinched, the correct impulses are not being transmitted by the nerves, thus causing problems elsewhere.

It now accepted that chiropractic treatment can be effective where other treatments have failed to provide relief. Typically a chiropractor will find certain problems in particular areas, and will be able to identify the cause; this advice means that in many instances the owner/rider should be able to prevent the problem recurring. Typical findings of a chiropractor are:

In the lumbar region: Signs of strain (overwork), which may be the result of increased lateral work as a horse learns new movements, a saddle that is too long for its back, a rider who sits incorrectly, and problems with the sacroiliac joint.

In the pelvic region: The pelvis can be tipped forward or backwards or rotated as a result of the muscles on one side of the horse pulling on the hip (*tubae coxae*). If the 'pull' is in an upward direction, this causes a pelvic rotation (one hip is lower) but a pull towards the head causes a pelvic tilt (one hip is further forward); the pelvis can be rotated and tilted at the same time. Some horses do have uneven hips as a consequence of an old injury, so you need to be familiar with your horse and what is normal for him.

In the thoracic region: Often the result of an ill-fitting saddle pinching the withers, or the stirrup bars impinging on vertebrae further along the spinal column.

In the cervical region: Atlas rotation is often caused when a horse pulls back sharply when tied up, or has been worked in an incorrect or false outline, particularly if forced to do so by mechanical means (for example the inappropriate use of draw reins). A rider will often try to correct a head tilt by lifting one rein, but of course this won't put a vertebra back into line.

The muscles: Under or over-development of muscles is also detected although you may need the services of a physiotherapist or Equine Body Worker to resolve these issues. The muscles and ligaments of the spine keep any adjustments in place. They must be in good condition (toned), otherwise adjustments won't 'hold' and the chiropractor will be returning.

Note: It is against the law for an unqualified person to treat a horse. Furthermore, before any complementary/alternative therapy can be effected on your horse, permission must be sought from your veterinary surgeon.

Kissing Spine

Kissing spine is diagnosed as being when the dorsal spinous processes of the vertebrae are

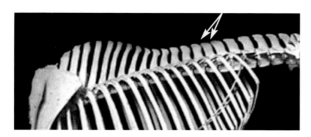

Fig. 2.30   Dorsal spinous processes: the arrows indicate where two DSPs are closer together than the others. In some horses such closeness may never cause discomfort, while in others it could be the cause of pain when ridden.

too close to each other. It is now recognized that quite a large number of horses actually have a kissing spine to some degree, but do not exhibit any particular issues such as pain or reduced performance until they have a fall or even roll too enthusiastically. Kissing spine can be responsible for a slow deterioration in the horse's performance; at worst it can cause extreme behaviour.

Much depends on the number of vertebrae involved, their exact location, and the extent of the impingement of the spinal processes, as to what treatment is effected, whether the use of anti-inflammatory drugs, shock-wave therapy or surgery. Veterinary advancements now mean that many horses that were once written off can be treated, and resume a positive working life. Horses with 'low grade' kissing spine happily race as they have the appropriate section of the spine medicated.

Treatment

In mild conditions, chiropractic treatment can help to maintain movement between the affected vertebrae; the addition of a joint supplement to the feed can help to decrease inflammation. Acupuncture and magnetic therapy have also proved to be successful in mild cases – anything to improve and increase blood flow to the affected area.

The affected joints can be medicated with anti-inflammatory and pain-relieving drugs: corticosteroids are injected deep into the affected area and act like a nerve block. This treatment has to be carried out at intervals, so the longer the period between injections the better.

With the advances in veterinary techniques, kissing spine operations are now carried out with the horse standing upright; this allows for much more accuracy and so a better prognosis. The offending dorsal processes are re-shaped so that they no longer impinge on each other.

IN SUMMARY

The purpose of this chapter has been to provide insight as to how certain injuries can impact on a horse and his way of going. Armed with this knowledge it will enable you to better understand the implications, and to make a realistic appraisal of what you can achieve with your horse.

Whilst some of the above may have made scary reading, it is important that everyone is aware of what can typically happen within the racing world. This is not a criticism of any individual, but a fact of racing. Unfortunately the racing world isn't always able to give a horse the time it needs to recover because the costs are so high. In any equestrian sport injuries are incurred, but they are not so widely publicised.

We must be realistic, and no horse should ever be put under duress to achieve something that he physically can't; nevertheless with careful, rehabilitative work, much can be attained, especially if time is allowed. Nature is also a wonderful, great healer and never ceases to amaze. Of course trust has to be put in veterinary science, and we should always work in consultation with our vets; but just as in the medical profession where patients have defied the odds, so too have horses.

3 Adapting to 'Life on the Outside'

There are people who are quick to criticize the ex-racehorse as hot-headed and wild, but in fact the majority are extremely well behaved whilst in training, and with patience and time, readily adapt to 'life on the outside'. There are many aspects of his new life that the ex-racehorse will find different, but armed with a little knowledge of the way of life your horse has been used to, you will be better prepared to help him make the transition from one life to another.

UNDERSTANDING CHANGES IN BEHAVIOUR

Whilst a horse may not have shown any signs of excitability, napping or aggression when in training, a new home with a new routine and new people around him may cause him to react less favourably. You may be on the receiving end of behaviours that are not usual for him, and you may find yourself having to deal with situations you haven't encountered before. This is quite normal, and in time he will settle down – provided proper attention and consideration is given to his needs.

Like a first day at school, it probably all feels very strange and he doesn't understand what is happening and why he is in unfamiliar surroundings, but we expect him to take it all in his stride – and whilst some do, others don't. While we should not be guilty of anthropomorphosis, clearly horses are capable of a wide range of emotions, and allowance should be made for this. The racehorse starts his adult life at a very tender age so becomes conditioned to certain stimuli; some of these reactions cannot always be fully eliminated, although they can be successfully managed.

Fig. 3.1　From the day the horse steps into your yard his life changes quite dramatically; he will understandably feel very insecure. (Photograph courtesy of Jon Fullegar, Sandown Racecourse)

Fig. 3.2　Georgie (Leosaid) was a challenge but with patience and very clear, consistent handling, he made the transition from racehorse to riding horse.

Despite best practices to create relaxed environments, racehorses can also exhibit stereotypical behaviour – box-walking, weaving, cribbing – because they are not psychologically happy or can't cope with their environment. This is not true of every horse, and there is no reliable data establishing that the incidence of 'stable vices' is greater in a racing yard than any other competition yard. However, it is assumed that it is so because racehorses spend more time stabled, and their management routine is further from what nature intended than for the majority of other horses. New owners routinely report that their new charge has a 'vice'.

Even though your horse may not actually have had a 'stable vice' (the display of stereotypical behaviour) when in training, he might develop one simply because he is out of his comfort zone: having left his familiar (racing) environment, in a strange home with someone he doesn't know, he is now feeling very insecure. However, once he begins to settle in and adjust to his new way of life, such behaviours should significantly reduce if not disappear altogether as the change of diet, more turn-out time and the slower pace of life gradually take effect.

When in training the racehorse leads a structured life with a strict routine, and certain things are done in a specific way. The change of routine and lifestyle can also be a cause of stress and stress-related symptoms until he settles down, and however keen you are to get him started on your regime, you must give him adequate time to adjust to all the changes occurring in his life. Life in larger racing yards is busy and time often short, so the horse may not be used to the affection you now wish to show him – in fact to begin with he may appear to be quite grumpy, with ears back, neck stretched out, head lowered. However, don't be alarmed at this: just give him time to adjust and settle in, and he will soon realize that you are good company.

ADJUSTING TO A NEW ENVIRONMENT

Whilst some horses are perfectly happy in larger, busier yards, others prefer the quieter surroundings of a smaller training establishment. Some new owners may be keeping their ex-racehorse at livery in a large yard, and they must be aware that even though life on the racing yard was busy, it would probably never have been as busy as a large livery yard, or as noisy, as the various owners

Fig. 3.3   Reassuring scratches and interaction with you will help the new boy settle in.

Fig. 3.4   The thoroughbred requires plenty of mental stimuli, so don't stable the horse 'round the back' where he can't see anything! Providing horses with an interesting outlook keeps the mind occupied.

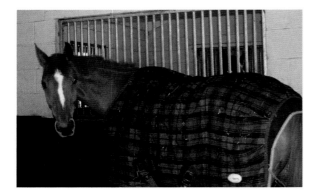

Fig. 3.5   Small grills between stables allow horses to interact if they wish but don't put a horse permanently 'on show'.

come and go at different times of the day. Traditionally racing yards shut down for two to three hours during the afternoon so that the horses can relax and rest in peace and quiet in their stable; yard staff have their lunch and a break before evening stables commences at around 3.30pm.

Some livery yards have younger children around, who can be particularly noisy; whilst most horses that have been in training are very familiar with dogs, they may not be accustomed to children.

Your horse will need time to adjust to all this.

Changes in Stable Routine

The day-to-day routines of grooming, tying up, mucking out, rugging up and clipping are bound to be carried out differently in a private home or a livery yard as compared to the racing yard, and the ex-racehorse might take some time to get used to these changes. Equally his new owner should make every effort to understand the level of care and daily routine his new horse has been accustomed to, and initially at least may have to adapt his stable management in order to help his horse adapt and settle in.

- Your horse is used to a meticulous grooming every day as part of the evening stables routine. Be careful – the thoroughbred is thin-skinned and often ticklish; use softer brushes especially on the face and under the stomach!
- Your new charge will have been kept very warm spending more time with a rug on than off. Even on seemingly warm days, racehorses are worked with exercise sheets on to keep toned muscles warm. As a very fit athlete, he won't be carrying excess fat, and you will initially need to keep him rugged up. Some horses come from yards where there is heating in the stables and their water is warmed in the cold weather. Similarly in the summer, there are cooling systems.
- Just because a horse has been clipped, that doesn't mean this is an easy task as he may not have enjoyed the experience. In racing, horses that are not happy to be clipped are usually sedated to avoid the risk of injury both to horse and staff and to save time.
- He will definitely not be used to being tied up outside his stable. This just isn't done in racing. Any attention a horse needs, including being tacked up, is done while he is in his box. Nor is the horse out of training used to being cross-tied.
- Racehorses are used to really thick beds, so if you only sprinkle some bedding in a corner your horse may be reluctant to stale or lie down.
- Sometimes stables are mucked out while the horses are being worked, so initially your horse may be a bit wary of this process; however, he will be accustomed to being 'picked out' – usually with a muck-sheet rather than a barrow.
- Some horses dislike the 'goldfish bowl' effect of the stabling system found in most American barns, whereby the stables have bars as opposed to solid walls between them and the horse is on permanent view from all

round. The shy or timid horse can find this disconcerting, resulting in him not eating properly, dropping weight, etc; it can also lead to behavioural issues or the development of vices such as box walking. Give your horse some privacy by boarding over some of the bars.

Adapting to a New Diet

How often have we heard a worried owner saying: 'He won't eat up!' This is because you are trying to change his feed to something he isn't familiar with.

The racehorse is fed a high energy diet, primarily comprising concentrates with only small amounts of fibre, so if you give him bowls of chop or chaff he may well leave these. Given that the horse can only consume so many kilograms of feed in a day, for the racehorse the larger proportion of that quota has to be hard feed, as opposed to forage, in order to provide the energy necessary to race competitively, as forage just cannot fulfil the desired energy requirements.

As the new owner your first task is to alter the type of energy food the horse receives – the racehorse diet may have caused digestive problems, such as gastric ulcers, but now that he is not having to race he can be fed a high fibre diet as the basis to his ration, which should help to restore his digestive tract to good health. However, as he won't have been given much forage at all, in the early days impaction colic can be a real threat, so whilst understandably you will be keen to attend to matters of diet, it is essential that any changes are introduced gradually.

Horses are fed at the same time in racing yards, so if your horse is at livery and this is not the practice on the yard, then try and at least arrange for him to be fed at the same time as the horses on either side of him so as to avoid unnecessary stress.

Fig. 3.6 Miniature Shetlands make great field companions.

Adapting to Turnout

Whilst increasing numbers of trainers are realizing the benefits of a degree of regular turnout to keep horses more relaxed, it still isn't the norm for racehorses to be turned out to grass for the afternoon, as the risk of injury is too great. Your ex-racehorse will therefore have had little, and possibly no turnout other than during his holidays; however, racehorses are put on a horsewalker, or perhaps are led out for a pick of grass, or allowed a spell in a grazing pen.

Much as you want your horse to go out in the field, do not expect him to leave the (race) training environment one day and then happily graze in the field all day the next – the change will be too much for him to cope with, so access to stabling is initially essential. However, some turnout time is preferable as soon as possible, even if just for half an hour. If he seems particularly edgy, stressed or over-exuberant, or is recovering from an injury, it may be sensible to administer a small amount of sedative before turning him out. If in doubt, consult your veterinary surgeon.

He will need time to adjust to being outside for longer periods: natural as it may seem, not every horse actually enjoys being out for long periods, particularly if the weather is bad. His digestive system will also need time to adjust to larger amounts of grass.

It is unlikely that your horse will have been turned out alone, apart from in a grazing pen; equally he may not be used to group turn-out. As horses are very social there should always be a companion, but if this isn't feasible another horse (or horses) should be on the other side of the fence for communication and reassurance.

The ex-racehorse is unlikely to have encountered an electric fence, since post and rail/post and wire fencing is the norm in racing environments. This means that he may not realize that the white/green tape is his

Figs 3.7 and 3.8 At the 'Breeze Up' Sales, the young horses show off their racing paces in front of potential buyers before going in to the Sales Ring. (Photographs courtesy of Doncaster Bloodstock Sales/Trevor Jones)

> **RE-ESTABLISHING GOOD MANNERS**
>
> The horse out of training should have good manners; however, a change of environment with the associated stress and anxiety can cause a horse to forget them for a while, so you may need to re-establish a few rules.

boundary, so attach bits of cloth or strips of plastic to the tape to ensure that he sees it if he is racing around at speed. It has also been known for some horses fresh out of training to react to white fence tape and posts – a connection with the white rails of the racing paddock being the most likely explanation.

Until he acclimatizes, even on a relatively warm day your horse will need a lightweight turnout rug since he has no excess body fat to provide an insulating layer to keep him warm naturally. Be mindful when fitting rugs that have leg straps on: racehorses are well accustomed to fillet strings, but some may not be familiar with straps around their hind legs.

THE FIRST STEPS IN RETRAINING

Old Head on Young Shoulders

Compared to most other horses, the ex-racehorse – in particular the flat-raced horse – will have had almost a lifetime's experience by the time he is three years old. For example, at barely a month old he may have travelled back to stud with his dam; as a foal and/or yearling he may have gone through the sale ring; he may have been sent to a pre-training yard to be backed – if destined for flat racing this will be when he is just eighteen months old. After backing he will have commenced his training, and then as a two-year-old may have been sent to the 'Breeze Up' sales.

Figs 3.9 and 3.10   Compare photograph on the left of Fred working De Marco (owned by Beverly Dyer) with that of a young racehorse being long-reined at Bryan Smart's. (Photograph courtesy of Bryan Smart Racing)

The schooling process for racehorses is limited compared to most other disciplines. The yearling is long-reined, but for how long depends entirely on a trainer's own system. Long-reining obviously acclimatizes the young horse to the feel of the bit moving in his mouth, he is taught to turn left and right, to go forwards and to stop, but he is not taught to turn with the 'correct lateral bend', nor is anyone particularly concerned where he places his head, hind feet and so on.

In other words the racehorse is not taught about suppleness, proper contact with the bit, flexion, or working in an outline, and a racehorse trainer is not looking to teach his yearling to engage, step under, or move away from the leg, he just wants him to run (fast) effectively in a straight line.

Introducing Changes in Tack

So you are ready to ride your ex-racehorse – but beware when tacking him up, as he may not have had a 'conventional' saddle on his back before – or even a saddle on at all for a while if he had a lay-off prior to being rehomed. So he may react the first time (or for the first few times) you put the saddle on, by kicking, humping his back or bucking. Always use a nummah as opposed to a saddle cloth to limit concussion.

You should also bear in mind that he will keep changing shape as he puts on weight, so you will need regular consultations with a saddle fitter in the early months.

Finding a suitable bit is often difficult as racehorses don't have a 'mouth'. The single-jointed bit is the choice of most racehorse trainers, so your horse will probably have been backed, trained and raced in one – but he is unlikely to respond to its action in the way that a non-racing youngster would. It is better to use something completely different and to 're-educate' the horse's mouth. However, there are always exceptions.

Not all racehorses are used to wearing boots, so be careful when removing them as those fastened with Velcro may startle the unprepared horse.

Fig. 3.11 When racehorses are held, generally the handler stands in front of the horse. When that person then moves to the horse's side, it is the signal to walk on. So think about this when you come to get on board for the first time.

Getting On: What to Expect

Of course the ex-racehorse is used to being ridden, but this whole process is somewhat different for both you and him. First of all, he probably won't stand still to be mounted, as this is not general practice for the horse in training as the rider is legged up, usually whilst the horse is on the move; he may even attempt to hop off the ground if you try to stop him from walking off. Also you may be the heaviest person he has ever had on his back, so this might surprise him. Nor is a racehorse used to his rider tightening the girth, so to begin with it

may be advisable to ask someone to be on hand to do this for you from the ground.

Riding Away: A Different Experience

Although he is used to being ridden, the young racehorse is certainly no riding horse in the conventional sense of the term. To start with, he probably won't know anything about contact; his 'braking system' may be limited or non-existent; and he will probably be completely ignorant of the aids, whether hands, legs, seat or bodyweight, other than a squeeze or kick to

Fig. 3.12   Racehorses can behave calmly hacking out. (Photograph courtesy of Clive Cox Racing)

make him move forwards, and a letting go of the reins to slow him up. Physically he is likely to feel stiff and 'rigid', simply as a result of not being supple, because racehorses are never schooled on the flat to be so.

Bear in mind, too, that it may well be that no one has ever ridden him with longer stirrups: although more and more horses are now used to the rider having a longer leg position, this may be another thing that he will have to get used to. It is often the different position and use of the leg that can cause a reaction in some ex-racehorses.

Another important factor is that the horse that has been in training has a greater dependence on the company of other horses as he has always had plenty of friends around him, whether he is working – racehorses are

invariably ridden out in a string – or resting in the yard. Inevitably this gives him a sense of reassurance and security – so if you ride him out on his own he will almost certainly feel nervous and insecure, and will react accordingly.

As a new owner you may be reassured that most racehorses are in fact quite used to hacking out. For some yards the gallops are on the doorstep, but for the vast majority of racehorses reaching the gallops can entail quite a long hack. Thus horses trained in Lambourn hack out on to the Downs, whilst those trained in Newmarket go out on to the Heath. Many of us would probably think twice about taking our horses into such an expanse of open space; however, this clearly indicates the security the horse feels in the company of others, as well as the confidence he feels in his rider.

Fig. 3.13 It is when they are unleashed onto the racecourse for the canter to the start that some can become rather fractious. (Photograph courtesy of John Pike, Racing Images)

Schooling Work: Making a Start

You will need a safe, enclosed area in which to start schooling work – it isn't practicable to expect your horse to settle to schooling in an open field initially. Covered canter tracks are routinely becoming part of the facilities in the larger yards so that horses can be kept working whatever the weather, so you shouldn't encounter any particular upsets when going into an indoor school.

Bear this in mind when you think about having a canter in an open space in the early stages of retraining: your horse may think he is off down the racecourse to the start!

THE FIRST EXCURSIONS

Getting There

Racehorses usually load well, but note that it is customary for racehorses to be loaded via a loading ramp, as this drastically reduces the risk of loading-related injuries and any difficulties with reluctant loaders.

Your ex-racehorse is unlikely ever to have travelled in a trailer, and you may well have to accustom him to travelling in it as you would a young horse. Nor are racehorses used to standing in the horsebox: once at the racecourse they are stabled.

Not all racehorses will have seen traffic, depending on where they have been in training.

Settling Down in Company

Even when the racing life has been left far behind, going to a show can trigger certain behavioural reactions. The ex-racehorse is used to being in company, but when attending a competition he may get excited, tense or stressful because he is anticipating racing again. As attending shows becomes more routine, he will invariably settle down – though some horses will always become tense or excited.

Unlike other young horses, whose owners will spend time gradually familiarizing them with new situations, the young racehorse is rather

Fig. 3.14   *Most horses cope with the pre-race build-up very well, bearing in mind they know exactly what is about to happen. (Photograph courtesy of Jon Fullegar, Sandown Racecourse)*

thrown in at the deep end – he goes to a racecourse to work, whether for a workout or to actually race, and is never led around just to 'soak up the atmosphere' or allowed to stand quietly in the horsebox with a trusty companion. Feeding a calming supplement may work, but cannot be guaranteed to produce the desired result with every horse.

We recommend a 'reconditioning' process, so you gradually build up from working with one horse around, to two, three and four, whether in the school at home, or going to another venue for an outing. Then he might be taken to quieter shows. As we have said, most horses are good to hack, though some understandably lack confidence on their own, whilst others become more excitable in a group.

Putting your horse in a group situation too early can merely add to tension/excitement and may cause him to react in a negative way, not

because he is being naughty but because he just isn't ready to cope. Ideally hack out with just one other horse until he is comfortable with his new lifestyle.

Fig. 3.15   *This horse enjoys a leisurely hack out as much as he does hunting and showing. (Photograph courtesy of Claire Bowers)*

4 Managing the Horse Out of Training

Ensuring a horse's wellbeing is a matter of addressing his psychological welfare as well as his physical fitness. If he is happy in his surroundings he is going to be happier in himself and consequently in his work. We therefore owe it to our horses to provide them with an environment in which they feel secure, and which provides for their nutritional, mental and physical wellbeing.

ACCOMMODATION FOR THE EX-RACEHORSE

A horse's living space is as important to him as ours is to us. Whether you elect to keep your horse out the whole time, predominantly stabled, or a mix of the two, doesn't matter as long as due consideration is given to the quality of the environment in which he is kept.

The Stabled Horse

Keeping the stabled horse content isn't difficult with a little thought: he will be happier if his stable has an interesting outlook, is big enough for him to move around easily and lie out comfortably, and is light and airy – a dark stable is depressing. He needs company, preferably of his own kind, so he can communicate visually, vocally and telepathically even if he can't have physical contact with his neighbour. And if it isn't possible to have a companion horse close by, fit a stable mirror: a horse doesn't realize he is looking at his own reflection. And there are all

Fig. 4.1   Stables with rear-opening windows are invaluable.

sorts of horse 'toys' on the market to help occupy an active mind.

Signs of chewing around the stable are not always due to boredom: the horse has an in-built desire to chew, so make sure that he is fed plenty of bulk to satisfy this urge.

The atmosphere within the stable is very important: even on cooler days it is better to have fresh, circulating air, so keep him warm with another rug.

The Horse at Grass

There are numerous books available with advice regarding acreage, grassland management and fencing for the field-kept horse, but his basic requirements are having enough to eat, water, shelter and a companion. Thus when the grass

Fig. 4.2 It is unkind to keep a horse alone; he should have company.

dies back or when the field starts to get bare, keep an eye on your horse's body condition: it will probably be necessary to provide supplementary feeding, particularly if you wish to ride, and definitely during the winter months. Also watch for signs of crib-biting.

There should be an adequate supply of clean water at all times.

Horses will need shelter – from trees, a high hedge, an adjacent building – from flies and the heat of the sun in a hot summer as much as from cold winds and rain, because they can suffer from sunstroke. In the winter, if your horse isn't carrying enough condition or just naturally feels the cold it may be necessary to rug him, even if the field is sheltered or has a field shelter.

Signs of chewing might indicate that he is bored, although this could also mean there isn't enough for him to eat in the field (lack of fibre), or that he is lacking in minerals.

Companionship is important: if it is not possible or practicable to have a second horse, provide an alternative such as a sheep or goat.

HEALTH MATTERS

If you didn't have your horse vetted when you bought him, then a veterinary check is recommended so that an assessment can be made of his physical condition, and any specific issues brought to your attention.

FEEDING AND NUTRITION

Equine nutrition is a much more in-depth subject of management than it used to be years ago, though fortunately every feed company now has in-house nutritionists ready to help the baffled owner comprise a suitable diet – 'baffled' because there is an absolutely dazzling display of feeds and feeding products these days, and it can be very confusing trying to compare them all. And feeding appropriately is of the utmost importance because no matter how well trained a horse is, if he is not receiving the appropriate nutrition for the job he is being

Fig. 4.3 The old adage, 'feed according to the work done' should be uppermost in the mind. (Photograph courtesy of Hurlingham Polo Association)

WHY A HORSE CRIB-BITES

It is increasingly thought in the circles of equine research that cribbing and similar 'vices' (the so-called stereotypical behaviours) are actually less attributable to boredom and rather more of an instinctive reaction by the horse, because saliva is produced when these vices are executed – and saliva neutralizes the constant flow of stomach acid. This may be why such 'vices' are often seen in horses whose diet is proportionately higher in concentrates than in forage (fibre).

---

asked to do, then he won't be able to perform to the best of his ability, and ultimately his health may be compromised.

The Way Nature Designed the Horse

In his feral state the horse has evolved to browse and graze for up to eighteen hours a day, ingesting up to 2 to 3 per cent of his bodyweight; his digestive system is designed to eat and process low quality forage (fibre) in large quantities in a virtually non-stop activity known as trickle feeding.

The horse is designed to digest fibre in the hindgut, where millions of little micro-organisms are responsible for the breakdown of the digestible fibre the horse ingests – microbial fermentation. These 'friendly bacteria' or gut flora need the right environment in which to live; it is somewhat a chicken-and-egg situation in that a horse needs his digestive system to work correctly for maximum health and for that he needs an abundance of these bacteria, yet if the gut is not healthy the bacteria cannot survive or the numbers are significantly

reduced. The horse has a small stomach, so food passes through it quite quickly into the small intestine. However, stomach acid is constantly produced whether food is there or not. This is why an almost continuous supply of food is important in order to stop a build-up of the potentially damaging acid that causes ulcers. Horses have an instinctive desire to chew, and constant chewing produces the saliva that is vital to neutralize harsh stomach acid. As fibre takes longer to chew than cereals, providing a high fibre diet is one way of reducing the risk of ulcers. Another benefit of a high fibre diet is that during the digestion process thermal energy is created, with the greatest amount being produced in the hindgut, where fibre is digested; this energy is effectively an in-built central-heating system providing warmth – hence the reason why horses that live out should be provided with adequate forage, both to sustain them, and literally keep them warm.

The Racing Diet

The horse in training is usually fed a high energy diet in which the concentrate/starch (for quick-release energy) is often in excess of 7kg per day, and the fibre content relatively low – often less that 5kg per day – certainly by comparison to that fed to horses in other sports, or the fun horse. To the racing industry, a horse that reacts to this high concentrate diet by exuberant behaviour is not a problem, but just a part of normal, everyday life. So when the horse you have just acquired is termed 'a bit lively' by his lad or lass, it is quite possible that at least to begin with he will put in a buck or two, and tend to be excitable.

In order to fulfil the racehorse's energy requirements, grain-based feeds – concentrates such as oats, maize and barley – are given, as other feeds do not provide adequate carbohydrate to meet demand. However, such high levels of starch can contribute to colic, tying up, ulcers, even laminitis.

Although tradition has been for a cereal-based diet, rations higher in oil are becoming more popular. Oil provides more energy than carbohydrates and although it cannot be directly utilized as a fuel source for high intensity work, it is thought to have a glycogen-sparing effect at low intensities. This simply means that the horse will utilize oil as an energy source when working at low intensities, leaving full stores of glycogen (derived from starch in cereals) for when the work intensity increases. This reduces the amount of cereals required in the diet which has additional health benefits.

The Starch Effect

Some horses react to starch, and a diet that is starch-based does generally seem to make horses excitable.

Starch, along with fats, sugars and proteins, is digested and absorbed in the small intestine. The passage of food through this section of the digestive tract, which accounts for approximately 20 per cent of the complete digestive system, is very rapid (typically less than an hour) so the energy released is readily available.

Figs 4.4 and 4.5 (top) Pretty Officer on the day of her arrival here three weeks after her last race. Her appearance is typical of a flat-raced horse – not an ounce of fat, with once-toned muscles dropping away. With a change of diet, she soon began to put on weight. Combined with correct re-training, the musculature appropriate to the riding horse is building (bottom).

However, the horse has a limited absorption capacity in the small intestine, and feeding too much starch in one feed can result in some passing into the large intestine. This is not an ideal place for it to be, as the presence of starch, especially in larger quantities, causes a disruptive influence and actually kills off the desirable bacteria that live in the digestive tract, keeping it healthy. This results in poorer digestion of fibre, leading to digestive upsets such as diarrhoea and colic. High starch diets are also now believed to be a significant contributory factor in the formation of gastric ulcers.

THE IMPORTANCE OF FIBRE

Increased awareness has resulted in more and more owners realizing that the equine diet should comprise as much fibre as possible, for the following reasons:

- It is what nature intended
- It keeps the gut healthy, in that the acid that is produced by the breakdown of fibre (which takes place in the hindgut) is much weaker than the acid produced by starch from cereals
- Munching on fibre prevents boredom and relieves stress
- Plenty in the diet significantly reduces the risk of digestive upsets
- Fibre helps to create a reservoir of water in the digestive tract, and therefore helps against the risk of dehydration, particularly important during warm/hot weather or when competing, especially in eventing and endurance.

A prebiotic provides the gut flora with a food source so that they can flourish and help to maintain the right environment for them to live in, enabling them [the bacteria] to do their job of eliminating nasties. A healthy digestive system is a properly operating one ensuring that received nutrients are suitably broken down and absorbed and fully utilized. Stress upsets the beneficial gut flora, and often manifests as loose droppings. A horse that passes loose droppings is also losing fluid, so if the situation persists over several days, there is the possibility of the horse becoming dehydrated, particularly in warm weather. Although the feeding of a prebiotic can't inhibit the passing of loose droppings, it will help to negate the threat of harmful bacteria taking advantage of the disrupted good bacteria.

A probiotic is a yeast culture that contains live yeast cells. These help to keep the environment in the gut healthy for the bacteria to work in and are also involved in helping bacteria to digest fibre. YeaSacc1026 is one of the most popular yeast cultures.

The Task in Hand

The horse in training is superbly fit: he carries no excess fat, so when the training regime ceases, along with the high-powered racing diet, the taut racing muscles start to relax (and diminish as they are not being worked) and the horse might appear underweight. Obviously if the right diet is not implemented straightaway, the horse can readily become thin and indeed undernourished.

As the new owner your primary task is to alter the type of energy the horse receives, as he can now be fed a high fibre diet as the basis to his

Figs 4.6 and 4.7   Two horses of the same size but they have completely different nutritional needs.

 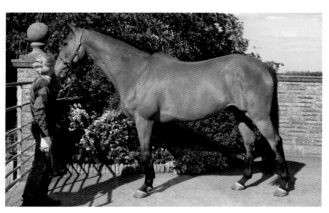

Figs 4.8 and 4.9   Whilst the quantity and constituents given will be vastly different, the miniature Shetland has the same nutritional requirements as the racehorse – he must receive a suitably balanced diet for optimum bodily function.

ration to restore his digestive tract to good health. It will probably be necessary to feed additional feed alongside the forage to promote weight gain and physically prepare him for the building of a different musculature.

Good nutrition is also important to help the horse's body recover from the rigours of racing. Obviously a totally different feeding programme is required to the regime that the horse has been used to, and this in itself can sometimes be a source of additional stress for some horses – and their owners in the quest to find what suits!

The diet of each horse should be individually assessed depending what his bodyweight or target weight should be; once you have established a weight, coupled with your horse's temperament and his workload, a suitable diet can be formulated.

Because of the way in which his digestive system is designed, any changes to the horse's diet (and that includes introducing grass, as in turnout) must be introduced gradually. Furthermore, what you normally feed may well be totally alien to your new charge, so don't be alarmed if feeding times are initially an exercise of trial and error whilst you encourage the horse to eat a more acceptable diet.

If you have elected to let your horse have a few months in the field prior to commencing work, if it is summer, the grass should provide all the nutrition he needs. When he is brought back in, however, bear in mind that the hay/haylage may not have the same high levels of nutrition that fresh grass had, so a balancer may need to be fed, particularly when he first comes in and his new feeds are not up to optimum levels (because you are introducing these gradually).

A Horse's Nutritional Requirements

Whatever a horse's breed and whatever his level of work, whether he is a 12.2hh show pony or a four-star event horse, a balanced diet is essential in order to meet his energy requirements, and to provide all the other nutrients required to keep him fit and healthy.

It is often thought that only the working horse requires energy, but all horses have a basic energy requirement in order to survive, energy being the result of the breakdown of certain nutrients from food that enables the body to carry out its basic daily functions. When a horse is asked to perform tasks that require energy over and above his maintenance needs, more energy is required either by ingesting more grass, or by what his owner gives him.

The essential components of a balanced diet are as follows.

Water: Absolutely vital for life; a horse needs access to clean, fresh water at all times. The quantity each horse drinks varies so you should become familiar with what is normal for your horse; a sudden increase or decrease in water intake can be a sign that all is not well.

Protein: Essential for the production of new body tissues and cell repair. Individual amino acids comprise protein and while horses can synthesize some of these, others must be incorporated in the diet. If a feedstuff has good levels of essential amino acids it is known as a quality protein source. Note that cereals are very low in quality protein. Protein is often mistakenly thought of as a 'high energy' source, although a diet should not have a too high a protein content. For maintenance and light work an 8–10 per cent protein content diet is sufficient. Medium to hard work increases the requirement to 12–14 per cent. Excess protein in the diet can be used to provide energy, although this conversion is not an efficient process. Higher levels of protein are usually only fed to lactating mares, developing youngstock and horses in training.

Carbohydrates: Sugars, starches and fibre that can be disgested to provide energy that is utilized for bodily functions and exercise. Carbohydrates are disgested at different rates, sugars and starches being the most quickly digested in the small intestine, hence the energy provided by starch feeds being termed 'quick release' as it is easily digested in the small intestine and is stored in the muscles as glycogen ready for instant use.

Oil: An excellent source of energy – up to 2.25 times more than oats, but without the heating effect; it is termed a 'slow-release energy' feedstuff and is easily digested by the horse. Oil/fats also boost the calorific value of the diet, which equates to weight gain and improves condition, but don't have to be fed in large quantities.

Fibre: After water, the next most important constituent of the diet as it is vital for efficient digestive function. Fibre is also an excellent energy source and for horses in light or even moderate work, additional feeding may not be required.

Figs 4.10 and 4.11 Two thoroughbreds with completely different nutritional requirements. While the gelding (left) doesn't want to be gaining any more weight (training will alter his musculature), the mare (right) needs to fill out all over.

Vitamins: Support all the bodily processes.

Minerals: Come in two forms – macro minerals (calcium, phosphorous, potassium and magnesium) of which the horse needs quite high amounts; and trace elements (iron, zinc, copper, selenium and manganese), which are required in much lesser amounts.

Assessing how Much to Feed

It is universally accepted that horses require 2 per cent of their bodyweight for maintenance and when in light work. This is increased up to 2.5 per cent for those that are either underweight or do not maintain their weight well, and decreased down to as little as 1.5 per cent for the 'good doer'. Generally a thoroughbred weighing 500–550kg will require between 10–12kg feed per day, comprising a per cent ratio of concentrate to forage, the composition depending on the workload of the horse.

When deciding how much to feed your ex-racehorse, start with the forage, remembering that a minimum of 1 per cent of the horse's bodyweight should be fed as forage; thus a 500kg horse should have 5kg of hay, at the very least, each day.

The best basis to the ration is ad lib forage, and if this is sufficient to maintain your horse's weight and provide enough energy for the work he is doing, all you need to feed alongside is a balanced source of vitamins and minerals. Only the overweight horse needs forage limited, to approximately 1.5 per cent of bodyweight.

If ad lib forage isn't sufficient to maintain your horse, you may need to use more concentrated energy sources, although you should still offer your horse ad lib forage, particularly if he isn't holding his weight well.

The amount of concentrates you use will depend on the type of feed selected.

Compound feeds: Contain added vitamins and minerals that have been formulated to be fed at certain levels. Weigh your horse, weigh your feed, and follow the instructions on the bag to ensure the right amount is fed, as it is important to feed as per the guidelines otherwise your horse will miss out on a balanced diet. Nuts and cubes tend to be higher in fibre than mixed compound feeds, and are more palatable than straights.

Straights: If you decide to use straights – that is, feeds with no added vitamins and minerals – you must use a supplement or balancer alongside them to ensure the diet is balanced.

The maximum amount of straight cereals that should be fed to a horse per meal is 1.5–1.8kg (3.5–4lb); thus if you can only feed twice a day, the daily ration equates to 3–3.5kg; feeding more in the two feeds may cause harm, particularly if his racing diet has predisposed him to gastric ulcers.

Using a weight-tape can help you more correctly assess your horse's bodyweight, although body condition scoring is preferred by those who like to visually assess a horse's weight. Each horse is different: some gain weight very quickly, others take longer,

Fig. 4.12 All too often horses are actually overfed for the work they are doing.

particularly if other issues present, such as gastric ulcers. You should be particularly aware of weight loss, as this not only indicates that something could be wrong, but could also affect the fit of the saddle.

The method below was typically used to determine the balance of a feed ration, concentrate to forage, for a horse in work:

25:75 per cent	maintenance/light work
30:70 per cent	light/medium work
40:60 per cent	medium/hard work
50:50 per cent	hard work
70:30 per cent	the racehorse

Other factors must also be considered when deciding how much to feed your ex-racehorse.

● His temperament and metabolism – is he highly-strung or stressy? He will burn off nervous energy so may lose weight, and would require a higher conditioning element in the feed ration.
● Does he need to gain weight/condition? More calories need to be provided in the diet, so feed more calorie-dense energy sources such as oil. It is always preferable to use a more concentrated ration than to feed more volume.
● Is he a poor doer? Feeding more small meals is vital, as this allows more feed to be fed in total without risking an overload. Use highly digestible fibre sources such as sugar beet and alfalfa to boost calorific intake safely.
● Is he stabled or at grass (or a combination), rugged or unrugged? As we have seen, the process of fibre digestion generates heat, which helps to keep the horse warm. So it follows that an unrugged horse living out in the winter will need a greater amount of forage than his stabled, rugged counterpart just to keep warm.
● His workload.
● His age: As a horse gets older the absorption of nutrients is not so efficient so a greater

quantity is required in order to ensure he receives enough to meet his needs.
● Forage quality: Hay/haylage can be deceptive in its nutritional content, so it is important to have it analysed periodically. A pleasant smell does not necessarily equate to good value.

So What to Feed?

If your ex-racehorse is in good condition, then a high fibre, low-energy product fed at the recommended levels should provide all the nutrients needed for good health. So just work out your horse's bodyweight and hence the recommended amount (volume) of feed to give; then use the per cent ratio guide above to determine the concentrate-to-forage feed levels.

Whether you elect to feed straights or compound feeds is personal choice.

Feedstuffs

Fibre: Traditionally chopped straw and/or hay, but now there are chaffs that comprise just pure dried grasses. Good fibre sources are alfalfa, sugar beet and straw (usually oat straw, as used in some chaffs and pelleted feeds). Alfalfa also provides energy and protein, and is a source of vitamins A, B and E.

Energy feeds: These feeds are starches/carbohydrates, and are usually cereal based; if used correctly and in moderation they will not cause problems. Whilst many horses can maintain their weight and carry out their workload without needing cereals at all, the harder working horse or one that has a limited appetite may require a cereal-based feed to consume sufficient energy.

Cereals should be fed cooked; micronizing and extrusion are methods used to improve digestibility. Both increase the amount of starch that is absorbed by the small intestine, helping to reduce the risk of starch reaching the hind gut. If using a compound feed, cubes generally contain less starch than a mix.

Good energy sources are oats, barley and maize. Oats actually contain less starch than other grains, and are usually crushed, rolled or bruised to make them easier for the horse to digest. There are also 'naked oats' which are more energy dense than traditional oats. Barley is higher in energy but lower in fibre than oats, and should be fed crushed, rolled or boiled, as it is such a hard grain. Maize is very high in energy but low in fibre and protein, and must also be processed before feeding.

Protein: Sources of protein include peas, soya – which also has a high oil content – and beans. Alfalfa is also a source of protein.

Oil: Good sources of oil are rice bran, soya and linseed, the latter two being rich in Omega 3 and Omega 6, which the horse cannot synthesize so must be provided by the diet.

Feeding Scenarios

Feeding for Weight Gain

The horse coming straight out of training will not be carrying an ounce of fat, so the first task is to adjust the diet and get some meat on those bones! This is done by feeding high calorie but non-heating feeds; for example, oil provides 2.25 times as many calories as a cereal, so is great for weight gain. A feed high in oil is preferable to actually adding liquid oil, which some horses dislike.

Small feeds given throughout the day are better than a large feed morning and night, so if possible feed the horse that needs to gain weight at least three times a day, four being ideal.

The suggested ration to promote weight gain for a TB in light work (bodyweight 550kg): 2.5kg alfalfa and oil fibre feed (e.g. Dengie Alfa

A with Oil/Dengie Alfa A Molasses Free), 1kg dry weight alfalfa and sugar beet blend, and ad lib forage. This ration should be divided into three or four feeds per day as large feeds pass through the digestive tract too quickly, resulting in less efficient absorption; don't increase the workload until bodyweight has been gained. Other factors that can contribute to a horse not carrying the condition it should include:

- A heavy worm burden
- Poor dentition
- Stress
- Temperament
- Illness
- Not enough feed, or the wrong feed being given
- The horse is not warm enough, or is overrugged and too warm.

Feeding the Excitable Horse

These horses need their energy intake reducing, as excess starch is probably reaching the hindgut and upsetting the digestive process.

Soaking hay for a few hours prior to feeding may reduce its sugar content, though other useful nutrients may also be lost. Otherwise increase the fibre levels of the diet with a chop/chaff and/or low-energy cubes as the longer digestion time equates to slower energy release; significantly reduce or eliminate any concentrates.

However, excitable horses tend not to carry their weight well, so usually a conditioning feed is required. Such feed needs to provide calories for weight gain, but not to put more fuel in the tank; this is done by feeding fibre, oil-based feeds and (cooked) barley. Feed manufacturers produce specific conditioning mixes/cubes which work very well, especially when fed in conjunction with (unmolassed) sugar beet and/or a fibre feed. Look for the MJ/Kg on the bag, as the higher this figure, the higher the calorific value.

The suggested ration for a stressy, over-excitable TB competing at Intro or unaffiliated level (bodyweight 550kg): 2kg alfalfa and oil fibre feed (e.g. Dengie Alfa-A Oil), 0.5kg alfalfa and sugar beet blend (dry weight of sugar beet), and ad lib forage. A broad spectrum vitamin/mineral supplement or Balancer should be added to the feed and ideally a prebiotic/yeast supplement. The ration is based on fibre and oil to keep quick-release energy to a minimum.

Feeding for Performance

Performance horses need feeding to maintain their condition as well as provide energy. Nutrition needs to provide quality protein to keep the body functioning at optimum levels and support muscle function, with a controlled starch intake to provide fuel.

The suggested ration for a 16hh intermediate event horse, level temperament (bodyweight 550kg): 2.5–3kg alfalfa and oil fibre feed (e.g. Dengie Alfa A with Oil), 0.5kg alfalfa and sugar beet blend with a performance vitamin/mineral supplement. Or if the horse won't eat this amount of Alfa A Oil: 1–1.5kg alfalfa and oil fibre feed (e.g. Dengie Alfa A with Oil) and 3–4kg of a fibre-based conditioning/performance mix. This should ideally be divided into three feeds a day.

Feeding for Energy

For the lazy horse, starch and carbohydrates are required to provide energy (not protein). The diet that contains more starch provides quick-release energy because starches are digested, and hence absorbed, much more quickly.

However, before altering the feed levels, be sure that the horse's lack of energy is not being caused by some other issue, such as a locomotive problem, physical weakness, or discomfort from the tack used, or shoes – or if he is unshod, perhaps shoes are needed? Is he receiving the right feed, enough of it, and in the right proportions? Is he fit enough for the work you are asking of him?

The suggested ration for a 16hh horse in medium work (bodyweight 550kg): .25kg alfalfa and oil fibre feed (e.g. Dengie Alfa A with Oil), 0.5kg oats, with a performance vitamin/mineral supplement. Or replace the oats with a balancer that has a high oil content (such as Dengie Alfa A Balancer) as well as glucosamine (ideal for the working horse). The energy content of the ration can be increased by adding more oil to the diet if the horse lacks stamina rather than energy, but if it is actual energy that is required, the addition of oats to the diet should solve the problem. Remember that alfalfa is as equally high in energy as cereal-based rations.

Note that, depending on the individual, Dengie Alfa A with Oil may be replaced with Dengie Alfa A Molasses Free.

Feeding the Good Doer

Some thoroughbreds maintain their condition and energy to work without the need for conditioning feeds, and can sometimes be fed less than the recommended 2 per cent of bodyweight per day.

For example, Indie, a 16hh TB gelding with a bodyweight of 550kg, only needed a basic feed

Fig. 4.13 Throughout his training period with us, Indie always maintained his weight well, hence the very basic feed.

comprising 1.5kg Dengie Alfa A Lite and 0.5kg alfalfa and sugar beet blend (Alfa-Beet), with added broad spectrum vitamin/mineral supplement. Hay/haylage was approximately 8kg per day. Dengie Hi Fi Molasses Free is also ideal for the good doer.

The Horse at Grass

The nutritional levels in grassland vary considerably depending on the area of the country, and even if grass quality is good, not all essential nutrients are provided in sufficient quantities, such as zinc (which affects hoof condition). If the grass quality in your pasture is not good, then feeding a balancer is a good way of ensuring your horse receives adequate nutrition without additional calories. However, if your ex-racehorse is lacking in condition and the grass quality of his field is not good, then you should give him a supplementary conditioning feed.

It also goes without saying that if he is to live out through the winter he will need supplementary feeding to ensure he maintains his weight, and this amount will need to be increased as the weather gets colder and the grass loses its nutritional content.

WORMING

Recent research has confirmed that there is an increase in resistance to worming products mainly because, if anything, horse owners have a tendency to over-worm. It is actually far better to worm only when a worm count indicates.

Worm counts cannot indicate the levels, if any, of tapeworms; this is done by an ELISA test, which involves taking a blood sample from the horse, which is then analysed. Such a test should be done every eighteen to twenty-four months.

If a worm burden is suspected it is better to give a course of wormer spread over a period of three to four weeks rather than one powerful

Fig. 4.14 *Colic obviously has numerous causes but a worm burden can be one of them.*

dose, as this in itself can cause colic as there can be such a strong reaction in the gut.

Despite routine worming a horse can still be carrying a worm burden, and this is something that should be considered if he doesn't gain weight despite being fed appropriately and his teeth are in good order, or if he has recurrent bouts of colic.

EQUINE DENTISTRY

Everyone is aware of the need to have a horse's teeth checked, particularly as trouble in the mouth can be the cause of numerous riding problems and resistances.

Domestication of the horse has impacted on its teeth! In their natural environment horses grazed on a wide range of forages, which not only kept them in good health physically but also took care of their teeth. The horse's teeth are hypsodont (i.e. they continue to erupt). Nature has adapted the jaw design so that the teeth wear down on the teeth of the opposite jaw; this coupled with munching on grass which is quite abrasive (it contains silica – a component of glass) kept their teeth sufficiently balanced (naturally worn down). And grazing

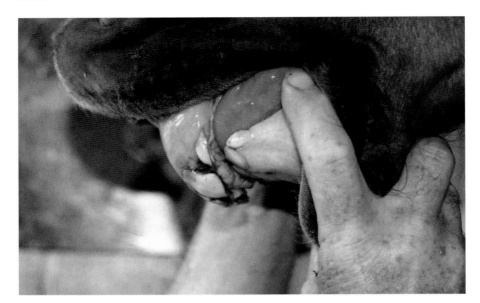

Fig. 4.15 Horses with any form of mouth abnormality should be carefully monitored to ensure they are not having any problems eating.

on various feedstuffs with differing abrasive qualities countered the fact that the teeth also grow at different rates.

The diet upon which horses are now fed actually causes a greater rate of tooth eruption, primarily because hay and haylage are not sufficiently harsh in their make-up to be natural filing tools. When grazing, the jaw has a circular action akin to a figure-of-eight pattern, facilitated by the upper jaw being 30 per cent wider than the bottom jaw, which brings the surfaces, known as tables, of the opposing teeth into contact with each other. To eat hay, this circular action is not required, or is much reduced, so wear is uneven, resulting in sharp edges, hooks, etc. The feeding of concentrates also alters jaw function, as does feeding from haynets/hayracks as this is not a natural stance for the horse; hooks and ramps consequently develop more quickly than in the horse fed off the floor.

Any alteration in jaw function has a knock-on effect on the muscles responsible for mastication and can lead to temporomandibular (TMJ – jaw joint) tension, dysfunction and discomfort. This in turn leads to dental imbalances, creating further tension which passes to the entire horse. Subsequently other joints and muscles are compromised, which can lead to pain and lameness.

There are numerous indications that dental attention is required; if a horse displays any unwanted behaviour, apart from a visit from the chiropractor and saddle fitter, an EDT should also be on the call-out list. It is generally considered that a yearly check from an EDT is sufficient, but a horse should have his teeth checked at least twice a year.

The EDT should check that:

● the temporomandibular joint is not sore or has restricted movement.
● the masticatory muscles (i.e. the muscles that the horse uses in order to chew) are not sore and/or swollen.
● the mandible (lower jaw) has normal lateral movement.

The incisors are routinely overlooked by some EDTs but they should not be omitted as they provide an important balance point for the molar arcades and TMJ.

THE FARRIER'S ROLE

Thoroughbreds are well known for having flat, poor quality feet, often with shallow heels and usually thin soles. When you first acquire your ex-racehorse, getting his feet into better condition may be a lengthy task. In racing, hoof condition is not helped when farriers have to plate regularly – swopping ordinary shoes for racing plates.

Problems with the foot/shoeing can radically affect a horse's way of going, so your farrier is a valuable member of your 'management team'. In the short term he may have to effect some remedial shoeing to take account of poor quality horn and foot imbalances, which although not impacting on the horse when it was in training, may subsequently cause gait abnormalities and/or lameness now that he will be working on a variety of surfaces.

MIS-SHAPEN FEET

A mis-shaped foot can be the cause of lameness. And long heels can be the cause of a horse refusing to jump as this causes the pedal bone to tilt upwards pushing its tip into the sole making it painful when a horse lands over a fence.

Racehorses are invariably cold shod, mainly because it is a quicker process and therefore less expensive, so be careful when your ex-racehorse is hot shod for the first time as he may be alarmed by the steam!

Going Barefoot

Going barefoot with a thoroughbred depends on the strength and condition of the individual's horn. By changing to a more suitable diet and with good general foot management, many thoroughbreds have successfully adopted the barefoot way of life.

Before electing to go barefoot with your horse you should consult with your farrier (and possibly your veterinary surgeon also) as foot structure has to be taken into account, as does a horse's basic conformation. After having had shoes for a period of time, the digital cushion actually shrinks because the hoof mechanism doesn't operate as effectively as it does without shoes. When shoes are removed, a horse will feel very tender because the digital cushion isn't thick and strong enough to support the coffin bone. The transition to barefoot is a time-consuming exercise and much attention is required to hoof conditioning over a period of up to a year – but ultimately it is, of course, the most natural thing in the world.

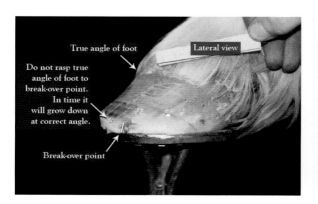
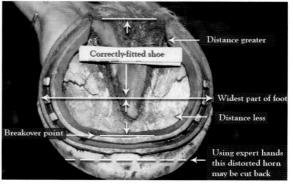

Figs 4.16 and 4.17   A correctly fitted Natural Balance shoe. (Photograph courtesy of Cecil Swan)

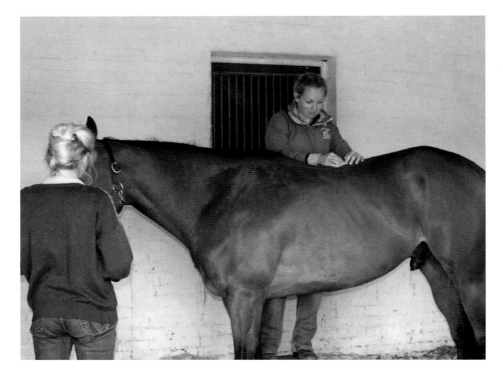

Fig. 4.18 Chiropractor Georgina Sim is a regular visitor to our yard, addressing the numerous issues that routinely crop up or come to light prior to and during retraining.

Natural Balance Shoeing

This type of shoeing used to be called 'square toe shoeing': when the horse is in motion, breakover is sooner, changing the timing and the flight pattern of the hoof (as a stride is taken). Thus Natural Balance shoes shorten the breakover point, bringing it more towards the centre of the foot, so this improves the horse's way of going as it is more in line with what nature intended.

The quicker the breakover, the less stretching of the tendons, which is good for horses with tendon problems. And squaring the toe also reduces the stretch on tendons and muscles, which is of great benefit to the performance horse, whilst long toes behind can be the cause of over-reach injuries as well as back, pelvic and hock issues.

Natural Balance shoeing can therefore be the answer for the seemingly problematic feet of the thoroughbred. A Natural Balance shoe basically sits back off the toe, leaving an area of hoof with no shoe, creating a breakover point that is further back. With a traditionally fitted shoe the breakover point is effectively the tip of the shoe.

ALTERNATIVE THERAPIES

Chiropractic assessment and treatment play a very important part in a horse's health in ascertaining, treating and then maintaining the spinal column. A checkover from an equine chiropractor is particularly helpful to rule out, or establish the presence of (and so treat), any sore spots prior to retraining work commencing. As a chiropractor records each visit, this 'service record' can be helpful at a later stage should a physical issue come to light.

It is recommended that a horse has a chiropractic check twice a year, and it may be that he also needs physiotherapy; moreover, other 'alternative' therapies can play a positive role in keeping your horse in optimum health. There is a whole range of massage therapies that come under the head of 'equine bodywork', such as TTouch/ TTEAM, Equine Touch, acupuncture, Bowen, reiki and shiatsu.

You should seek proper advice from recognized practitioners to establish whether such a therapy would be of benefit to your horse. They all assess muscle tone, noting asymmetry and abnormalities in the superficial layer of muscles. Such therapies can also determine which side of the horse's body is the dominant side; if one side is particularly dominant, that side's hind leg is working harder and this can lead to locomotory disorders if not corrected.

Magnetic therapy is very popular as it is non-invasive and pain free; it is proven to relieve pain, ease stiffness and help promote the healing process by removing inflammation and restoring circulation by improving blood flow and supplies of oxygen to the site of an injury. Activo-Med rugs are proving very popular in professional circles as magnetic therapy also promotes relaxation.

Massage therapy has been used on horses for centuries and provides the benefit of improved length and quality of the stride, increased circulation (reduction of swellings), improved joint mobility, relief of muscular tension, stiffness and spasms, improvement to muscle tone, stamina and performance, aiding the healing process and boosting venous and lymphatic drainage as well as the release of toxins. Massage also releases tension thereby promoting relaxation. Massage can be done by a therapist or by using pieces of equipment enabling a horse to have physiotherapy at a time of day to suit his work and management routine. Regular use

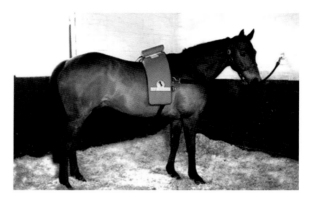

Fig. 4.19   Horses soon become accustomed to the Equissage system. As with anything new, a carefully managed introduction is all that is required.

of Equissage, for example, provides all the benefits of hands-on therapy.

We have found that regular use of Equissage eliminates stiffness and swellings, especially in horses undergoing early training and backing as their bodies adjust to work and weight. Its use is also invaluable in our work with horses out of training as these horses are, effectively, no different to young horses except there is often a known physical issue to be worked through. Equissage is also of great benefit to horses suffering from muscular tensions or dysfunctions, respiratory conditions, leg injuries and haematomas; the cycloidal massaging (horizontal, vertical and circular motions all at the same time) improves the circulation, and hence venous and lymphatic drainage, aiding joint mobility and generally helping with bodily flexibility and suppleness. The horses evidently enjoy the relaxing yet stimulating effects.

There is other massage equipment available in the form of an Equilibrium Pad or a Cyclossage 'head to tail' rug. Although we are not familiar with them, both have considerable amounts of very positive feedback and many satisfied customers.

5 The First Few Days

The following information is a guide to managing the arrival of your ex-racehorse, and his first days in your care. The situation may well be as stressful for you as is it for your horse, as you do your best to help him settle in to his new surroundings; but how you manage him at this time is crucial to his future happiness and your relationship together.

Every horse is different, so there are no hard and fast rules: suffice to say, patience is a virtue. Watch your horse closely and he will tell you all.

Whilst you may intend him to have a period of rest and relaxation (usually two to three months is recommended) before starting his retraining, some horses actually get bored being out in the field all day, and want something to do; leaving them out in fact stresses them more than coming back into a simple yard routine of some sort.

We have worked with horses that have come straight out of racing and which haven't had a period of turnout for a particular reason, and have successfully introduced them to their new training straightaway without any problems. However, this is not something we would recommend as the norm, particularly if you have no previous experience of retraining a racehorse.

WHEN YOUR RACEHORSE ARRIVES

Your horse has arrived, and much as the temptation may be to take him for a walk to show him his new home, the moment he steps off the lorry is not the best time. Make sure that his stable is ready before he arrives, suitably

Figs 5.1 and 5.2   It is impossible to say how long it will be before your racehorse becomes a riding horse. Much depends on the nature and temperament of the individual as well as the environment you are bringing him into. (Photographs: left courtesy of John Pike, Racing Images; right – unknown)

Fig. 5.3 For the horse that gets bored with full-time turnout, a few hours a day in a smaller paddock with a friend can be just as beneficial.

bedded, with fresh water and some hay or haylage. Try to arrange an arrival time when the yard is not too busy or noisy – thus preferably without barking dogs, squealing children, delivery vehicles coming and going. Arrival after dark is not recommended in a strange yard.

Take your horse straight to his box, show him where the water and forage is, and then just leave him be; watch from a distance to see if he has a roll (which is a good sign) and stales (a very important sign). Also make sure that there is a companion horse in the stable next door, preferably a laid-back character, which won't react when a new horse arrives.

Even if it is a cool day, let the horse have a roll before you put a rug on, as he may well 'break out' if he is anxious. Try not to keep bobbing in and out of the stable for the first few hours: understandably you want to comfort him, but for the horse that is a little anxious it is usually best to leave him alone to settle quietly in his own time.

If after a while he is still rushing around the box, tie him up with a haynet; this will help him settle, as being tied in his box is something he is

used to from his racing yard routine, and strangely enough, will provide some comfort.

The following day you can begin to get to know each other, and the horse to familiarize himself with his new surroundings.

When he arrives at his new home, a horse is quite likely to call out in his attempts to seek

Fig. 5.4 However settled he seems after a couple of hours or so, don't be tempted to take your new horse out for a walk; better to let him continue to relax for the rest of the day.

security and comfort, as well as trying to establish if he hears anything familiar. It can be upsetting to hear a horse constantly whinnying, but usually after a couple of hours this ceases. However, it can sometimes last for a few days, and is often coupled with the horse not eating properly and possibly also box-walking. Again, avoid 'pestering' a horse that is clearly fretful; by all means give him a short groom, as that will be something familiar to him and is the starting point for the building of your relationship, otherwise let him settle in his own time, which he will do eventually.

Only give him very small hard feeds to begin with; don't overface him with new, unfamiliar feedstuffs, otherwise you may put him off eating altogether for a while.

THE FIRST WALK OUT

For your first walk out, remember that at this point the horse is an unknown quantity to you, just as you are to him: you will be as apprehensive as each other. For safety, put a bridle on with a three-way coupling attached to the bit/noseband and a lunge line, as you need to be prepared for excitable behaviour. A standard-length leadrope can soon be pulled out of the hand if he rears up unexpectedly.

Much as you may be disinclined to use a bridle, certainly don't be tempted to try out your new training halter for the first time, either. Horses must be given the chance to learn how a training halter works, and if a horse suddenly feels pressure on his poll in a way that he isn't used to, he may be very upset and react badly. Initially keep to what he is used to.

Keep your first walk to just a few minutes, and try and do this when the yard is at its quietest. And although your horse may seem perfectly settled for that first walk, it is best to remain in a 'safe' area – so for example avoid walking past fields with other horses in.

The thoroughbred usually has a brisk walk compared to other breeds, so let him walk out as he is used to doing: this is not the time to try and train him. If, however, he should get rather too forwards, or tries to drag you off in another direction, then stop, push him backwards for a few steps, and then walk on. The lads in racing yards are well used to handling fit thoroughbreds, and usually make no attempt to stop jig-jogging and sidling, as the horses are in the yard to be race-trained, not taught social skills. So provided he doesn't drag you all over the place, make allowances for a few days; thereafter you can begin to correct things.

THE FIRST TURNOUT

Turning the ex-racehorse out for the first time can be a fraught experience, though more for those watching! Ideally you don't want him rushing about at racing speed, otherwise he is likely to damage himself (or aggravate an injury), and will just increase his stress levels and take longer to settle. Therefore turn him out in a small paddock, rather than the ten acres which is your normal turnout; the restricted space will discourage him from too much frantic rushing about, and will prevent him from building up too much speed.

Whilst you cannot always guarantee the best footing, try at least to remove any stones that may be evident. Make sure the fencing is secure and of a reasonable height; don't rely on electric fence tape unless the horse is familiar with it, otherwise he may well just go charging through it, not only getting loose, but possibly damaging himself at the same time.

It makes good sense to use some protective boots for the first few days, especially if your horse has recently recovered, or is recovering, from a leg injury. Turning him out in a headcollar is also good practice, just in case he needs to be caught quickly.

Fig. 5.5 If you are unhappy about a larger companion, then a small pony makes an ideal pal in the field. Should there be kicking, a small pony is less likely to do as much harm as a larger horse.

If possible, turn him out with a companion that is usually calm and unflustered; ideally this should be the horse stabled next to him, so there is already a degree of familiarity. It should most definitely not be a horse that is known to be bossy or grumpy in the field, otherwise your horse may run the risk of getting himself hurt. Remember that he may not be used to interacting, or know how the pecking order works. Obviously at some point he will need to learn, but he can do without his first turnout experience being a painful one, literally.

There is bound to be squealing and snorting, and bucking and kicking, but unless they clearly show no sign of settling down, it is best to let the two horses sort things out for themselves. If you are particularly concerned about how the horse may react, a small amount of sedative would be the best course of action.

Don't leave your horse out for hours – the length of turnout should be gradually built up, not only to allow his digestive system time to adjust to the intake of grass, but also so that he is not too overwhelmed. A long turnout time is not normal practice for the racehorse, so this is another change to his lifestyle. For the first turnout half an hour may well be enough.

Some horses will adapt very quickly and it will take only a few days to build up to your horse having several hours, or even the whole day out. Others will take longer to adjust. Use general calmness, attitude and weight gain as a guide to how settled the horse is becoming.

Be sure your horse knows where the water trough is. Also, he may be worried by the self-fillers that invariably start gushing the moment the float moves, so you may need to provide water in a separate bucket until he is brave enough to tackle the trough!

MOVING TO A LARGER TURNOUT GROUP

Introducing a new horse to an established group can cause some excitement. The stranger will naturally be wary and unsure, whilst the group will be curious and keen to make sure the newcomer knows his place; even a normally placid horse may present a challenge to the new arrival. Equate the situation with a family moving to a new area: the children have to forge new friendships by being accepted into already formed groups.

Before turning your horse out in a larger group make sure he has bonded well with his initial companion. The two of them can then be turned out in the group, and at least your horse will have a friend to turn to if he is shunned by the others for a while. Ideally your horse should be introduced to the larger field with his trusty companion but without the others horses being in there, so that he can familiarize himself with the change of surroundings in his own time.

On the day you decide to go for group turnout, put your horse and his friend in the field first, then add the others. This means that your horse will see the field as his, so he will feel more confident when the others come in. More often than not it is the stranger that causes confrontation because he lacks respect for his fellows and doesn't know the rules. Again there is likely to be kicking and squealing, but the situation should settle down reasonably quickly.

Many people report that their horse is 'fence walking', and this is as distressing to witness as it is for the horse himself. A horse will do this for various reasons: usually when he is turned out alone; a gelding will often do this when there are mares nearby; if he does this whilst with another or in a group, he is clearly not happy and is stressing, and needs to be put with a different horse; if he is not familiar with turnout he is telling you that he is unsure and lacks confidence.

Turn him out with another horse, one that he can feel safe with, so not of a flighty nature. If a companion horse is not an option, then find a sheep or a goat. Otherwise you will need to spend some time sitting in the field for a while to allow your horse the chance to gain confidence in being in the great outdoors.

INTRODUCING OVERNIGHT TURNOUT

Turning your ex-racehorse out overnight for the first time should again be done with his trusty

Fig. 5.6 Left to their own devices, horses often settle much quicker than might be expected once they've introduced themselves to each other.

friend. Choose a time when the weather conditions are favourable – a dry night, with no howling winds and no sub-zero temperatures.

As your horse will be used to coming in and being fed, then even if feeding is not really necessary, put a small quantity in his feed bucket and put some hay/haylage out. This is doing something that he is familiar with, rather than abandoning him – as he might consider – without any tea!

The field should be sheltered, and preferably with a field shelter, because, however warm it feels to us, your horse – who has never had a night out under the stars – will be more susceptible to feeling the drop in temperature. If he is used to having a rug on, then leave it on. However, don't introduce a turnout rug for the first time on the first night out.

HOW TO PROGRESS

How the next few weeks or months turn out is entirely dependent on whether the horse you have rehomed needs time to recover from an injury, or just needs a let-down period to relax tired muscles and gain condition. As long as the horse is sound, there is no reason why he can't be walked out in hand. Otherwise spend time grooming him, or just be with him; use this time to get to know every inch of him – not just the lumps and bumps on his body, but his sensitive spots, his ticklish spots, his temperament and character.

You may not want to give the horse weeks out without handling, in which case a little ground training can commence.

He may have already had a let-down period so if he is a sensible character then some gentle hacking is a great way to get to know each other.

If he does prove to be excitable, throws his head about, or doesn't seem to understand the braking system too well, and you wisely decide that some schooling is the order of the day first, then that is fine.

Read the situation for yourself, how you feel – not how others tell you and certainly don't be cajoled into doing something that you are not comfortable with.

Work at the pace you are happy with, and seek the advice of someone well versed in reschooling the thoroughbred – there are plenty of people who will sit on the fence and tell you what you should do, but can't show you how to do it!

ABOVE: *Fig. 5.7 It doesn't matter whether you elect to compete or not; the main thing is that you and your horse have fun. (Photograph courtesy of Tik Saunders)*

LEFT: *Fig. 5.8 Spending time with your horse doesn't always have to be about working him or grooming him. We hear so much about spending 'quality time' with our loved ones and families – your horse is no different.*

6 Fitting New Tack

Having settled your horse into his new home and ensured that he is as physically fit as possible, the next step is to fit suitable tack so that the retraining programme can begin.

BITS AND BITTING

For the horse that has been in racing, getting him happily bitted and willing to drop his head, let alone seek a contact, is one of the biggest challenges facing the new owner. When you first get on and pick up the reins, invariably you meet resistance – poked out nose, tossing head stuck in the air – because he has no idea how to respond.

When riding work, jockeys often have to take a very firm hold in order to remain in control, so the horse you rehome can seem hard and unresponsive in the mouth; however, these horses can also be very sensitive in the mouth, which will invariably have suffered some bruising. Most racehorses are raced in a single-jointed snaffle, which has a nutcracker action. These bits can easily pinch the tongue, bruise the roof of the mouth, as well as chafe the corners of the mouth; these are occupational hazards of racing and can be hard to avoid, particularly if a horse 'runs a bit free' with its head up.

There is a huge array of bits on the market today, and deciding just which one is right for your horse is a difficult task. Moreover the bit that is most suitable in the early stages of retraining doesn't necessarily remain so as training progresses, and a horse will often be

transitioned through several bits before the 'right' one is found. Some people think that periodically changing the bit will keep the horse responsive and light in the hand; however, whilst this can be a helpful, some horses can become quite upset by a change, so if he is generally comfortable with the bit you are using, why risk upsetting him?

Although it is acceptable to experiment with different bits, before doing so, be clear as to the reasoning behind its choice and be sure that you are competent enough to use it (e.g. not relying on the hands to retain balance). However, don't change bits by the day; a horse must be given the chance to adjust to the action of a new bit, especially if it is totally different to that which he has been used to, e.g. switching from a double-jointed bit to a combination bit.

Fig. 6.1 This bit from Hilary Vernon (Informed Bitting) is light, beautifully balanced and makes a perfect curve in the mouth. Once in the mouth, the broader side of lozenge lays flat on the tongue.

Bit Evasion

Evasions are too often 'fixed' by the addition of a flash or dropped noseband when the horse is simply trying to communicate his discomfort or dislike of a bit. This may be because it is too small, is incorrectly fitted, doesn't suit the conformation of the horse's mouth, or has an action that doesn't suit him. Evasions include head tossing, mouth opening, drawing the tongue back, poking the tongue out, leaning, hollowing, inverting, high head carriage, refusing to going forwards, running backwards and even bolting.

More subtle signs – such as lack of salivation, or incorrect muscle build-up – may be missed by the less experienced rider, and they may not pick up changes as to how their horse feels down the rein, how he is carrying his head, and in particular not coming down on to the bit correctly. Horses can give their riders the impression that they are rounding correctly, when in fact they are not. Moreover a strong horse can actually be leaning, and a horse that leans isn't using his back. Also, such a horse isn't necessarily strong in the mouth, but is using his neck and shoulder strength against the rider – often an evasion to using his back.

A horse may evade the bit to escape unsympathetic hands.

Mouth Conformation

Before making a decision on which bit to use, it is important to consider the conformation of your horse's mouth, as this is the primary influence on bit choice. You should observe the following points:

The bars: The gap on each side of the mouth between the front and back teeth comprising tissue-covered, sensitive cartilage where the bit lies. Can be broad, flat or v-shaped, so this area is influential in how a bit fits and the resultant reaction to its action.

Fig. 6.2 Assess your horse's tongue thickness by gently parting the lips; if the tongue bulges between the teeth, the horse has a thicker tongue.

The tongue: Thicker bits are deemed to be milder due to their greater bearing surface, but horses with a relatively large tongue and/or quite small mouth can't cope with a thicker mouthpiece. With a thicker tongue, the bit comes into contact with the bars much later than in the case of a thinner tongue, therefore influencing bit action. Also, in order to swallow, the horse draws his tongue up to the palate so a bit that presses too sharply onto the tongue restricts this movement therefore inhibiting swallowing; if a horse isn't swallowing, he isn't salivating and if he isn't salivating, he is not relaxed generally, but certainly not through the jaw (and so isn't flexing properly at the poll).

The palate: The roof of the mouth. It is important to know palate height, because if this is shallow, there is less space to accommodate the tongue and so less room for the bit.

Mouth corners/lips: An extremely sensitive area: sustained damage – from a bit being too high, the rider see-sawing with the hands, or the horse resisting (for whatever reason) – results in a loss of that sensitivity.

Width: Mouth width can be deceptive and it is best to use a bit measure to assess the bit size

Fig. 6.3 *In this horse, the lower jaw is perfectly formed, but the upper jaw has grown too long. In such cases, the mullen mouth is the bit of choice, not only to facilitate easier insertion and removal of the bit, but also in regard to comfort to provide more tongue room as the palate is lower.*

you need. A bit should not be so small that it presses against the sides of the mouth/face, nor so wide that it hangs out at the sides.

Length: Take the length of the horse's mouth into account when considering a bit with a lever action – for example when dressage or show horses move up to a double bridle.

The jaw: An overshot or undershot jaw can affect how the bit sits in the mouth and may present a bitting issue.

Teeth: Teeth that have grown inwards will affect the amount of mouth space available for a bit and its action; outwards will affect comfort, as sharp edges can cut into the side of the mouth.

Choosing a Bit

The bit is a directional piece of equipment; it must be correctly shaped and fit properly (whether or not the reins are taken up) so that is an effective communication tool. However mild, any bit can cause discomfort if incorrectly

fitted (e.g. too high in the mouth, too small, doesn't suit mouth conformation) especially if the hands behind it are harsh and unyielding. Don't be misled into thinking that just because you now own an ex-racehorse, you need a stronger bit. Far from it: a milder bit is required in conjunction with retraining. Of course you need to be able to steer and stop, but remember that your horse will have no comprehension of the aids as does the riding horse – it is your task to teach him, so don't be tempted to use something stronger until the basic aids are in place!

The range of bits available is extensive, with straight, curved, single- or double-jointed mouthpieces, all with different cheek styles, and you may find it difficult to decide what is best for you and your horse. If you are experiencing any particular issues once other possible contributory factors – teeth, sore back, tightness in the muscles – have been eliminated, then we recommend seeking the advice of a bitting clinician.

A bit works hand-in-hand with correct, sympathetic training and accurate riding; rider ability and experience are very influential factors when choosing a bit.

Fig. 6.4 *Lozenge bits abound in their variations (design and shape of the lozenge, shape of joints, length and shape of the bit arms), but are all very influential in the action of the bit in the mouth, particularly on the tongue.*

Mouthpieces

Mouthpieces vary in both shape and thickness and come in a variety of materials, but basically there are two types: straight – a solid bar which can be straight, exerting a direct action on the tongue, bars and lips or slightly curved, which lessens the pressure on the tongue; and jointed – single- or double-jointed. Double-jointed bits are often referred to as 'lozenge' bits. The French link is considered to have a mild action. However, if a horse isn't particularly still in his head carriage or the rider isn't quiet with the hands, the joints will slide from side to side causing bruising. Also the combined length of the link and joints may prove to be too long for the horse with a narrow mouth. Laying flat on the tongue, the link has contact with a larger area than many other lozenge bits, which some horses don't like.

Cheek Style

Apart from the actual mouthpiece, cheek style is also influential. Cheeks help to keep the bit stable in the mouth so the mouthpiece doesn't slide from side to side, providing the bit isn't too big; this is particularly useful with horses that are not very still in their headcarriage, otherwise there would be considerable friction on the tongue and bars as the bit slides around.

Loose-ring cheeks: The mouthpiece moves on the cheek ring; it more readily follows the angle of the tongue as the horse's outline alters, therefore remaining comfortable, encouraging mouthing, but discouraging blocking and leaning. Signalling is less clear and rein contact may be delaying his responses to rein aids.

Eggbutt cheeks: The mouthpiece is fixed to the cheek rings so there is no movement, giving the horse a more stable feel in its mouth. It is particularly useful for the horse that is tentative about seeking a contact. The fixed cheek assists with the turning signals.

D-ring cheeks: Fixed cheeks that lie even flatter against the face than the eggbutt cheeks; they assist in turning because the aid is clearer.

Fig. 6.5   Loose ring cheeks.

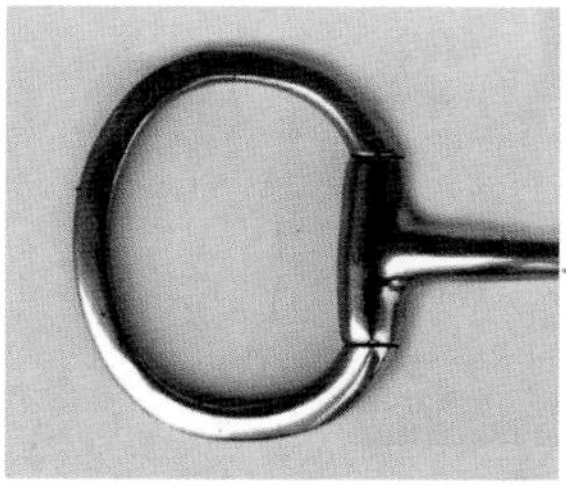

Fig. 6.6 Eggbutt cheeks.

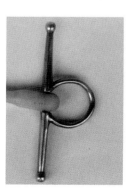

Fig. 6.7 Full cheeks.

Fig. 6.8 D-rings.

Fig. 6.9 Baucher/ hanging cheek.

Full cheeks: Help in turning, especially with horses that tend to drift or hang into corners. The long cheek helps keep the bit stable as the mouthpiece hardly moves, preventing friction. A variation is the fulmer cheek where the bit rings are loose, so while there is help with the turning aid the actual mouthpiece can move.

Baucher/hanging cheeks: The action of these cheeks has the effect of lifting the mouthpiece, thereby reducing pressure on the tongue and bars. It also creates a mild pressure to the poll, which can encourage some horses to lower their heads and work in a more rounded outline, but its real effectiveness lies in the reduction of the weight of the bit on the tongue and increased stability in the mouth.

Bit Material

The material that bits are made from also provides multiple choice these days.

Rubber: Rubber bits tend to be a little too thick for many horses, and can be readily damaged if the horse chews at it. These bits give a less direct directional cue, so their use is somewhat limited.

Plastic: Thickness can vary, as can the degree of flexibility. While there are horses that are happy with these bits, some riders consider they can't get enough 'feel' for more advanced work.

Vulcanite: A very hard plastic so these bits have virtually no flexibility; they also tend to be too thick for the thoroughbred mouth.

Sweet iron: Horses generally mouth well with sweet iron, as it oxidizes with use and produces a sweet taste; the fact that the bits go rusty is off-putting to some people.

Stainless steel: The most commonly used metal, but can create a dry mouth as it is tasteless and

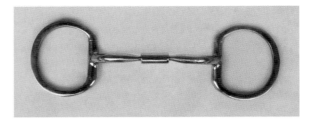

Fig. 6.10 The Myler MB02 is a super bit for encouraging a horse to confidently seek the contact.

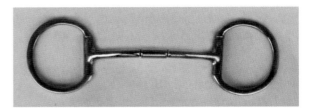

Fig. 6.11 The traditional mullen only has a slight curve to the mouthpiece.

Fig. 6.12 A fleshy-mouthed horse will benefit from a mullen with a more slender mouthpiece and with a more forward curve, as designed by Hilary Vernon (Informed Bitting).

feels cold. However, many trainers consider that if the horse is comfortably bitted and working through the back then he will salivate and relax his lower jaw anyway, hence allowing correct poll flexion.

Copper/copper alloys: These metals are warmer in the mouth, encouraging salivation and bit acceptance.

Bitting Suggestions

Everyone has their own preferences as to what they consider is the most suitable bit to use.

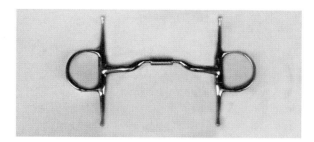

Fig. 6.13   This bit, the Myler MB04, encourages the horse to relax at the poll by virtue of the slight port which reduces pressure on the tongue. As it works off the lips and bars too it is good for helping to create lateral bend. It also has independent sideways movement.

Fig. 6.14   Neue Schule produce a super Waterford with slimmer, smoother links than often seen and has a 'shelf' for the lips to rest on, which prevents rubbing.

Fig. 6.15   The 'Team Up' from Neue Schule is a super little bit for introducing the concept of a lozenge bit.

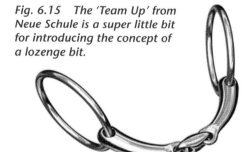

Fig. 6.16 The Myler Combination bit – a valuable piece of equipment in any tackroom.

However, initially we recommend starting retraining work with one of the bits detailed below. But as with anything equine, the ultimate choice lies with the horse, so let him decide – after all, he is the one who has to carry and respond to the bit.

A wide-barrelled bit: A straight bar creates greater pressure on the tongue and less on the bars; however, a central barrel (often coupled with a slight curvature to the bit arm) disperses the pressure over a greater area of the tongue, but the central barrel restricts how much the bit can close, eliminating too much pressure being placed on the sides of the tongue, and exerts a milder pressure to the bars.

A mullen mouth: A shaped/curved mouthpiece relieves tongue pressure to a

certain degree so is deemed to be milder, but creates more pressure on the bars, giving a better directional cue. Such design helps to eliminate the horse getting behind the bit or inverting as well as encouraging him to be stiller in the mouth as the curve goes with the tongue not against it. It discourages heaviness in the hand and as there is no 'closing' effect, it can encourage the bit-shy horse to take the bit. These bits are often regarded as being best suited for a horse that is already at a certain stage of its training, but remember you are working with an ex-racehorse not the perfect, unspoilt young horse.

A slight port: The small upward curve provides more room for the tongue, and most thoroughbreds respond well to some tongue relief.

BITTING THE EX-RACEHORSE
BY HILARY VERNON, BITTING CLINICIAN

I have over the years been able to work with racehorses in training as well as racehorses that are being re-trained, so have seen quite a few aspects of the industry. As a general rule, and I can only go by what I have seen, the young racehorse is normally put in a thick mouth, loose ring, single-jointed snaffle which is very thick for a thoroughbred mouth to hold easily, and there is usually very little schooling done (if indeed any) for the acceptance of contact.

The horses I have seen have been ridden to the end of the rein in walk and trot normally in convoy, and then as they go forward into canter and gallop they are accustomed to pulling forwards into a strong contact. This is the way they are trained and ridden so they think this is normal. So when we come to re-train them for another element of equestrianism we have to go back to basics. And in particular this involves teaching them to carry a bit without wanting to avoid it, and to learn to yield so that they learn to accept and soften to a contact.

Time, patience and repetition are the key to training and re-training, coupled with good physical and mental horse management. Choosing the most comfortable equipment that fits well is crucial to encourage the horse to relax into what is required rather than resist.

As far as a new bit goes, several things need to be taken into consideration; conformation is very important. Thoroughbreds, even the larger ones, have elegant faces and bone structure, and bits should fit the conformation of the mouth and give the rider the ability to signal the horse clearly and humanely. They frequently have a very sensitive tongue, and can avoid contact with the centre of the bit by lifting the lower part of the tongue high into the upper part of the mouth so that the tongue makes as little contact with the bit as possible. From a contact and signalling point of view this makes re-training very difficult, as the tongue is the only part of the inside of the mouth that is the least likely for us to damage and the part that allows for the easiest signal and reward. Also if the tongue is continually lifted the mouth is open and the jaw gapes, which overworks the jaw joint and the horse spends most of its time working the mouth and avoiding the pressure of the bit.

Breaking bits with keys, in my opinion, do not start re-training in the correct way. If you encourage a young horse or a horse that you are re-training to work and fuss with the bit in its mouth and play with it, we are probably giving it the wrong signals at the start of its training.

You simply want a young horse to accept a bit in its mouth without any fuss, and in the early stages of training to hold the bit comfortably in the mouth, come to the end of the rein and learn to balance itself while carrying a rider and obey instruction without anxiety. So if we train the horse in these early stages and lead it to believe it is an everyday occurrence to flip the head and fuss with the bit, but then a month or two down the line

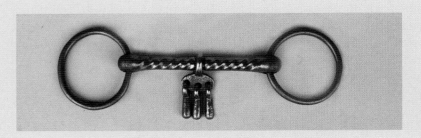

Fig. 6.17 A key bit which has traditionally been viewed as the bit to start the mouthing process.

when we are riding the horse onwards in its training will we not regard this as a nuisance or evasion and be going down the route of restrictive nosebands to close the mouth over the problem we have created?

Mouthpieces should allow for tongue room and follow the conformation of the inside of the mouth. Single-jointed mouthpieces can really pinch and do not give much release of pressure, so round, flat or half lozenge and barrel mouthpieces are very suitable if you are going to go down the jointed mouthpiece route; and if you feel the horse is not responding well to a jointed or collapsing mouthpiece, then forward-curved mullen, Hartwell and medium-ported mouthpieces allow for more tongue room without the horse being able to feel any joints, or a mouthpiece that collapses around the tongue and lower jaw.

Slim mouthpieces have in the past been thought to be severe, but the truth is that the horse's tongue is designed to fit its mouth perfectly, and despite thousands of years of domestication it has not developed a groove for us to place the bit in! Therefore anything placed in the mouth is sandwiched between the top of the tongue and the roof of the mouth. So in most cases a slim bit with a forward curve fits the inside conformation of the horse's mouth much better than a thick one that bears no resemblance to the round shape of the tongue.

For strong horses, re-training in a controlled environment is much better than going down the restrictive noseband and severe bit route. But if you feel that you do not have as much control as you would like, then choosing bits with a small amount of leverage and transferring some pressure on to the jaw with a leather jaw strap is a humane way of gaining just a little more signalling ability. Butterfly Hartwells, medium ported Uxeters and slotted-cheek Myler snaffles used with a leather curb make a good choice.

A lozenge: Horses that are not happy with the 'fixed' mouthpiece of a straight-bar bit are often more comfortable in a lozenge. On a loose ring cheek we particularly like the 'Team Up' lozenge bit (Neue Schule) as the curved arms and design of the lozenge make this a very comfortable bit with even weight distribution in the mouth. There is no one particular pressure point, making this an ideal introductory and general purpose bit, especially for the horse that is fussy in the mouth and reluctant to take the bit forward. However, other styles of lozenge bit do work well, especially when on a baucher cheek.

Waterford: Although these bits look severe because they resemble a chain, they are in fact mild as there is no nutcracker action. The mouthpiece is flexible, which encourages jaw relaxation and hence mouthing (salivation), but discourages leaning, helping the horse to learn to carry himself and use his hindquarters. It can also assist in controlling horses prone to getting strong in the hand. It is particularly effective with baucher or full cheeks.

Myler combination: Although sinister-looking, this is one of the kindest bits due to the way pressure is dispersed over the poll, nose, jaw, tongue and the bars (of the mouth) all at the same time; and likewise, when the horse responds, the pressure is released from these five areas simultaneously – thus horses learn about the 'pressure and release' concept. It gives a stable feel in the horse's mouth, and is good for horses that are sensitive and finicky.

The Myler combination should be carefully introduced, and it is recommended that specific advice is sought with regard to this bit.

Single-jointed bit: Not recommended for initial re-education primarily because of its head-raising effect (the majority of ex-racehorses already carry their heads too high). When a contact is taken, the mouthpiece slides forward closing the bit, which then squeezes the tongue

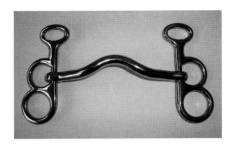

TOP RIGHT: *Fig. 6.19* The action of this Uxeter bit is milder than a pelham due to the lack of shank length.

TOP LEFT: *Fig. 6.18* Butterfly Hartwell.

RIGHT: *Fig. 6.20* The slotted-cheek bit can also have a curb chain fitted to afford greater control and signalling ability.

and lifts the central joint up to the extent that it can bruise the palate. If the horse isn't in the correct outline or the rider isn't quick to release the rein when the horse responds, the joint can readily bruise or at least rub on the palate. And for the rider that has the habit of lifting one hand in an attempt to correct head tilt, crookedness or some other evasion, this just drives the joint into the tongue creating discomfort.

Butterfly Hartwell: With butterfly cheeks there are two rein options: with the reins fitted to the top ring the curb is not activated; fitted to the lower ring the curb is activated, which gives a much clearer signal to the horse to lower his head, and affords greater control. Ideal for soft-mouthed horses that require more tongue room as the mouthpiece not only has a small port but also a forward curve. Use of a leather curb is recommended rather than the traditional chain. This bit suits horses that back off the contact, but not those that lean.

Uxeter (slotted Kimblewick): Unlike the traditional Kimblewick, the cheeks of this bit

have rein slots to vary the amount of pressure exerted on the poll: the lower the slot used, the more pressure that is exerted. The low-ported mouthpiece gives a little more tongue room; the bit cannot collapse on to the bars.

Slotted-cheek Mylers: For clearer signalling or if your horse is too forward-going, you can attach the reins into the slots in the bit rings to create a more consistent and clearer contact; this keeps the bit stiller in the mouth – useful for a horse that tends to head-toss – and exerts a slight poll pressure.

The Myler bitting range is extensive and there are variable cheek styles to accompany the various mouthpiece designs.

Going Bitless

Many bitting issues can be resolved by using no bit at all; the hackamore is the best known of the bitless options in the UK and Europe. Hackamores and bitless bridles work very well

Figs 6.21 and 6.22 The Dr Cook Bitless Bridle (™) is available in both English (left) and Western (right) versions. (Photographs by kind permission of Dr Robert Cook, The Bitless Bridle™)

Browband cannot ride up and scrunch delicate ears due to design of headpiece

Softly padded headpiece

Noseband padded for additional comfort

Fig. 6.23 A perfectly fitted bridle – except that the bit is a fraction large for this horse. While we elect to use the Barnsby Padded Head Comfort bridles as the shape and fit are superb, there are numerous brands on the market, so it is a matter of personal choice.

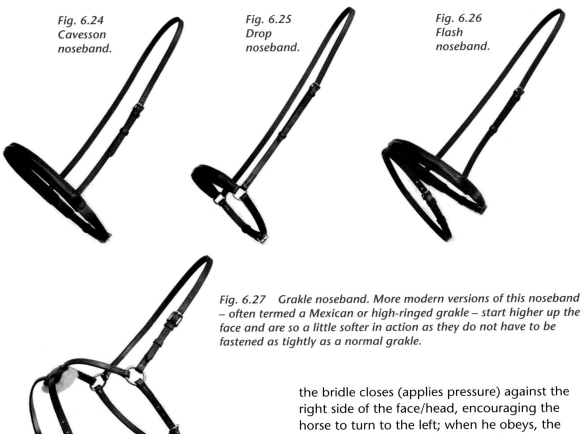

*Fig. 6.24
Cavesson
noseband.*

*Fig. 6.25
Drop
noseband.*

*Fig. 6.26
Flash
noseband.*

Fig. 6.27   Grakle noseband. More modern versions of this noseband – often termed a Mexican or high-ringed grakle – start higher up the face and are so a little softer in action as they do not have to be fastened as tightly as a normal grakle.

and can be the right option for some horses; they also offer an effective braking system. However, the various bitless options require the rider to have very good hands and be effective with the leg, seat and weight aids, i.e. have an independent seat. The true bitless bridle (the Dr Cook™) allows the less experienced to ride their horse without a bit as it is very forgiving, even when the rider may not have proper control of their hands. It applies pressure which is distributed over the nose, under the chin, over the poll and along the side of the face. For example, when the rider takes up the left rein,

the bridle closes (applies pressure) against the right side of the face/head, encouraging the horse to turn to the left; when he obeys, the pressure is released, which is his 'reward'. These bridles are also effective in cases of headshaking and in all manner of 'napping' problems.

A horse should be introduced to this concept quietly over the course of a few days in a safe environment.

FITTING THE BRIDLE

The fit of the bridle is also important, but is often given little consideration. For instance, ensure that the browband is long enough to fit comfortably around the base of the ears without pinching or riding up the ears, and avoid using cheekpieces that are too long and so have to be fitted on the highest hole, as again, this can cause the browband to ride up. A padded headpiece alleviates poll pressure.

Nosebands

We prefer to use a plain cavesson. Crank nosebands are a variation of the cavesson but broader across the nose and with padding behind the jaw as they are fastened very tightly compared to the basic cavesson. Such nosebands have no place in racehorse re-education. Similarly nosebands that restrict lower jaw movement should most definitely not be used to mask other problems, although their use may be necessary in the short term for retraining purposes. For example, a horse that habitually gets his tongue over the bit can be re-educated with the help of a flash noseband, in combination with other factors such as a bit change.

Whatever the choice of noseband, ensure that it is fitted correctly as appropriate for its use.

The cavesson noseband: Used for cosmetic purposes, particularly in the show ring to enhance appearance. It has no action in relation to the bit. Not to be confused with the **crank noseband**, favoured in the dressage world as its tightness can discourage a horse from crossing its jaw.

The drop noseband: Helpful with a horse that opens its mouth too much, has a tendency to lean, or is a little 'dead' in the mouth, as pressure is exerted in the curb groove as well as across the nose. Some horses object to them as they do not like the pressure exerted on the nasal bone. If fitted too low and fastened too tightly a drop noseband can restrict a horse's breathing and prevent him from being able to move his tongue to swallow.

The flash noseband: Not designed to put pressure on the nose (hence it is fitted at the same height as a cavesson), but the lip (flash) strap helps to keep the bit up and still in the mouth, which is helpful for a horse that is not settled in the mouth, gets his tongue over the bit, or plays with it.

Note: If the flash strap is fastened too tightly it pulls the cavesson down, thus loosening the flash strap and defeating the object of using it.

The grakle noseband: Helps to prevent a horse crossing its jaw and also to keep the bit in place – in the corners of the mouth. It has to be fastened quite tightly and some horses resent this. It also discourages a horse from running a bit free.

Fig. 6.28 Conformationally thoroughbreds are known for their high withers; some also have a long wither, making a comfortable saddle fit more tricky to achieve. Note the saddle position may not directly sit in line with the girthing area due to the positioning of the scapula.

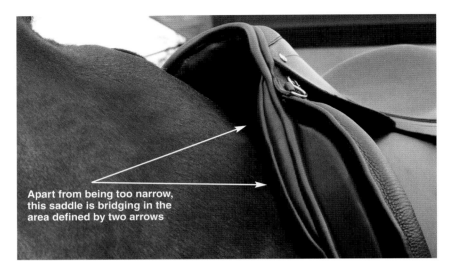

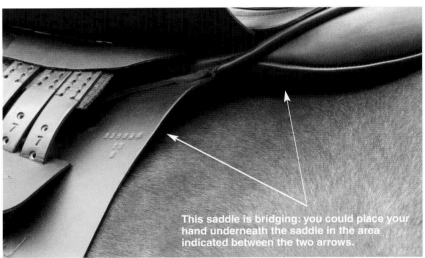

Apart from being too narrow, this saddle is bridging in the area defined by two arrows

This saddle is bridging: you could place your hand underneath the saddle in the area indicated between the two arrows.

Figs 6.29 and 6.30 A correctly fitting saddle is of vital importance to the comfort and performance of your horse.

SADDLES AND SADDLE FIT

The horse that has just arrived will significantly alter in shape in the ensuing months: he will carry more weight and gain a completely different muscle structure to when he was in training. Racehorses are usually loaded with Type I muscle fibres, known for their endurance. After different training, these muscle fibre types are often combined with a higher degree of Type II fibres, which are highly oxygenated but bulkier for shorter bursts of power. Due to these continual changes in muscle structure, you may need several saddle adjustments and even different saddles. The saddle that fits your horse when he first arrives will be very different on him a few months down the line.

In the early days there are several options: you might use a synthetic saddle, or have a leather saddle adjusted as much as possible. Opting to fit a slightly wider saddle and using a combination of thicker numnahs or a riser pad can ensure comfort. However, bear in mind that the latter should only be used with your saddle fitter's advice and for a short term only, as too much thickness under the saddle can cause pressure points due to tightness or poor saddle tree balance. This is a topic that must be discussed openly with your fitter.

A saddle that is alterable in the tree may also be an option. There are several saddles on the market that can be altered at the headplate; financially this is an appealing option, but it is worth thinking that if the front width of the saddle is altered it may mean that the rear gusset height may also need to be altered to maintain optimum saddle balance. Your saddle fitter can advise on which meet these requirements.

Most people do appreciate the requirement of a well fitting saddle. However, the subject is a little more involved than just checking that the saddle doesn't press down on the withers or lose contact on the under panel (bridging: *see* box). Remember that a saddle may seemingly fit well when just sat on the horse's back, but add a girth plus the weight of a rider, and everything can change quite dramatically – and even more so when the horse actually moves; hence it is very important that the saddle fitter can see the horse in motion, where possible. An

ill-fitting saddle not only causes a sore back, possible lameness and behavioural problems, but can inhibit correct muscle development of the back. The saddle that fits correctly stays central and doesn't move whatever the horse's pace, both with and without a rider. So if yours is moving, get it checked! It is always recommended to use the services of a Society of Master Saddlers qualified saddle fitter as saddle fitting is not just a case of adding a bit of flocking to a saddle. The saddle fitter has to consider all of the following.

- The saddle should not be too long for the horse's back. It should extend no further back than the last rib as there is no structure within the skeleton to support the weight of a rider. Significant internal muscular damage can be done if this occurs.
- The saddle has to be the correct width to accommodate the horse's spine: too wide and the saddle will sit down onto the spine itself; too narrow and it will pinch the spine. Thoroughbreds can be misleading and will more often than not taker a wider fit of saddle than you think.
- The cut of the saddle should not restrict the shoulder blade, otherwise the foreleg action, can be impinged and the trapezius muscle may be hindered in developing.

Hence it is important to allow a saddle fitter to check the angle of the points of tree are suitable for the individual. The tree shape should follow the line of the horse's back and be symmetrical so that it carries the rider's weight evenly.

Thoroughbreds often need saddles that are open-headed to allow adequate clearance of the bony structure of the wither area. Many individuals have long withers so this is even more important. The panels of the saddle, i.e. the weight-bearing surfaces, should be as broad as possible so as to distribute weight over a greater area. Being of slimmer build, it is often thought that the thoroughbred doesn't want a

BRIDGING

A saddle that bridges makes contact with the horse only at the points of the tree and at the rear – there is no contact with the horse throughout its middle bearing surface section. This can be illustrated by placing your hand underneath the panel where it and the flap connect. If you run your hand on the under panel from front to back there should be even contact with the skin throughout. If you lose contact this is termed 'bridging'. Significant discomfort is apparent for the horse, and muscle wastage and poor performance are inevitable.

broad panel; in most cases he does. He is now adjusting to the weight of a rider sitting down on his back, so he wants to be as comfortable as possible.

A saddle fitter continually strives to distribute as much weight over the largest surface area possible to enable the muscles to work as effectively as possible. Saddles may need greater/shallower gussets (the underside of the saddle) to achieve an even symmetrically balanced saddle on the horse's back. Often a fit thoroughbred can have a raised spine, so it is important that the saddle fitter takes this into account with the width of the gullet.

And finally of course the saddle has to fit the rider too. Seat size is often a difficult conversation to have with the rider, but is paramount to a horse's comfort. If the seat size is too small for the rider, the weight distributed across the horse's back is more weighted to the rear, which may cause discomfort and poor muscle performance. If the seat is too long for the rider, they will feel unsupported and may alter the weight distribution too. Sometimes the rider is too large for the saddle seat size necessary to fit within the space behind the scapula, and in front of the final rib. At this stage, the saddle fitter may ask the rider if they would like to think about whether it is appropriate to compromise the horse's comfort.

Fig. 6.31 If you have to use two numnahs, make sure they are pulled well up into the gullet. And be mindful that you may have to keep adjusting them during exercise.

Another factor that comes into play, particularly with the thoroughbred, is that of the stirrup bars as these can be a source of aggravation, especially with the 'long-withered' horse. Despite a seemingly superb fit, if for some reason the horse is just not happy, perhaps in rising trot, popping a small fence, etc., the stirrup bars can often be the culprit as, when the rider rises, the bars can exert some additional pressure. So sometimes it is necessary to have them 'opened' slightly away from the tree, if feasible.

Please note: to maintain warranty and safety standards, alterations to saddles should only be done by a Master Saddler.

Numnahs

Thoroughbreds are notoriously sensitive on their backs, especially in the first few months after

Fig. 6.32   Using elasticated girths adds to the comfort of your horse. The one pictured is a Barnsby Humane Girth. With soft padding and subtle shaping, these girths have an 'Equaliser system' – sliding elastic at both ends, which makes them supremely comfortable, especially for the more sensitive horse.

Fig. 6.33   Hero Worship looks quite at peace with the world as he happily trots around; he has no intention of dropping his head.

coming out of training. However well fitting the saddle, using a concussion-absorbing numnah may be beneficial to the horse's comfort. Use a product that will absorb sweat and not irritate sensitive skin.

Avoid using two numnahs, as too much padding can be as bad as not enough. The front of a numnah should fit up into the gullet; if you use two numnahs there won't be room to fit both into the gullet, so the first placed one will invariably sit down on the withers, and during the course of exercise, exert undue pressure.

Girths

The girth must also be comfortable, and for this the horse's confirmation must be considered; for example, some horses haven't enough room behind the elbow for a wider girth, which will rub. This can also happen with a shaped girth if the shaping doesn't lie in the right place for the horse in question. Elasticated girths are best, but preferably at both ends so that the 'pull' is even, otherwise a saddle can be slightly twisted.

TRAINING AIDS

Training aid or gadget? Opinion various enormously depending upon which piece of equipment is being talked about and it's a topic

that divides the equestrian world. In a perfect world there would be no need for any additional aids or 'gadgets' to be employed over and above perhaps a running martingale when out hacking. The racehorse, however, has never been taught the same aids as the riding horse – acceptance of contact, working over the back, engagement and so on – and can be easily confused and seemingly unwilling to co-operate when asked to conform to a new set of rules. Despite your best efforts to communicate with your horse, what if he just does not respond in the desired fashion?

For example, when you commence lunge work, your horse is quite likely to trot around with his head in the air and not take any notice of your requests to drop his head and stretch his neck forwards – in fact he could happily trot around like this for what seems like hours because he doesn't know any different; he has muscles on the underside of his neck to support

NOTE

Before using a training aid, ensure that you are not compromising any physical issues your horse may have; there may be good reason why he can't do what you are asking of him.

him doing this, and he simply doesn't understand your requests. Also your horse may have had an injury that has caused a tightness/stiffness somewhere, which is initially restrictive. However experienced you may be and know exactly how to ask the trained horse to 'drop', you may not have the skills to teach a horse that hasn't a clue what you are requesting.

While his head is up in the air, the horse is certainly not going to learn to use and work his back properly. In such circumstances, it is better to try to show him what you are asking for by employing the assistance of a training aid. A host of people will throw their hands up in absolute horror at this, but as a short-term measure, to help get a horse on the right track some training aids can offer great assistance. Strictly use of a training aid isn't necessary and not in line with classical training; time and correct training are all that is required. But it must be borne in mind that not everyone is suitably skilled in the art of lungeing or long-reining to teach a horse to accept the bit, seek a contact, engage, etc., so temporary use of a training aid can be invaluable.

The training aid argument will always rage on; where is the line between 'vital piece of equipment' and 'training aid' crossed? A flash noseband is seen by some as a training aid as it helps restrict mouth-opening and so disguises an evasion, yet the flash is allowed in dressage. And the double bridle in the wrong hands can readily cause discomfort and distress to the horse.

There is an assortment of training aids on the market, and many of the world's most eminent riders do use certain pieces of additional equipment over and above a lunge line. You should look at all the options available in line with your own groundwork skills, your horse's stage of training, and what you are trying to achieve, and then seek professional advice as to the most suitable piece of equipment for you, your horse and your objectives in relation to your experience.

A lowered, stretched outline with free, forward movement is the starting point for all future schooling work, so any training aid that does not promote this principle has no place in equine training.

When electing to use any training aid, *always* seek proper guidance on how to fit and then use it correctly.

Apart from side reins – which should be used with extreme care – we have found that two training aids in particular are helpful pieces of equipment for racehorse re-education: the Harbridge and the Equi-ami Lunging Aid.

Fig. 6.34 The Harbridge is easy for the less experienced person to use and achieve positive results.

Fig. 6.35 The Equi-ami comes complete with a useful instructional DVD.

The Harbridge

The Harbridge can be used for both ground and ridden work, and is invaluable for all disciplines and stages of training. It is simple to use and to fit. It encourages a horse to work with a lowered, stretched outline, developing softness and suppleness over the back; it can be adjusted as the horse's musculature and balance develop to help promote lightness and self-carriage, improving engagement and the paces. It does not pull the horse's head down, but introduces him to the idea of working in a simple outline and, through correct adjustment combined with proper training, a more elevated frame.

Correctly used, the Harbridge does not fix the outline, nor does it prevent a horse from flexing laterally; it does, however, discourage a horse from leaning.

The Harbridge can also be used for ridden work; this not only helps the horse continue his education under saddle but allows a less experienced rider to develop feel and softer hands as well as helping to promote a better riding position.

The Harbridge can be used for work over trotting poles as well as small grids and fences.

The Equi-ami

The Equi-Ami is unique, with a very simple and logical application. While many training aids work by pressure or restraint, this is not so with the Equi-Ami. It comes in an option for lunge work only, ridden work only, or a combination of the two. Working in harmony with the horse, when he responds in the desired manner (a rounded outline), the Equi-ami loosens so the horse learns the concept of the aids. The Equi-ami developes lightness and self-carriage. It encourages a soft, consistent contact, yet there is no restriction on giving away the reins so the horse can have proper relaxation periods within a training session.

When used for ridden work, the Equi-ami encourages the horse to accept the hand with a soft, consistent contact, discouraging leaning and resistance, thus promoting engagement, lightness, lift from the wither (i.e. correct development of the trapezius muscle) and self-carriage. There is no restriction on giving away the reins so the horse can have proper relaxation periods within a ridden training session. The Equi-ami can safely be used for polework under saddle but not jumping.'

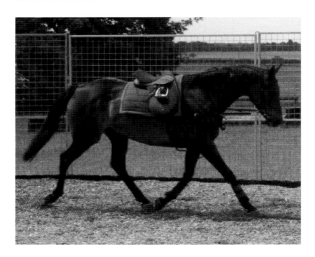

ABOVE: *Fig. 6.36   This horse is starting to work out what the side reins are encouraging her to do. She is stretching her neck forwards and as she is encouraged to keep stepping up to the bridle, she will begin to drop her head down.*

Side-reins

Used correctly, side-reins can be very beneficial in certain situations and with certain horses; used wrongly, and they can most definitely do more harm than good. Side-reins are intended to mimic the rider's hands and introduce the horse to the idea of contact.

Their disadvantages are that they don't allow the horse to stretch forwards and down, nor do they allow lateral flexion. In walk and canter they actually block the natural movements of the head and neck; and the doughnut inserts that some side-reins have bounce up and down,

Figs 6.37 and 6.38   Incorrect (right) and correct (below) use of side reins.

jarring the horse's mouth. Used incorrectly, a horse can readily invert and come above the bit and so develop the wrong muscles, or go behind the vertical which results in tightness and a choppy stride.

In their favour, they help to relax the jaw and encourage a light contact and a more rounded outline, and ultimately self carriage. However, they should never be fitted too tightly, thus pulling the horse's head down or in; they should be gradually shortened over a period of time as the horse becomes more supple, and develops balance and the muscles to carry himself. If necessary, advice should be sought on how to fit and use side-reins correctly.

In the Fig. 6.38 Hero Worship is drawing himself in as the side reins are too tight so he can't move forwards and step into the bridle. (Fred has purposely not adopted the driving position, as this photograph is purely for illustration.) In Fig. 6.39 the side reins are at the correct length, and Fred has adopted the driving position to encourage Hero to reach into the bridle, which he is starting to do very nicely.

Always let a horse loosen up properly first without the side reins attached; then having carried out your exercises, unclip them so that the horse can really stretch out.

The success of side reins is dependent upon the skill of the trainer to keep the horse seeking the bit and moving actively forward. All too often horses are seen going round and round in endless circles, not actually doing themselves any good except getting fitter!

Martingales

Martingales are viewed by some as a training aid as they 'hold a horse's head down'. However, this is not the case.

PLEASE NOTE!

In any situation where there is a rider/horse communication breakdown it is always best to seek hands-on assistance to help you both.

The running martingale: Correctly fitted, the running martingale can prevent a horse from getting his head up too high and beyond the angle of control. For hacking out and cross-country jumping we always recommend the use of a running martingale as a safety precaution.

The Market Harborough: This is not an aid we use ourselves, but it can be useful for horses that carry their heads extremely high, before re-education has really begun. It is not a replacement for schooling work, but is a temporary measure to aid control. Many people are keen to hack out their ex-racehorse for a few weeks before commencing school work, and the Market Harbourgh can be more effective than a running martingale.

The standing martingale: Probably the most misused of martingales, and often seen on smaller ponies that carry their heads very high. It is thought by some that a standing martingale can help to create an outline, but in fact a horse evades it by inverting. Horses in standing martingales typically have more muscle on the underside of their necks than topline as a horse invariably sets itself against the martingale thereby building the wrong muscles.

7 Working from the Ground

'The horse is capable of learning if we are capable of teaching him.'

Ground training encompasses much more than just leading a horse around or tying him up: it allows for the building of trust and a sound relationship with your horse so that you work with, and not against, each other. In the world of 'traditional' horsemanship, ground training was considered to be lungeing or long-reining work, and 'working a horse in hand' or 'in-hand training' was associated with teaching more advanced movements such as half pass, piaffe and passage. However, with the growth and popularity of the 'Natural Horsemanship' movement over the past ten to fifteen years, it is now universally accepted that 'ground training' encompasses absolutely everything that a horse is taught without a rider on its back: it is the foundation upon which ridden work is built.

UNDERSTANDING HORSES

Although the horse has been domesticated for many years, his natural instincts continue to influence his behaviour and reactions. We must therefore do our best to see the world as the horse sees it, and appreciate why he reacts as he does, so that we are then better placed to train him successfully, in a way whereby he remains happy, and feels confident and secure.

In the wild the horse is a food source for other animals, and his survival depends on his ability to detect danger (a predator) and flee from it – which is why horses are termed 'flight animals'. Horses will flee from any sensory stimulus with which they are not familiar, and they don't trust anything until they feel confident about it. The instinct to flee can be the hardest aspect to

Fig. 7.1 Fred working Mr Bojangles, an ex-racehorse competing at Advanced Medium Dressage.

WHAT IS NATURAL HORSEMANSHIP?

Natural Horsemanship is basically a method of training and communicating with horses which works in harmony with their basic instincts and psyche. The techniques used have been developed by observing horses' behaviour in the (wild) herd, and mimicking these during training to build a harmonious relationship between horse and trainer to produce a horse that is calm, confident and co-operative.

Natural Horsemanship training is not new, and many people are using their techniques on a daily basis without realizing they are doing so – they just go about horse training and handling according to Natural Horsemanship principles, with consideration, confidence, competence, clarity and consistency.

Whether you wish to follow Intelligent Horsemanship (Monty Roberts), Parelli, Klaus Ferdinand Hempling, Mark Rashid, John Lyons or the Dorrance Brothers (or whoever – there are endless variations), the basics are the same: to get a horse responding to your cues willingly and enthusiastically, without stress or argument.

Fig. 7.2   The horse has to be taught to move away from pressure.

largely via body language. They are not by nature aggressive, but are 'inter-pressure' animals, meaning they have an instinctive response to push into pressure. For example, a horse pushes against you, you push back, and he actually pushes back against you more! But he is not being naughty, that's just the way nature made him.

Fig. 7.3   Spend time with your horse giving him a groom or a good scratch – interact with him. It is important that whenever he sees you he doesn't only associate you with food or work!

overcome when working with horses, as this is where nervousness stems from. The horse doesn't stop to think – he runs away first, and only stops later to take a look back.

Horses are herd animals, and they rely on the company of, and interaction with, others in order to survive. Herds also have a hierarchy (pecking order), with the leader commanding great respect and trust – the herd trusts the leader to keep it safe from danger, and will take direction without question.

Horses also have a highly developed system of communication, and show their emotions

So how do we train to maximize a horse's understanding, co-operation and happiness? First of all, by using our own body language in a way the horse can equate to, thereby opening up the lines of communication. Then by building trust, so that we become the one in whom he can put his trust – as the handler we become the equivalent of the herd leader. And also by providing comfort: horses mutually groom each other, as this is pleasurable and provides reassurance of friendship and safety, and in the same way we must take time to interact with our horses.

Consistency in training is absolutely essential. Lack of consistency gives a horse mixed signals, and he will get confused very quickly. You can't do something one way one day and expect the horse to do it a completely different way the next because you have changed your mind. Whilst it is perfectly acceptable to use a different approach if progress is not being made, the horse must be given the chance to understand that you have changed tactics.

It is important to concentrate: you can't expect your horse to concentrate his attention on you if you are not paying attention to him. Training time is your horse's time, so be as attentive to him as you want him to be to you. If his attention begins to wander (as would a child's), then it is your task to bring his focus back on to you.

Fig. 7.4 Don't be afraid to let your horse know when he has been a good boy.

You must remain above your horse in the pecking order. Horses are very intelligent, and those of certain dispositions will routinely try and 'push the boundaries' to see just what they can get away with – to see if they can 'train' you to act and react in the way they want you to! Constantly watch for the subtle signs your horse gives you, praising the slightest hint that he is doing what is being asked.

Be quick to praise your horse verbally as well as physically. Horses are sensitive, and readily respond to gentle tones in the voice, so communicate verbally, to praise as well as giving a good scratch to reward a horse for doing right.

Make training fun. It can't be all work and no play when it comes to training, so keep your training sessions varied in order to keep a horse's interest. The horse that gets bored doesn't learn: he switches off and looks for other ways to be inspired.

Repetition is another important aspect of training: it takes roughly sixty repetitions for the horse to understand exactly what you are trying to teach him.

The Trainer's Responsibilities

As trainer/handler, you are basically responsible for the ultimate behaviour of your horse. He will react to your moods, and sometimes even to your thoughts if you are truly in tune with each other.

You also have the responsibility of enabling your horse to lead an enjoyable life, whether this is time in the field, in the stable, or during exercise/training: you should make every effort to understand him and his needs.

When a horse acts 'out of character', or becomes unsettled, frightened or even uncontrollable, it is our task to comfort him, calm him down and restore the status quo. Bear in mind that such behaviour might also indicate that he is unwell or hurting.

'Pressure and Release'

Although a term we dislike, 'Pressure and release' is a fundamental concept in the training of horses that people are familiar with. For example, the trainer applies a 'pressure' (stimulus) or gives a directional cue for the horse to take some kind of action, such as to move in a given direction; the moment the horse responds, the trainer 'releases' the pressure (removes the stimulus). For example, in ridden work when you put your legs on (apply pressure) to ask the horse to move on, you stop applying the leg (release) when he responds. If the horse doesn't respond, a little more pressure is applied until he does. (Note that pressure is not force.)

On the ground, the horse, when gently 'pushed', reacts by beginning to move his feet. This positive reaction, however slight, can then be built on so that the amount of 'pressure' is reduced until the horse will move when the trainer simply moves to his side, or gives a hand signal, or whatever the ultimate cue is to be. Everyone has their preferred cues, whether a swing of the rope, the voice, or a hand movement.

The trainer must be quick to release the pressure the moment the horse responds in the desired manner, or attempts to make a response, however slight. If the pressure is not released the horse will not learn, and may become resentful and increasingly 'dead' to cues.

It is also important to bear in mind that negative experiences for horses are stressful: they raise excitement levels, resulting in a tense horse; the tense horse is not learning, and in fact looks for escape routes either by shutting down or by reacting explosively. To learn, a horse must be relaxed.

By communicating with a horse in this way arguments stop and co-operation is encouraged.

TEACHING GROUND MANNERS

The fundamental aspect of teaching ground manners is that it helps a horse to overcome some of his natural instincts so that he becomes gentle and co-operative: if he is not good mannered it is generally because he doesn't trust those around him. The horse out of training is perfectly familiar with being tied up, standing for the farrier, being led and so on, but placed in an unfamiliar environment with a person he is not sure about, he may forget his manners at times.

Teaching ground manners gives you both the chance to form a working relationship, and for your horse to build up trust and confidence in you before proceeding to ridden work. A horse can be taught new concepts and challenges from the ground, for example, learning about moving his body in ways he will not have been used to, prior to being ridden. Working from the ground helps to overcome fears and resistances – because the horse puts his trust in you to look after him, not put him in danger; it is your job to keep your horse safe and protect him. Your horse should want to be with you, put his reliance on you, and not run a mile as soon as he senses your approach.

He will look to you for guidance, particularly when he is unsure, and a confident handler/rider can significantly reduce instances of

Fig. 7.5 The horse, when gently 'pushed', reacts by beginning to move his feet; he has reacted positively – even if only very slightly – and he can now be praised.

Fig. 7.6 The horse with good manners will stand patiently awaiting instruction from his trainer.

spooking and general disobedience. When a horse plays up for one person but is impeccably behaved for someone else it is generally because he doesn't trust or respect the person he seemingly misbehaves with.

Teaching ground manners also promotes co-operation, with the horse learning his boundaries and to respect your space unless you allow him into it – he will learn not to crowd you. Besides, the horse is a large animal with a lot of weight to throw about if he gets stroppy, so having a polite horse is very important for the safety of everyone around him, and indeed his own.

Finally it opens the lines of communication between you, and without clear communication no successful, harmonious training, and hence learning, will take place.

With good manners in place a horse will be safer to handle and altogether more obliging. It is important with ground training that the handler has feel and softness, along with a firm/positive manner, coupled with accurate timing; training can be severely hindered because the trainer doesn't 'release' at the right moment.

Ground work is a perfect advanced warning mechanism as it provides an ideal opportunity to look for any changes in a horse's gait, behaviour and attitude; much is learnt about a horse by watching his reactions to specific stimuli, his body language, etc.

Equipment

The equipment that you will need to teach the horse the basics of ground manners includes the following.

Training halter: It is perfectly acceptable to work your horse in a headcollar, but many people feel more comfortable using a training halter of some description to afford them more control if required.

Training halters work on the horse's instinctive response to pressure. Although horses generally push into pressure, if such pressure comes from a sharper object the horse will respond positively by moving away from it. When correctly fitted, the pressure from the halter is applied to pressure-sensitive areas of the head – the poll, cheek, and bridge of the nose – thus stimulating the instinct to move away from a sharper pressure. The very moment he responds as you want, the pressure must be released.

Note: your horse should be taught to understand the concepts of a training halter in the safe environment of an enclosed area, and you should also be familiar with its usage and techniques required. If this is a new concept to you, then please seek instruction before attempting usage.

Lunge line: Using a lunge line is preferred to a standard lead rope as these are too short; a soft rope of approximately twelve feet in length is better still as you don't have too much held in your hand.

Other equipment: For practising exercises other than those associated with everyday handling such as leading, it is recommended that a horse wears protective boots or bandages, particularly if he has shoes on.

Ideally you should wear gloves, and a hard hat is also recommended when teaching a horse something new.

Fig. 7.7 It is important that horse learns to lead quietly in hand. Don't hold the lead rope too closely under the chin, it should be slack while the horse is behaving himself, i.e. no pressure on it.

Fig. 7.8 Teaching a horse to step backwards is a very useful exercise as it can be used to stop him from barging and pulling you about.

GROUND-TRAINING EXERCISES

The following are easily executed exercises to help you train your horse. During any of the exercises, should the horse move his head up or down, do not pull his head back into position, just keep a firm hold of the lead rope until he brings his head back to an acceptable position, releasing your hold the moment he does so. Remember to reward your horse as soon as he makes any attempt to respond, however slight the movement may be, by releasing the pressure of your hand and giving him a stroke or a scratch.

Leading

The horse in training usually leads very well; however, some do dance around on the end of the lead rope, but stable staff are well-used to this sort of behaviour and no-one is at all concerned by it. With you, in a completely different environment, good ground control is essential, especially if you are on a yard with other people and horses and children running about.

Some trainers advocate that the horse should be behind the person leading him, but the best position to be is just in front of the shoulder;

Fig. 7.9 Although this horse hasn't inclined his head, he has nonetheless responded to the slight downward pressure on the rope by moving his feet.

this affords the greatest control should the horse either try and run past you or drop back.

Backing Up

A horse that can be backed up is more readily controllable. Our preferred method for teaching a horse back up is to face him, positioning yourself slightly to one side rather than directly in front of his head. Use your fingers to press gently on his chest (at a point mid-way between centre and the point of the shoulder), and say 'back' at the same time. Add a little more pressure if there is no response, but praise any positive response.

With practice you will only need to lift your hand to convey your wish for your horse to move backwards. Then just facing your horse, and indicating with your body language what you want him to do, will achieve results: thus as you take a step towards your horse, he will step backwards.

Alternatively, stand in front of your horse and gently wiggle the lead line, taking a step forwards (towards the horse) as you do, and asking him to 'go back' at the same time. This will indicate to him to move away, backwards.

Another option would be to stand just to the side of his head and move the left hand in a downwards direction but slightly towards the horse's chest so that his nose is moved a little closer to his body. If this 'pressure' doesn't encourage the horse to move his feet, give a couple of sharp downward tugs on the line (*see* Fig. 7.9).

Moving the Hindquarters

Teaching a horse to step to the side is a part of

Fig. 7.10   Position yourself mid-way along the horse's body and hold the lead rope softly in the left hand. Place the right hand on the hindquarters and gently push with the fingertips. As the horse responds (and it doesn't matter to begin with how he moves as long as he moves), then coax his head to the left which further encourages and indicates the requirement to move his hindquarters by moving his hind feet.

Fig. 7.11   This horse is responding positively – he has moved his off hind. Correctly, the near hind should have moved first, but at least the horse has made a positive attempt.

Fig. 7.12   Next time, the horse has a better understanding of the exercise, and is stepping correctly with his near hind leg (he is stepping across and under his body with the inside hindleg). A little more practice will see him soften through the neck.

good manners, for instance when you want him to move over in the stable as you are mucking out, or when grooming, rugging up or tacking up. Being able to disengage the hindquarters puts you in control. Being able to move and control the hindquarters is invaluable as it helps with all manner of suppling exercises, as well as enabling the rider to take control of the horse that gets a little 'nappy'.

Once the horse understands what is being asked of him, you can move your hand from his quarters and place it on his side, in preparation for the leg aid when under saddle.

Some people teach the horse to move the hindquarters by swinging the end of the lead line in a circular motion near to the hindquarters; this can be useful initially for horses that are worried about being touched, or are likely to kick out.

Moving Sideways

This exercise can help suppleness and general responsiveness.

Position yourself midway along your horse's length facing his body. Put your left hand on his shoulder and your right hand on his quarters or his side, whichever is most comfortable. Gently apply pressure with both hands and at the same time say 'Over'.

Place a pole on the ground and stand the horse over it, with his forelegs on one side and hind legs on the other. Use the same cues as above. The pole helps to keep the horse straighter, which aids his co-ordination.

Exercises with Poles

The horse in training has no experience of polework, and might become excited or flustered by poles on the ground. By doing some in-hand work with poles prior to work on the lunge or long-reining, you can help him realize that they are nothing to be worried about, and indeed can be fun.

These exercises not only provide variety and interest but aid suppleness and co-ordination of the horse; they also test the handler's skills.

Work in hand over poles: Initially the horse can be introduced to poles by being led over them in walk and then in trot. The poles can

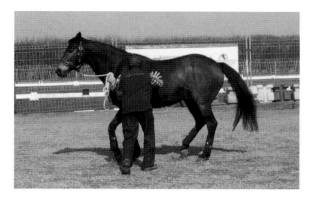

Fig. 7.13   Your horse should respond by moving his whole body sideways as if he was doing a full pass, i.e. his body is straight and his front and hind legs cross together.

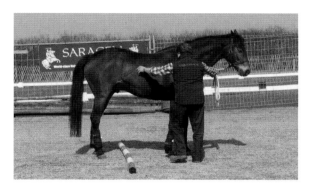

Fig. 7.14   Using a pole on the ground can help horses better understand what is being asked.

also be laid in a fan shape so that stride length can be adjusted. Such exercises are a sound introduction to polework on the lunge or when long-reining.

Tram lines: This exercise tests the horse's obedience, and the handler's accuracy in directing the horse. Lay two poles on the ground approximately four feet apart. Back your horse between them, keeping him as straight as possible. Increase the difficulty of the exercise by laying two poles end to end on each side and backing him over a longer distance.

Fig. 7.15 This exercise can help develop a straight rein-back under saddle.

Right angles: Lay some poles on the ground to form an L-shape. Back your horse between the poles, negotiating him in reverse round the corner. The exercise can be made more difficult by laying down enough poles to create two corners to negotiate.

Ground-training exercises form the basis for in-hand work. If you are already familiar with working a horse in this way there is no reason why you can't progress to teaching your horse leg yielding and shoulder-in, or indeed any of the more advanced movements such as travers.

Fig. 7.16 Narrowing the distance between the tram lines further tests accuracy.

PROBLEM SOLVING

You should be able to lead a well mannered horse anywhere without question or argument. It is important that the horse knows how to behave, as inappropriate behaviour can be dangerous, especially if he has to be led on a public road. (Note that a horse should have a bit in its mouth when on a public highway, but if you prefer not to lead a horse off the bit, then use a training halter over the top.)

Don't struggle on in a tricky situation, as it can escalate, and don't be afraid to seek practical help.

Fig. 7.17 A horse should be polite enough to be led from a simple headcollar without fuss.

Problem: My horse won't lead
This problem usually means that the horse jogs and jibs or perhaps hops off the floor when being led. It is acceptable for a horse to look around whilst being led, but he should still have his focus on you.

Barging, dragging you: Don't keep constantly tugging on the lead rope but adopt the position for 'Leading', as described above.

Exert a pressure on the lead line by means of a quick, sharp tug. If he ignores you, then stop and back him up for several steps. Step backwards yourself and 'tug and release' the line so that he moves with you. For the first few times he may throw his head up or out, but that

Figs 7.18 and 7.19   By moving the horse backwards you are making him do the opposite of what he is trying to do.

is just in response to the initial 'pressure'. Ignore this and pull him backwards – you may have to be quite firm to begin with.

Lagging behind: Avoid turning to look at him as this will produce a 'stand-off' between you. And if one or two sharp tugs don't have the desired effect, avoid pulling constantly as he will probably just plant himself. Nor should you be tempted to flick his side with the end of the lead rope as this may cause him to leap away from you.

Reposition yourself so that you are just behind his shoulder. As he has been lagging behind you, step away a little from his side to give him a space to walk into, and at the same time offer

Fig. 7.20   The horse that lags behind needs encouraging to come up to the leader's shoulder.

your right hand forwards and step forwards yourself. Once the horse is walking on you can adopt the correct position.

If this doesn't work, give a sharp pull on the rope in your direction, thus pulling him on to a circle so that he has to move his feet.

Walking into you: If your horse is distracted and keeps walking into you, then you have to refocus his attention to you. Try giving the lead line a few wiggles, or a quick, sharp tug; repeat if necessary. Alternatively flick his chest with the end of the lead rope, or carry a small cane or carrot stick, and when the horse comes too close just tap his shoulder with it.

The idea is *not* to inflict pain, but to regain the horse's attention so he concentrates on you rather than everything else around him.

Rearing when led: If your horse tends to rear up when you attempt to lead him, use a training halter (be sure to have introduced him to such a halter first).

When he rears up, give one very firm pull on the lead rope: this puts pressure on his poll, which a horse doesn't like, so he will move in order to release this pressure. Repeat if necessary.

Avoid keeping a steady pull on the lead rope as this will encourage a more negative reaction from the horse, and will increase the risk of him going over backwards or running backwards. If you take the pressure away immediately, you put him in 'no man's land'.

Problem: My horse won't load

The method of blocking one side of the ramp to encourage a horse to load is not favoured by everyone as it is seen as restricting his freedom of choice – he should load because he is happy to do so, not as a result of 'pressure'. However, with the horse out of training it is better to use tactics he is familiar with, rather than trying to adjust too much, too soon. Once he is loading confidently you can gradually adjust the way you do things.

Fig. 7.21 *Given that the vast majority of racehorses are loaded via loading ramps, use similar tactics initially to load him yourself should he be at all hesitant. Parking by a fence or wall to block one side will simulate, to an extent, a loading ramp. (Photograph courtesy of Fellowes Farm Equine Clinic)*

The racehorse never travels by trailer so it is a small, scary place for him to enter, plus the flat-raced horse may associate the narrow space with starting stalls and be reluctant to go in. (Trailer practice with the ex-racehorse is much the same as you would train a young horse, hence we will not go into detail here.)

Loading by putting a rope around the hindquarters – which can work, as it is similar to the handlers at starting stalls loading by using a quoit – should only be done by those experienced in loading horses this way; if the horse objects the rope risks becoming entangled in his legs, and this method can cause some to rear up.

Problem: My horse pulls back when tied up

The horse out of training is used to being tied up, so pulling back would not be normal behaviour – though having said that, he is not accustomed to being tied up outside, so if something startled him on his first experience, breaking free might become a habit.

There are various solutions you might try to resolve this problem: first, always practise in an enclosed area, and when you tie him give him a haynet to keep him occupied. Use a rubber stretchy tie that applies a pressure, but which releases when he steps forwards. Although you should never tie a horse up using a training halter, if he is familiar with poll pressure, when he feels the pressure of a normal headcollar he should yield to it.

Initially tie a quieter companion next to him (but out of kicking distance), and practise at a time when the yard is at its quietest. Stay close to him to reassure him, perhaps grooming him to provide a pleasant distraction.

If he is particularly anxious, a safe alternative is to put the rope through the tie-ring and hold it yourself, so you control the give and take. This method is particularly helpful as you can also gauge the pressure exerted before the 'give', and can use your voice to try and calm him. Use this method whilst grooming.

When he is relaxed you can gradually move further away from him, reassuring him with your voice initially if needs be. Stand just off his hindquarters and as the horse steps back, encourage him to go forwards again.

Then move out of sight – literally for a few seconds – and gradually build up the amount of time your horse can't see you.

8 Lungeing

The racehorse will almost certainly have been lunged, although this may have been some time ago, and most probably in a purpose-built lungeing pen. However, when you first attempt to lunge your ex-racehorse, assume that he must be taught what to do, then you are less likely to have him galloping around you at full speed.

Work on the lunge is valuable for many reasons. It:

- provides exercise if a horse cannot be ridden
- releases tension
- helps a horse to find his own balance and to establish/improve co-ordination without a rider's weight
- supples the horse, loosening the back and neck muscles, encourages engagement of the hindquarters (if carried out correctly) and improves/increases lateral flexibility

- strengthens the horse, encouraging him to 'step under'
- helps accustom the horse to new tack
- helps to build trust between horse and handler
- allows the trainer to assess a horse's physical and mental development
- is a good idea if a horse has not had a saddle on for a while
- enables the more advanced movements to be taught from the ground first.

ENCOURAGING THE HORSE TO STEP UNDER

It is the abdominal, dorsal and lumbar muscles that have to be strengthened first as a horse

Fig. 8.1 Hero Worship behaving in typical fashion of most horses when left to their own devices on the lunge line – head up, tail out and a run more than a trot.

Fig. 8.2 Proceed with caution if a horse hasn't had a saddle on for a while – just in case!

needs a strong central core to support his back. When these muscles start to take shape, the horse will naturally reach forward so he has to bring his hind legs more under in order to maintain his balance. The horse that begins to take weight behind lifts his forehand. Once a horse works more consistently through his back and steps under with increased activity and flexion in the hocks, we have the basis for collection – where a horse lowers his croup as if appearing to sit, i.e. his centre of gravity has moved back and he is truly taking weight behind.

Strengthening is achieved initially by letting the horse stretch – the nose reaching forwards and downwards as if he were about to start grazing. A fully stretched neck activates the muscles of the abdomen and back and allows the hind legs to step under, further activating the mucles of the hindquarters and stretching the hamstrings. As the back becomes more supple, the horse naturally lifts through the withers, arching his neck forwards (reaching into the bit) with his poll the highest point. If the poll is not the highest point a horse can't step under correctly; the overbent horse (where the nose is brought into the chest) is unable to take weight behind as he doesn't build the correct muscles.

Fig. 8.3   It can take time for a horse to relax and begin to respond on the lunge.

Whilst the horse in Fig. 8.3 is not stretching forwards and down, he is nonetheless stretching his body out and has a slight lateral flexion to the inside. Gently shaking the line will encourage this horse to drop his head. Note Fred's position in this photograph and the loose lunge line; he remains close to the horse so that it is less inclined to rush off.

GETTING STARTED

Where to Lunge

You don't need a lungeing ring or round pen in order to lunge successfully, but it is advisable to work in a safe, confined area, ideally a school. When teaching a horse to lunge, a restricted area automatically affords greater control; horses naturally drift outwards towards something solid, so even though your school may have rails all round it, this will not keep your horse working on a circle until he understands what is required of him, nor will it control his speed.

If the school is large, a smaller area can be made by squaring off a corner using jump stands and poles on the two open sides. A more contained area can be made in a similar manner in the corner of a field.

It is important to lunge on a sound surface; lungeing on grass is fine provided that it is level, free from stones, and is neither too hard nor too wet and slippery. No horse will move freely and learn if he feels that the footing is insecure: his whole way of going will change as he tries to balance himself, usually by shortening his stride, and a stride that is choppy or stilted has no positive effect on releasing tension (in fact it causes the opposite) or suppling the horse.

If you lunge on a surface, be aware that the surface material will gradually shift towards the outside of the circle so that after a while the track the horse is working on actually becomes sloped so he is no longer working on a level surface. A deep surface will compromise his ease of movement and may even damage his joints.

Equipment for Lunge Work

A horse can be lunged without a bridle, which is useful if he has a sore mouth, or just needs a leg stretch. However, ideally a bridle should always be fitted if the purpose of the lungeing work is as a schooling or training exercise. This is because the bit stimulates the flow of saliva, which results in the relaxation of the parotid gland muscles, which leads to suppleness.

There are no hard and fast rules: you can use a lungeing cavesson, or lunge directly or indirectly off the bit. However, lungeing directly off the bit is best left for when the horse is under proper control and fully accepting the contact, otherwise the risk of pulling the mouth is too great.

Attaching the Lunge Line

Using a coupling: A coupling is very useful when you need to control a very strong horse, or when you start retraining a more wayward character. We usually use the coupling when giving a horse a quick lunge prior to riding, or when putting a saddle on for the first time. Thereafter the coupling should not be used for lunge work.

Using a lunge cavesson: We do not favour the traditional lungeing cavesson because of the way the central ring bangs against the horse's nose. Also, if a horse should jump about or pull to the outside, the cavesson all too easily slips round his face. The traditional cavesson is popular because the trainer doesn't have to make adjustments each time he changes the rein.

A training cavesson is similar to a lungeing cavesson in basic structure but there is no

Fig. 8.4 *The three-way coupling provides an even pressure to both sides of the mouth as the central nose attachment prevents the bit being pulled to one side. A two-way coupling allows too much pressure to be put on the outside bit ring.*

Fig. 8.5 *This method of attachment is also good for the start of long-reining work, especially if you do not know how a horse will react, as a delicate mouth is less likely to get pulled about.*

central ring, just a ring on either side for the lunge rein to attach to. Hence the horse can be taught to lunge (and indeed long-rein) without any interference to the mouth. Such a cavesson can be fitted over a bridle so that the horse can carry a bit.

We have found this type of cavesson to be very useful with horses out of training if they are particularly bit shy or sensitive, as they can readily commence their retraining without having to worry about contact on the mouth; once certain basics are in place and the horse is moving freely forwards, working off the bit can be quietly introduced.

Using the bit ring and noseband: Securing the lunge line to the bit ring via the noseband affords control but without the mouth taking all the pressure (*see* Fig. 8.5).

We do not advocate fitting the lunge rein over the horse's head. Not only is pressure put on the poll, which some horses object to, it also has the effect of pulling the corners of the mouth upwards (as a gag bit does), resulting in the head and neck being raised. Furthermore if you are also using a training aid that aims to lower and stretch the neck, the horse receives conflicting instructions and is most likely to raise his head and hollow his back as he struggles to respond to both bit and training aid.

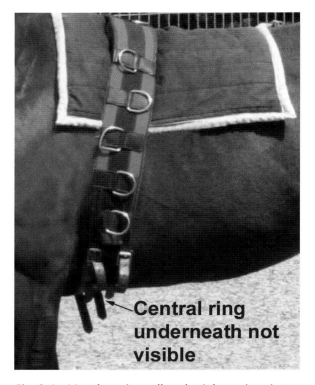

Fig. 8.6 *Most lungeing rollers don't have rings just where you need them and are often a little too close to the top of the roller and without a ring sufficiently low down for initial attachment of most training aids and for early long-reining work. This roller has been specially made with more rings.*

Other Equipment for Lungeing

Roller or saddle: Working with just a roller is a good reintroduction to something tight around the girth area if a horse has had a long lay-off, or if he has a sore back. However, it is actually better to put a saddle on with the roller fitted over the top: one of the purposes of lungeing work is to promote hind leg activity, which increases movement of the back muscles, which is further stimulated and increased by the weight of the saddle.

Boots: Horses should always have boots (or bandages) fitted for lungeing work to guard against injury; this is particularly important if the horse has shoes on and/or is recovering from a leg injury.

The lunge rein: Ideally lunge lines should be made of a web material rather than nylon or similar as the latter is too light and gets blown about in the slightest of winds, which interferes with correct aiding from the trainer. A lightweight hook is preferable to a buckle, as buckles can be bulky and take longer to undo in an emergency.

The lunge whip: The whip is not an instrument of punishment, merely an extension of your arm to enable you to give clearer instructions to the horse. With the more experienced horse it is often not necessary to carry a lunge whip, but when teaching a green horse it is very useful. When you don't need to be using it, hold the whip still and behind you. A horse may have been frightened by the whip in the past.

Yourself: Always wear stout footwear; gloves protect the hands from rope burn should a horse pull away sharply; and a hard hat is a sensible precaution, particularly when working with a horse you are unfamiliar with, or which tends to be lively.

Fig. 8.7   Fred has not given Call Oscar too much length of line as he will move around with him; if Oscar needs to be checked back this can be done quickly without the need to gather in a lot of lunge line.

The First Lungeing Session

There is no need to use a roller or saddle for the first lungeing session: you just need to find out what the horse does or doesn't know – some racehorses only encounter lungeing when they are introduced to the saddle, and not as a part of their training.

The most routinely adopted method for introducing a horse to lungeing is to first lead him around the lunge area (in a circle). When he is quietly walking by your side, step a couple of feet away from him; provided he continues to walk quietly you can gradually step further away from him letting the line out as you do so. We prefer to walk quite a large circle ourselves during early training so that the horse is being worked on a circle that is not too small for his physical fitness and balance.

It is quite likely that to begin with your horse will want to execute a few high-speed circles before settling down; this is perfectly normal. Advice on how to overcome this is given below.

If you are at all unsure, seek instruction, and practise with a horse that is already well versed in lunge work and the associated commands.

PROBLEM SOLVING

Racehorses are generally lunged in a pen or small enclosure, so in the open space of an arena they may be quite lively! It also often shows up their lack of balance, which often makes the situation appear to be worse than it is.

Typical lungeing difficulties experienced are not exclusive to the ex-racehorse, as problems are usually associated with the trainer not adopting the right position in relation to the horse, not giving clear communication, or not starting the process in the most appropriate way.

It is also important to remember that working on a circle is hard for any horse, let alone one that hasn't done this before, so it is essential to allow time for his muscles to build up – don't expect too much, too soon.

Problem: My horse races off

If your horse rushes off or races around when you lunge him, there are two ways you can get him under control, both unconventional in terms of horsemanship – but they work!

Walk the horse on a very small circle, then turn to face his shoulder but take a couple of sideways steps so that you adopt the lungeing position. Do not increase the size of the circle until the horse has accepted your position without reacting. You can gradually step away

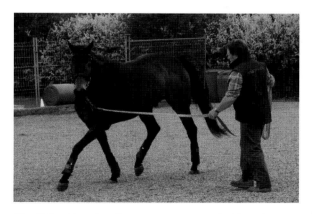

Fig. 8.8   Note Fred's stance – an easy hold of the lunge line and positioned mid-way along the horse's length so that he can readily move towards the shoulder to steady him or stop him turning in, or back towards the quarters if he tries to drop back.

TOP PICTURES: *Figs 8.9 and 8.10   Don't worry at this stage how the horse is positioning or using his body. It is control you are after; refinement can come later on.*

LEFT: *Fig. 8.11   Using simple tactics can avoid confusion on the part of the horse and frustration for the trainer.*

from him, but maintain the correct position in relation to his body as you do so, otherwise you will influence him to react in a way you do not want him to. The trainer's position and body language is very important in order to maintain control on the lunge.

The simplest way to address rushing off is to hold the horse close to its head and virtually push the hindquarters where you want them to go – like a turn on the forehand. Once the horse will step round you, you can very gradually let the line out. Be sure to keep your position just behind the shoulder: if you are too near the quarters then the horse can more easily turn in.

Some horses will persist in this behaviour however correct your position and accurate your commands seem to be; they will continue to turn to face you and generally dance about when you try to urge them forwards, and will either keep moving sideways away from you or running backwards. This unruly behaviour stems from the fact that the horse doesn't see you as his 'leader', he doesn't trust you, or you are not conveying your commands correctly.

Figs 8.12 and 8.13   We introduced Hero Worship to lunge work in a Harbridge so that his owner would have more control over him once she took him home as he could be quite exuberant.

Fig. 8.14 Lay a few poles on the ground in a fan shape; position yourself in the centre. The poles will stop your horse cutting in so he will learn to stay out on the circle. If necessary, make another fan on the opposite site of the circle.

For the horse that is really determined to tear off you might fit a Harbridge, side-reins (although these must be relatively loose) or similar: these can exert a steadying influence as the horse can't get its head up too high. However, ideally practise one of the techniques described above until the problem is resolved.

Problem: My horse cuts in on the circle

Often horses will not stay out on the length of lunge line given to them, preferring to cut in and then invariably rushing about, often in trot, but more usually in canter. To stop him doing this, first make sure that you are not adopting the 'driving' position by being too far behind his shoulder. 'Shaking' the lunge line in a wave-like action is often enough to encourage the horse back out on to the circle, and point the lunge whip towards his shoulder. Re-establish the walk before proceeding to trot.

Problem: My horse turns in on me

This habit often occurs when the trainer is lazy on rein changes and 'reels in' the horse.

Make sure you are not inadvertently creating a pressure/tension down the lunge line which is signalling to the horse to stop, or that you are not actually pulling him in. Check your position: ahead of his shoulder 'blocks' his forward movement so he stops and turns in; too near the tail allows him to come round in front of you. Try shaking the lunge line at him,

and pointing the whip at his shoulder, as above. Always watch him carefully and anticipate his moves so that you can be one step ahead of him.

Every time he turns in, put him back out on the circle and continue.

Once a horse has been introduced to side-reins, attach the outside side-rein only. If all else fails, work him with two lines.

Problem: My horse rushes off when the line is let out

Some horses will rush off, snatching the line out of your hand the moment it is let out. This habit often develops as a consequence of poor handling when lungeing was initially taught, and/or the horse had a fright of some sort. Do not be tempted to pull the horse too sharply,

Fig. 8.15 Fred doesn't pull at Call Oscar, but gradually reduces the length of the line so that he has to slow down.

just gradually shorten up the lunge line so that he has to come on to a decreasing circle – you are spiralling him in, and he will have to slow down otherwise he will lose his balance.

For the horse that generally rushes, just reduce the size of the circle.

If he is still travelling rather fast even on a small circle he is likely to slip, so stop him, back him up, and start again.

Problem: My horse turns away and kicks out

This problem usually occurs when the trainer is not in control, the horse is not paying attention and is going too fast, or when he is just feeling happy and full of himself.

Slow everything right down, even coming back to walk if necessary. Bring him back on to a much smaller circle; as you let him back out again, give a jiggle on the line every time he is distracted, or a quick tug. Be sure you are positioned more by his shoulder.

Should this basic over-exuberance continue for any length of time, check what you are feeding your horse, and increase his turn-out time if possible.

Problem: My horse turns his head to the outside

A horse that is unbalanced or a young horse will usually trot around with its head inclined to the outside. With correct control from the trainer, the horse can be gradually asked to straighten, and finally to incline slightly to the inside as his balance and suppleness improves.

Turning the head in this manner should not be confused with the horse that is distracted and happily surveying the scenery as he trots round!

If a few wiggles of the lunge line don't invoke the desired response, then give a couple of short, sharp tugs to focus his attention.

Problem: My horse keeps cantering instead of staying in trot

Cantering is typical of the horse that is not balanced, as he finds it easier to canter than to stay in trot. It is a case of repetition: keep correcting him and bringing him back to trot.

When you get some good trot work, reward your horse by bringing him back to walk; then trot on again. Working on a circle is hard work for a horse, so by cantering he is easing himself.

Using a Harbridge or side-reins (and often just a single rein fitted to the outside) can help a horse to balance.

LOOSE LUNGEING

Loose lungeing your horse is an option if you have an enclosed pen or lungeing area, and is an interesting training method as the horse works out everything for himself without direct interference from his trainer. Loose lunge work can be advanced in progressive steps in the same way as lungeing on a line. Tack can be introduced, and the horse worked in side-reins or in a suitable training aid.

First of all, familiarize your horse with the working area by leading him round. When he is walking in a relaxed manner with you, let him loose; remain standing in the centre of the ring and let him investigate. Use your body language to encourage him to slow down and/or speed up, adding voice commands at the same time.

Fig. 8.16   Bobbie is newly introduced to side reins so Fred is encouraging her to work forwards into the bit. Note the lunge whip is just an extension of the arm.

To slow down: Position yourself in front of his shoulder in order to block his movement, and lower the tone of your voice into a drawn-out 'W-a-l-k', or whatever voice command you wish to train your horse to respond to.

To speed up: Position yourself just behind his shoulder in order to drive him forwards, and use a more clipped, snappy voice tone: T-r-o-t!/ T-r-o-t o-n!

To halt: Lower the voice and draw out your selected command word.

If at any time the horse ignores your body language and voice, then proceed in the ways described for work on the lunge line: thus point the lunge whip in front of his shoulder to slow him down, and towards the quarters to move him on. Be clear in your commands, and keep to the same ones so that your horse learns and understands; the same commands can then be incorporated into work on the line, long-reining and ridden work.

If he cuts in, step towards him and hold the lunge whip towards his quarters. If he tears around the pen, don't worry, just let him tire himself, then when he stops you can spend a few minutes making him work. However, don't punish him by working him for too long, even though he may have spent the larger proportion of the training time messing around. Equally don't let *him* dictate when he drops back to walk, but keep him going until *you* say he can walk.

It is most likely that the horse will rush around to begin with, despite having been led around first. However, allow him to 'let off steam': he will be excited at the prospect of running loose with no one seemingly having any control over him. And don't react to this too abruptly, but just stand quietly and do nothing, apart from letting him turn round (change direction). He will soon realize that rushing about is not achieving anything, and will stop. When he

Fig. 8.17   Hero Worship proves to be a little lively when the saddle is put on.

does, you must make him move on again – and in all likelihood he will go off with another kick and a buck; but just keep repeating the process until he moves on quietly in the pace you want.

Stop him when you are ready, and not when he decides; however, don't punish him, and don't keep him moving for too long, as a tired horse becomes a nappy, sour horse.

INTRODUCING THE SADDLE

Once the horse understands what lungeing is all about, then you can commence work proper with a roller or saddle. This can also be done during the course of loose lunge work. If it has been some time since your horse had a saddle on, then be mindful that he may buck about when it is put on his back again, and the girth tightened.

To test what his reaction might be, place the saddle on his back, and then from the near side, hold the girth against his stomach; then very gradually, gently pull it a little more firmly as if preparing to fasten it. Should the horse react in any way, take the saddle off and proceed as follows, as the safer option:

- Rub the horse's back and all around where the girth will lie, to warm the skin and relax the muscles
- Place a numnah with good concussion properties on his back
- Place the saddle – preferably an old one, and having removed the stirrups and girth – on his back; be mindful not to catch his side
- Hold the saddle in place with the hands, and then just move it slightly; this makes sure that the horse is fully aware that it is there
- Remove the saddle and attach the girth, then replace it on the horse's back in the manner described above
- Fasten the girth, but not too tightly; push the horse backwards a few steps, then tighten the girth a little more; push him back again, and re-tighten it
- Then walk the horse forwards a few steps, stop him, reward him, and repeat the process.

If at any time there is any sign of tension, stop and push him backwards, stop again, and reward him. If signs of tension persist, keep repeating this process until he is more relaxed about it. Continued tension/apprehension may indicate soreness in the back area, so if you have not yet had a chiropractic assessment, now is the time to do so.

Problem: My horse is grumpy to saddle
Any grumpiness on the horse's part will be due to a negative association:

- He is in pain or discomfort somewhere – possibly gastric ulcers, or a sore back/withers
- The saddle is uncomfortable, or pinching him somewhere
- When the saddle has been put on, it has been lumped down on his back
- The girth has been done up too tightly, too quickly, or soft skin has been pinched.

Initially just place the saddle on the horse's back, and remove it straightaway without doing up the girth. Do this a few times. When you do fasten the girth, do so very lightly, and tighten it only gradually, over the course of several minutes.

EXERCISES ON THE LUNGE

Assorted exercises can be incorporated into lunge work, both on a lunge line and with the horse working loose. They can be done with or without a roller/saddle. We feel there is no need to describe each of the exercises in detail as they are simply an extension of basic lunge work once you have your horse listening and under control.

They might include the following:

- Transitions
- Transitions within the pace
- Lengthening and shortening of the stride
- Spiralling in and out on circles
- Half-halts (but only with a skilled handler).

The aim of these exercises is to improve the horse's balance and suppleness, and to

Fig. 8.18 The success of carrying out lunge work is entirely dependent upon your communication skills. You have to keep your horse's attention and be very clear in your body language, voice commands and handling of the lunge line itself.

encourage the engagement of the hindquarters. It makes no difference that you are working an ex-racehorse as opposed to any other horse, except that it may take a little longer to achieve certain goals, and the circles may have to remain a little larger – at least to begin with!

The exercises can also be done when a horse is accustomed to the feel of side-reins, with certain training aids, and of course when long-reining (*see* Chapter 9).

LUNGEING WITH TRAINING AIDS

Use of a training aid in some situations can be helpful in the short term, but it should never be a means of short-cutting the horse's training programme: there are no short-cuts in the world of equine training.

When your horse is happily lungeing and is clearly more supple than he was, it is time to work him in a more rounded outline, as this lays the foundations to working on the bit. The 'rounded outline' comes from a back that is more lifted and has a swing to it, and which brings the hind legs more under the body.

Side-reins

The use of side-reins as part of the retraining

Fig. 8.19   Bobbie needed encouragement to understand what was required of her. She was happy to trot around all day with her head stretched out in front of her but allowing her to continue like this was of no benefit.

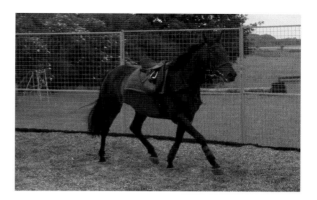

Fig. 8.20   Bobbie is introduced to the side-reins; they are loose and exerting no pressure on the bit and therefore have no influence.

Fig. 8.21   The side-reins are now a little shorter and Bobbie is reacting typically in that she has slightly tilted her head; although she is mouthing well, she is actually holding the bit rather than accepting it.

Fig. 8.22   By encouraging Bobbie to maintain a forward she gradually accepts the feel of the side-reins and after about ten minutes she has worked out that it actually easier and more comfortable to lower her head.

process for the horse out of training is the simplest way to teach acceptance of the bit. Correctly fitted, side-reins should form a straight line from the bit to the roller/saddle – they should not be angled upwards or downwards. The horse off the track needs to learn about contact, and using side-reins, together with correct lungeing technique, is the best way to achieve this and to teach him acceptance of the bit. They also help a horse to balance and to engage.

Fig. 8.25   Indie gets the idea to do something – he drops behind the vertical. By being sent on into a more forward trot, he will open his frame (see Fig. 8.26)

Fig. 8.23   Indie had become quite set in his head carriage with a rather thick muscle on the underside of his neck. When left to work on his own he literally propped himself on this muscle and could happily trot for hours without any attempt to lower his head.

Fig. 8.24   When the side-reins were first fitted, Indie still tried to maintain the head carriage he liked as indicated by the angle of the side-reins – they should form a straight line to the bit.

A horse should be allowed to get used to the feel of side-reins before he is expected to work in them properly; this may take just one session, or several over the course of a week. He must learn to accept bit pressure and to give to it, rather than work against it.

To start off, fit side-reins so that he is aware of their presence, but they don't offer any restriction. Once he is walking and trotting happily you can gradually shorten them, say a hole per lesson.

Initially the side-reins need to be set in a way to encourage a lowered, stretched head carriage – that is, exerting very little bit pressure. If at any time the horse stops, runs backwards or tries to rear or spin, if encouraging more forwardness doesn't have the desired effect, loosen them further as he is obviously feeling too restricted. He must not be forced to lower his head or to round: he must

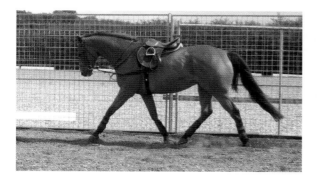

Fig. 8.26 *After a few more minutes of being up and down with his head carriage, the penny drops and Indie adopts a super outline and is stepping under much better. What a transformation in just one training session.*

Fig. 8.27 *Hero Worship hasn't quite accepted the Harbridge yet; although he isn't resisting it, he needs to lower his head and seek a proper contact with the bit. When this happens, don't be tempted to tighten the Harbridge; allow the horse time to work things out.*

work out that actually that is the most comfortable thing to do.

At this stage it is important to keep the forward impulsion, rather than letting a horse slow down too much, otherwise he will readily get into the habit of overflexing (dropping behind the vertical), which can be a harder habit to break. Any problems experienced whilst working a horse in side-reins, such as head tossing or resisting in any way, must be worked through and resolved otherwise they will persist when the horse comes to be ridden.

For the trainer, getting the ex-racehorse to seek the bit and work forwards into it is one of the main challenges.

If any of the problems above are experienced, once a horse is used to side-reins these often readily dissipate, as the side-reins act as a brake as well as aiding balance. Once the horse has the idea of moving forwards into the bit, then either the Harbridge or the Equi-ami can be introduced to help promote outline if you have difficulty.

Fig. 8.28 *With the Equi-ami fitted as it is here, the horse can stretch down if he so wishes but also work with a slightly more raised head carriage.*

encourage a lowered head carriage, and to strengthen the back, particularly after an injury. If a horse resists the Harbridge don't be tempted to tighten it, but allow him time (over several sessions if necessary) to work things out for himself.

The Equi-ami: Another training aid that should not be used in conjunction with any other. It is a very useful aid once a horse is established in his lungeing routine, understanding and obeying commands.

Other Training Aids

The Harbridge: Not to be used in conjunction with any other aid. It can be used initially to

FURTHER PROBLEM SOLVING

Problem: My horse is tossing his head

A little head tossing in the early days is acceptable as it is usually a sign of anxiety whilst the horse is working out what is required of him. However, if he persists, you will need to rule out certain issues as being the cause. First, be sure that he is not suffering any dental problems, or pain in his back or hind suspensory ligament.

Alternatively he may not like your choice of bit: if it is too thick it may be restricting his tongue; or if you have opted for a lozenge at this stage, the joints may be pulling to one side – especially if he tilts his head – or you are not maintaining a soft enough contact. Try a noseband such as a grakle to keep the bit a little higher and more stable in his mouth; if it doesn't have the desired effect, then go back to a cavesson.

If none of the above is causing the head-tossing, then the reason is simply that the horse has to learn to accept the bit, so the main thing is to maintain forward impulsion because he is obviously trying to avoid going into the bit. It can help to use a side-rein on the offside only.

Problem: My horse is overflexing/dropping behind the vertical

Very often the cause of this problem is that the side-reins have been shortened too much, too soon, and the horse is not moving forwards enough. Do not be tempted to attach the side-reins to a higher ring, as this can have the effect of encouraging the horse to lean even more – in fact he needs driving/pushing into a more forward, freer pace.

He may be need a different bit – the one you have chosen to use may be discouraging him from going forwards into the contact.

The reason could also be that the horse is finding the working surface too deep, or the work too strenuous for his stage of physical development.

Fig. 8.29   Some horses will drop behind the vertical as an evasion tactic, so be ready with the driving aid.

Problem: My horse carries his head too high/is tense and/or hollow

These issues are one and the same in that the horse that has his head up is a hollow horse, which is a tense horse. A hollow outline needs correcting quickly, and the horse encouraged to work out that actually it is more comfortable to work with a lowered head/neck.

First of all make sure that the saddle is not too tight and nipping the horse's withers.

Don't be tempted to force his head down by attaching the side-reins to a lower ring, as he will just pull his head up even more and set himself against them. In fact it usually works best to raise the side-reins very slightly, slow down the pace and work on a smaller circle.

If the horse really does persist in carrying his head too high, or if the underside of his neck muscles are over-developed, help him to establish the correct muscles by working him in a Harbridge or use an Equi-ami two to three times a week.

Problem: My horse lacks bend

If a horse is laterally tight or stiff, it is because the outside neck muscles require stretching, in which case ask for more bend with your hand – a soft hand. If using side-rein, don't shorten the inner side-reins; in fact using just the outside side-rein is often enough to encourage a horse to seek the contact simply by the weight –

Fig. 8.30 Attach the lunge line as a draw rein at the girth and pass it through the inside bit ring. This allows you to ask for a bit more bend with your hand – a soft hand.

THE WAY FORWARDS

If you continue to experience difficulties despite all your efforts at correcting them, it is could be that you are not being clear and consistent enough in your communication, so ask someone to come and work with you to ensure you are doing everything correctly.

Also a veterinary check is recommended, as there may be a subtle underlying issue which is causing the horse to react as he is.

albeit slight – that it exerts. Alternatively attach the lunge rein as in Fig. 8.30.

Problem: My horse lacks swing through his back

The 'swinging back' is a supple back as a result of lifted abdominal muscles and hind legs coming under the body. Horses are often seen that have indeed adopted a rounder outline, but they look stiff and stilted in their action: this is because the back is not soft and swinging.

To improve suppleness and therefore swing, use stretching exercises to strengthen the abdominal and back muscles.

Lack of swing is not the preserve of the ex-racehorse, but it is harder for the thoroughbred to achieve 'swing' as by their very breeding they are designed to run, not to perform dressage movements. Also many former racehorses will have incurred some sort of trauma to the back/pelvic region, which although might have little effect on their racing performance, may disadvantage them later on, when proper schooling work commences. This doesn't mean to say that they can't develop swing, but they need more time and a considerable amount of suppling work.

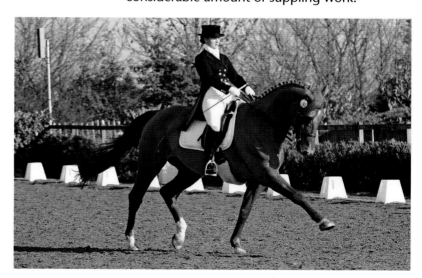

Fig. 8.31 Louis Feraud shows that the thoroughbred can indeed have plenty of swing. (Photograph courtesy of John Tyrrell Photography)

9 Long-reining

The early stage of long-reining is correctly termed 'double lungeing' as it is really lungeing with two lines. It progresses to being 'long-reining' when the trainer adopts a position more behind the horse for executing lateral work, and then on to the advanced dressage movements.

Working with two lines is better than working with just one, primarily because the trainer is able to control the horse's hindquarters – he can stop them from swinging out or in – and therefore has much more influence over the horse's way of going because the rein round the hindquarters develops a better 'tucking under' and increased activity of the hind legs, and a consequent lift of the forehand. It also improves balance.

Long-reining also helps to teach the horse the rein aids because the trainer has a direct contact with both sides of the mouth, allowing for an altogether softer contact; he can influence

flexion and bend where necessary, and can incorporate stretching into the work programme.

If you can work successfully with two lines, it will help with contact issues because you can be much softer in the hand. There is also a greater variety of work available, as you can now switch between circle work and work on straight lines, which helps with forwardness as well as building confidence, since effectively the horse has to take the lead.

If, however, you are experiencing problems when long-reining, either go back to lunge work until you are ready to progress to riding, or seek assistance, as it is easy to cause more issues than you are trying to resolve.

LONG-REINING EQUIPMENT

Equipment for the Horse

For long-reining, the horse should have his bridle on, with a training or lungeing cavesson over the top. Unless you are experienced in long-reining, we do not recommend attaching the reins directly to the bit for the first few sessions.

You can long-rein with a roller or a saddle. When using a saddle the stirrups should be pulled down and firmly secured under the belly.

Equipment for the Trainer

The trainer's equipment should be as for lunge

Fig. 9.1   Fred asks Mr Bojangles to work in medium trot. Bo could be more open in his neck but he is showing a good 'push' from the hindquarters and extension of the shoulder.

work: stout footwear, gloves, and a hard hat if working with a horse of unpredictable temperament.

GETTING STARTED

Probably the horse will have had experience of long-reining, but a long time ago, and you won't know how he reacted to it until you first bring the line round his hindquarters. As with lungeing, your position is of great importance, as is your initial reaction to the horse's reaction(s): thus if he leaps forwards when he feels the line around his back end, it is important not to be taken by surprise and let one of the reins go!

For double-lunge work, the usual lungeing position is adopted. When you progress to long-rein properly, always position yourself at a slight angle to the hindquarters, so the horse can see you.

Introduce the second line as follows – it is a task for two people. Attach a lead line to the cavesson (though we have used a headcollar) and a long line to the offside ring. Your assistant

Fig. 9.2   *The trainer should only be directly behind the horse for very advanced work.*

Fig. 9.4   *Having walked in a straight line, your assistant should quietly turn to the left. Be careful not to let the line actually touch the hindquarters. Ensure the horse he has you in his line of sight. Fred is deliberately holding the line away from the horse in an exaggerated manner so that the horse is aware of his presence during the turn. (Photograph courtesy of Matthew Roberts Photography)*

Fig. 9.3   *Position yourself at the horse's head on the off side. Your assistant should now lead the horse forwards while you work your way towards the hindquarters, gently releasing the line as you do so. (Photograph courtesy of Matthew Roberts Photography)*

Fig. 9.5   *The horse can now be fully introduced to the line along his offside. Don't worry if he steps a bit sideways as if to move away from the line; your assistant is controlling the head so you do nothing. (Photograph courtesy of Matthew Roberts Photography)*

Fig. 9.6   The horse may spook and his head come up and his quarters lower – adopting the 'preparing to flee' stance. Don't remove the line from his side; see if after a few moments he accepts it, as this horse has done. (Photograph courtesy of Matthew Roberts Photography)

should hold the horse whilst you position yourself on the offside. Work from the horse's head towards his hindquarters stroking his body as you do so, so that he is fully aware of your presence. Now repeat the exercise, but this time gradually release the offside long rein so the horse can see it, but don't let the line touch him.

If your horse does react in any way, keep walking him round the school with the line held off his side until he is relaxed; only then reintroduce it *gently*.

Continue to have your assistant lead the horse round the school to ensure he is completely at ease.

Fig. 9.7   As you turn the corner, the opportunity can be taken to move yourself to the near side which brings the line fully around the hindquarters. (Photograph courtesy of Matthew Roberts Photography)

Now is the time to attach both long reins. It is always easier and safer to gather the line in the hand, and feed the buckle end through the stirrup and attach it to the bit, rather than attaching it to the bit first and feeding the entire length of the line through the stirrup, particularly if the horse is tense.

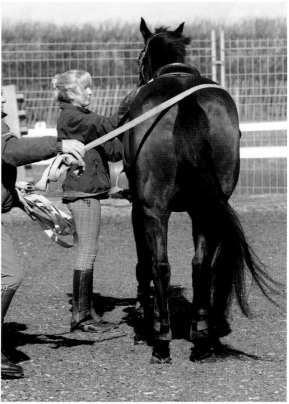

Fig. 9.8   With your assistant holding the horse, place the offside line on the back, just behind the saddle; gently feed the line over the hindquarters, making sure that the lines are gathered up and not trailing on the floor. (Photograph courtesy of Matthew Roberts Photography)

Let the horse stand for a moment so he can realize what is happening, and that nothing is actually different to the earlier exercise of walking round the school with the line round his quarters.

Have your assistant lead the horse round the school, being sure to change the rein. Horses all react differently, but most will reach this stage without too much fuss.

Now it's time to go it alone! When you are happy that all is going well, your assistant can gradually move further away from the horse until they are no longer of any influence.

Allow your horse to walk on without taking up a contact; he should remain relaxed, but don't be alarmed if he goes with his head up and his neck stiff, as this sort of reaction is not uncommon.

Your task is gradually to eradicate this tension by taking up the reins for a couple of strides or

Fig. 9.9   *Have your assistant remain close by to begin with so that he/she is on-hand to provide reassurance or quickly re-attach a lead line if necessary. (Photograph courtesy of Matthew Roberts Photography)*

Fig. 9.10   *This horse is showing the classical confused signals of a horse that has been taught to move on whenever any contact/pressure is put on the reins; his head has come up and the stride has shortened.*

so, and then releasing them, over and over again: it's a case of repetition, slowly increasing the number of strides taken. When you progress to trot, the whole scenario will be repeated.

This is where experience of long-reining is so important on the part of the trainer.

Fig. 9.11   *In a matter of minutes in Fred's expert hands, Oscar is already more confident to take the rein contact although his tension remains.*

Fig. 9.12   *After a few days, the improvement in Oscar is positive; he is more readily rounding and dropping on to the bit as he should, although the tension is still there as evidenced by the way he is holding his neck; a more active hind leg is also required but this will come as suppleness improves.*

An alternative way to attach the long reins
The long reins can also be used so that the outer rein is passed over the horse's back, rather than round his hindquarters. With this method the horse is more manoeuvrable, it is a better way to teach acceptance of the outside rein and a softer inside rein, and the trainer can develop more feel. However, without a lunge whip it can be harder to keep a horse moving forwards.

Work in Progress

With two lines attached, work no longer has to be restricted to circles – but this means that you do have to be fit in order to work a horse in trot and ultimately canter in a straight line! Working a horse on two lines enables the trainer to have much more control over the horse's way of going, as well as allowing work to become more demanding without the weight of a rider.

Nevertheless, however keen you are to make progress, you must allow time for the horse's muscles to soften and strengthen – and this can't be hurried, nor can it be forced, otherwise you run the risk of damaging muscles and joints. Trying to force the neck into an outline before the neck and back muscles are developed can result in tension and strain particularly at the poll. Similarly forcing the

hindquarters under (asking the horse to 'sit') can result in discomfort to the lumbar region as well as having a knock-on effect to the shoulders and even the withers.

Just as when riding, the trainer should be able to put the horse's head wherever he/she wants, and to influence the horse completely. As long reins don't keep the head in a fixed position, a horse can also stretch down – and this he may elect to do in his search for, and acceptance of, contact. When a horse really stretches it does wonders for his top-line muscles, as well as lifting his back, and 'stretch time' should be a part of the training session in walk, trot and canter, not just at the end of it.

Working with two lines opens up all manner of training opportunities, and you can teach your horse leg-yielding, shoulder-in, and ultimately – for the horse aimed at dressage – travers, half-pass, piaffe and passage!

Figs 9.13–9.16   In these four photographs Dora (black mare) and Light the Fuse (bay gelding) illustrate how the trainer should be able to influence a horse's head carriage when long-reining, just as when ridden. (Photographs below courtesy of Matthew Roberts Photography)

Fig. 9.17   Lateral movements, however simple, form the basis of straightening the crooked horse and teaching better engagement of the hind leg as well as the teaching of taking weight behind.

Fig. 9.18   Call Oscar has backed off – he needs sending on. By not correcting this immediately a horse can soon learn to drop back and this can lead to napping.

PROBLEM SOLVING

Most problems are highlighted or exacerbated when the lines are attached directly to the bit. The weight of the reins directly on the bit will equate to a 'pull', even though the lines around his body are signalling for him to go forwards, so this is a confusing time for the horse as he learns to accept a direct contact.

Problem: My horse won't go forwards/runs backwards/rears

First it is important to rule out a problem with the bit, as it may be that you are using a bit design that is not ideal for the individual horse; also check that the noseband is not too tight, or remove it altogether. Next you should check that his teeth are not too sharp, or that he is not in discomfort due to any other physical reasons.

If the horse persists in this resistance, then it is a trainer issue, attributable to inexperience, poor communication, lack of feel. The balance between maintaining a contact whilst encouraging forwardness is a fine one, and it is easy to give conflicting signals. However, a horse that continually rears is clearly distressed and trying to indicate something, and outside help should be sought before the situation gets out of hand.

Fig. 9.19   This is what you are aiming for during the early stages of re-training from the ground. Indie is already showing good lateral suppleness through his neck, although he does need to step under more. Note that even with such a light contact on the lines, Fred has complete influence on Indie's way of going.

Fig. 9.20   Call Oscar turns his head to the outside on the left side because his muscles are tighter down his right side. As Fred is very experienced in line work, he is able to correct this with half halts and gentle play on the inside rein without risk of upsetting Oscar.

Problem: My horse won't bend to the inside

A horse usually doesn't flex or bend to the inside because the offside muscles are tight and restrictive, so first of all it is important to rule out any possible causes other than general stiffness. Repositioning of the inside long rein can slowly encourage a softening of the outer muscles, allowing the horse to bend to the inside: attach the buckle of the long rein to the bit. Pass it through the bit ring and attach it to the roller or girth of the saddle. Note that only the inside line should be attached in this way.

If the horse should curl his head/neck into his chest or tilt his head with the rein attached in

Figs 9.21 and 9.22   How not to make a downward transition (above). There is too much contact on the left line and the horse is resisting. When the aids are applied correctly (below), he is much happier although there is still a long way to go as he needs to learn to lower his head and step under more.

this way, raise the line to a higher roller ring (or higher up the girth strap on the saddle); this can occur with horses that are very sensitive in the mouth, or if the trainer is not soft enough with the hand.

If the horse is carrying side-reins, don't be tempted to shorten the inside side-rein. A fixed rein is a dead rein and doesn't achieve a true softening. Fixing the head in this way sets the neck in the so-called desired position, but strains the outside muscles. The softening and building of muscles works by the muscle alternately contracting and relaxing.

Problem: My horse is resistant in downward transitions – he hollows

If a horse throws up its head when asked to do a downward transition it is often the fault of the handler because he/she is not light enough in the hand: the handling of long reins needs to be as soft and light as when holding the reins when riding.

First of all be sure that the bit you are using is not too severe, or pinching because it is too small, or hanging out of the horse's mouth because it is too large.

Then when you ask for a downward transition, initially work on it being a progressive change over the course of a few strides, rather than aiming for it to happen within a stride – in other words, gradually slow the pace first. This gives the horse the chance to understand what he is being asked to do, and allows for a smoother transition.

Give and release the reins a few times in succession, rather than 'holding' until the horse responds, as this prevents him just leaning into the bit and propping himself on you. The resistant horse is a hollow horse.

Practise downward transitions on a circle first, as you have more control and the horse is more focused than when working on a straight line.

Finally, remember that the elbows should be bent to provide an elastic contact, just as when riding.

Problem: My horse won't accept the contact/take the bit

This is a very common situation. Although you may have been lungeing your horse quite happily, the addition of the second line can temporarily upset things: with reins attached to either side of the bit working independently of each other, everything can feel strange and confusing. Whilst in walk, issues can be addressed more readily, but when you move into trot it is difficult to respond quickly enough with a given rein as well as maintaining impulsion. But if a horse won't accept the bit on lines, the same is going to be true under saddle, so it is better to resolve this issue from the ground.

To start with, the horse needs encouraging more forwards – be sure that you are allowing him to walk out actively. Thoroughbreds usually have a good walk, and any attempt at trying to contain it will result in him backing off and not actively seeking the bit.

Carry out lots of exercises in walk, but take care not to constrict the walk: different sized circles, serpentines, loops and zig-zags, walk over poles, leg yielding.

Flexing the horse's neck to the left for a few strides, and then to the right helps soften and stretch tight neck muscles – though be careful not to swing the horse's head (*see* Fig. 9.23).

Alternate between working on a circle and true long-reining, so that your horse gets more confident about taking the lead.

Problem: It all goes wrong in trot

The moment you ask the horse to trot – off he goes, much too fast and up comes the head! The simplest solution is to slow the trot right down so that the horse is moving in a seemingly lazy fashion, and to work on a smaller circle: he then has to drop his head in order to balance.

Once he has lowered his head you can quietly ask for more impulsion – not speed.

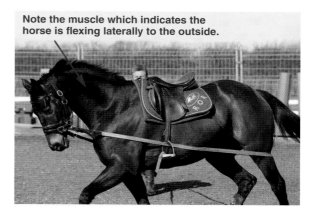

Note the muscle which indicates the horse is flexing laterally to the outside.

Fig. 9.23   Counter-flexion is a very useful exercise (in walk, trot and canter) at all training levels as the amount of flexion can be increased.

Problem: My horse takes off in canter

Asking for canter often results in an explosive leap forwards, sometimes with a buck. This happens because the trainer gives too forceful an aid with the outside line – a 'slap' as opposed to a 'flick' – or through lack of balance/suppleness.

Be reassured that cantering on lines is classed as 'advanced work' by many trainers, and remember that a horse needs to be reasonably muscled and fit to cope with canter work.

When asking for canter use your voice, as the horse will remember the voice aids from his lunge work. Be sure to keep a contact with the inside rein (don't let it go), and flick the outside rein.

The horse will undoubtedly canter too fast and you must steady him as quickly as you can, otherwise he may slip. If he canters too fast he is leaning.

Problem: My horse drops his shoulder

Often the trainer is at fault because he is too severe with the inside rein, and does not have enough contact with the outside rein (think riding), so the horse is being pulled round. Also the working circle may be too small for the suppleness and balance of the horse.

10 Groundwork over Poles

Polework is an important part of any horse's training, whatever his discipline. It provides variety and interest – thoroughbreds soon get bored, especially in the early stages of retraining – and achieves so much when done correctly: establishes rhythm, improves co-ordination and suppleness and activates the joints, increases athleticism, aids strengthening and helps relaxation.

The success of working a horse loose over poles depends on your control skills, as a horse will often try and rush. However, provided he is fully conversant with your commands and is confident in you as his guide, then all should progress well. When lungeing or long-reining over poles, control of speed is just as important, because without an even tempo the horse risks stepping on the poles or stumbling over them – he learns nothing.

Poles can be set in a line, or in a fan shape. The distance between poles depends on your horse's natural stride length, but is usually 4ft to 4ft 6in.

Be sure to use protective boots or bandages for polework and jumping.

GETTING STARTED

Start by leading your horse over a single pole: if he unexpectedly finds it in his path on the lunge line he is likely to cut in to avoid going over it.

Commence by lungeing as normal, but away from the pole. Gradually move closer to the pole until it is in the horse's path and he has to trot over it. If he tries to duck past the pole, lay a second pole at right angles as a guide; this is also useful if a horse habitually cuts in on the circle.

When he is relaxed and happy with this, add another pole (you may need to alter the distance to suit his stride). Gradually add poles until you have up to eight, and he is negotiating them in an even, rhythmical trot.

By varying the distance between the poles a horse can be encouraged to lengthen or shorten his stride; placing the poles in a fan shape allows you to do this without having to move poles.

A very useful exercise to encourage hock and general joint flexion is to work a horse over raised poles. They can either be raised just at one end or alternately at different ends, so that viewed from the front it looks like a giant X. Work over raised poles is a good exercise for the pelvis/hips.

Fig. 10.1   Be careful not to pull on the line, otherwise you will contribute to unbalancing the horse. If you are working over a row of poles, as opposed to a fan, gradually manoeuvre him back onto the circle; don't pull him in sharply. Note how loose Fred has the line so as not to create any interference. Note also the pole laid at right angles to the trot poles; this prevents a horse from cutting in.

Fig. 10.2   *When first using the the Equi-Ami for polework it is sensible to loosen it a bit from how you have been perhaps using it to date so that the horse has more freedom of the neck whilst he learns to negotiate the poles.*

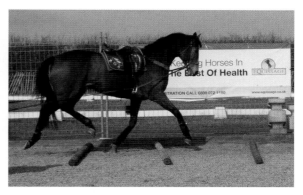

Fig. 10.3   *Long-reining over poles allows the trainer to have more influence in that the horse can be shortened up by get his attention so that he looks where he is going, his speed can be regulated and he can be kept straight.*

A horse can be worked over poles in side-reins, but only if he is very accepting of them and is already working in an outline to a certain extent. Side-reins fitted too early will restrict the natural 'forward and down' inclination of the head and neck. At a later stage of the horse's training side-reins can be used to encourage greater hock engagement and elevation, but the horse should be closely observed to ensure that the side-reins are not causing him to lose forward momentum. A horse can be worked over raised poles when side-reins are attached, but the trainer must pay careful attention to ensure they are not causing a restriction; such indication would be the horse inverting or shortening his neck.

A horse can also be successfully worked over poles with an Equi-ami, including raised poles.

The advantage of long-reining over poles is that you can more readily incorporate changes of rein into the training session, which is particularly useful for horses that get excited by polework. It allows the trainer to have more influence in that the horse can be shortened up by getting his attention so that he looks where he is going, his speed can be regulated, and he can be kept straight.

JUMPING FROM THE GROUND

Loose Jumping

Loose jumping is great fun for horses, though you do need to control the pace. Initially you will probably need to create a lane to encourage your horse to the fence and to help keep him straight; this can be done by placing poles on barrels to make a barrier. It is also helpful to have an assistant to keep the horse on the track, preventing him from changing the rein at will and controlling the speed.

First let the horse familiarize himself with the jumping lane, on both reins, without even a pole on the ground. Then lay a single pole on the ground, if possible keeping the horse in trot. Next raise just one end of the pole, and then introduce a small cross-pole.

Controlling the pace is important otherwise the horse may rush, so that when he meets the fence he makes an awkward jump or hurdles it, which rather defeats the object of the exercise, which is to improve his jumping technique. This is where the assistant is useful, as they can move around with the horse, positioning themselves adjacent to his shoulder, thereby acting as a brake.

Fig. 10.4   Tricky shows natural jumping ability but he is not folding up his forelegs enough nor lifting enough from the shoulder. However, jumps built in different ways and the use of grids will correct this.

Single Fence

Always start with a small cross-pole. To begin with the horse may be so excited that he makes a very awkward jump, but don't worry, just let him get rid of some of his excess energy, after which he will be more prepared to settle down and listen.

Use your voice and body language to control his speed, and don't position the jump too far off the corner – like that it will limit how much speed the horse can pick up down the long side of the school.

If the horse is rushing and hurdling the cross-pole, add a filler, because a solid jump has the effect of backing the horse off. A place pole 12ft from the jump also has a braking effect. It is not a good idea to place the pole any closer to the jump until you have better control, otherwise the horse risks treading on it whilst he is working out his striding.

The single fence can be an upright, but it is better to build an ascending oxer or a triple bar as this type of fence is more inviting and will encourage the horse to make a better shape, thus improving his technique.

Don't be dismayed if on your first attempt at loose jumping your horse doesn't make a very good shape over the fence: just be pleased that he is prepared to jump it at all – there is plenty of time to work on technique. And be sure to change the rein; horses nearly always favour one rein, and jump better in one direction than the other.

It is useful to loose jump a horse with tack on, as it accustoms him to the feel of the saddle and girth. It also allows the trainer to observe whether the saddle has a negative influence on the horse compared to how he jumps without it.

Fig. 10.5   A pole at the base of the fence provides a ground line making it more inviting for the horse new to jumping or lacking confidence.

Fig. 10.6   Call Oscar shows a boldness to his jumping as he is completely unfazed by the addition of the barrels.

Fig. 10.7   Initially the first jump should be an upright and the second an oxer, which can be widened as well as increased in height. Keep the first fence small and inviting; the second jump can be altered to test ability and boldness, and fillers can also be added.

Fig. 10.8   Always start off with simple grids to gain confidence; then you can become more ambitious.

Combinations

Once your horse is confidently jumping a single fence, a second fence can be introduced. Allow two or even three strides between the two, allowing 24ft for one stride – 6ft for landing, 12ft for a stride and 6ft for take-off. This distance may need shortening a little, depending on your horse's natural stride length. Initially the first jump should be an upright and the second an oxer, which you can widen as well as increase in height. Keep the first fence small and inviting; you can alter the second jump to test ability and boldness.

Don't be tempted to make the combination a bounce because you risk the horse tackling it as one fence, which whilst the jumps are low isn't so much of a problem but can risk serious injury once the height begins to increase.

Whilst a horse is building up his confidence and learning to jump don't make things harder for him by playing with stride lengths, but work with his own stride. Teaching lengthening and shortening of strides can be introduced gradually.

When you feel your horse is ready, the stride can be reduced to just one between the two

jumps. Lower the jump height initially just in case your horse panics or gets things a bit wrong; make it as easy for him as possible – you don't want to frighten him.

Likewise when you decide to try a bounce (12ft between the two jumps), the first jump in particular should be low (not so low that he practically steps over it) so that if your horse is focused on the second jump, the first jump is not high enough to cause any real problems.

Grids

If the horse is jumping confidently, and if space permits, you can introduce a third fence: this is the basis for gridwork.

The distances can be varied: thus between the first and second jumps you can have a stride or a bounce, and between the second and third jumps one or two strides. It is not good practice to use two bounces with just three jumps; if you are building a longer grid for the more experienced horse and have four jumps then you could have two bounces and a stride between the third and fourth fences. With a stride to finish the horse can regain impulsion if he has landed short over the previous fence.

With a grid, as with combinations, don't play around with distances until your horse is

Figs 10.9 and 10.10 The trainer must be careful not to interfere with the horse's mouth when lungeing over a jump; it is very easy to pull on the line and therefore put the horse off possibly causing him to stop or run out.

confident in what he is doing, otherwise you could put him off completely.

It will test his courage and ability to use fillers and to end the row with an ascending oxer; however, first be sure that your horse is happy and confident, because the last thing you want is to risk him refusing part way down the grid. Gridwork is the best way to build confidence and improve technique, but you should seek advice on how to construct grids depending on what you are trying to achieve.

Jumping on the Lunge

We prefer not to jump horses on the lunge, opting for loose jumping instead. However, if

you don't have a suitably enclosed area, then jumping on the lunge can be a very useful part of the training process, as long as you proceed carefully.

The aim of jumping on the lunge is not to see how high a horse can jump, but to encourage him to adopt a rounded shape. Don't try and catch him out – provide a true ground line to the jump. Spreads and parallels, rather than upright fences, teach the horse better technique in that they encourage a rounder jump.

Lungeing is a great way to introduce fillers.

Be very careful when jumping a horse on the lunge not to catch him in the mouth, particularly on the landing side, or to get in front of him as he is approaching the fence. You must be ready to move yourself about – and quickly.

Make sure there is no risk of the lunge line catching on anything; it is really only safe to lunge over single fences.

Jumping on Long Lines

Jumping a horse on long lines does require considerable skill, as it is very easy to put too much contact into the outside rein, and also to pull the horse up too sharply on landing. If it is not possible to organize a lane for loose jumping, then lungeing is the preferred option.

PROBLEM SOLVING

Problem: My horse keeps kicking out the raised poles
If a horse has difficulty flexing his joints he will more readily keep knocking raised poles. A horse that rushes over the poles is also more likely to knock them, as his strides will not be rhythmical.

First of all, slow the approach right down – to the point where the horse is almost breaking into walk if necessary – so that he has time to work out what to do with his feet. Just use two raised poles until he gets the idea of what to do, and make sure you are not raising the poles too high. If possible make the poles more stable using pole pods or jump blocks, so they don't knock down so easily.

Remember that working over raised poles is strenuous, so don't work for too long.

Problem: My horse keeps knocking the cross-pole down
Much as you want to keep the jump very low until you are happy that your horse is confidently going to go over it, some horses have absolutely no respect for poles and it is

Fig. 10.11 *When using more than one jump, be sure to prevent the horse being able to duck out between elements by using a raised pole as a guide rail. A guide rail into the jump will help keep the horse straight for take-off.*

better to have a more solid-looking fence. This can be achieved by using two or three straw bales placed end to end if you haven't any fillers.

Problem: My horse won't go to the jump when loose jumping
The best way to prevent a horse ducking out of a jump is to construct a long enough 'guide chute' towards it so that he learns straightaway what is expected of him.

You must be very clear in your instructions, and absolutely determined. Until your horse is familiar with loose jumping you have to be prepared to be very active yourself in guiding him towards the fence. This is a good time to enlist the help of an assistant.

A lunge whip is a useful extension of the arm to help convey your instructions, but it should never be used to frighten or chase the horse into a jump. Doing so will end up producing a horse that jumps through fear and not because he wants to – or worse, it could cause him to make an awkward jump and injure himself.

11 Basic Training Under Saddle

The time has come to actually start riding! It is important that riders are aware of the effect their body has on the horse, in terms of changes in weight distribution and their own tension. Horses also pick up the mixed signals that riders give out, which can be confusing for them. Most of the issues experienced under saddle are actually rider-related, and it makes no difference that you are on an ex-racehorse – in fact even clearer, more consistent aids are required.

Until you have ridden your horse for a few days you may not be sure whether your initial bit choice is correct, though the groundwork you have done with him should have established that he is happy in his mouth. However, it is not uncommon for a bit change to be required once ridden work commences. On the day you intend to get on him, don't do anything differently; tack him up with the same equipment you have been using for lungeing/long-reining work; if you want to introduce anything new, do this a few days prior to mounting. The day before mounting for the first time is not the best day to have new shoes fitted or attention from an EDT. It is simply a case of knowing that your horse is comfortable so that if he reacts adversely then there are fewer possible causes to rule out.

You will need an assistant, so if possible have this person present for a couple of days before you actually need them to do anything so that your horse is familiar with them.

Keep to your usual routine of lunge work (or long-reining), but stop a little sooner than you would normally.

Fig. 11.1   *Rider position in the saddle and the application of the aids are so important; riders can actually prevent a horse from achieving what he is being asked to do despite his best efforts. Line A = line of contact from bit to elbow; Line B = alignment of shoulder, hip and heel.*

GETTING ON

However calm and trusting your horse appears, and however confident you feel, it is a sensible precaution to lean over your horse's back prior to mounting in case he is reactive. (For the purposes of this book it is assumed that your horse has had a let-down period of two to three months.) The following procedure may seem pointless, but it is better to play safe and have a positive result than later wish you had gone through this process.

Whilst leaning over his back, have your assistant lead you about in a safe environment until the horse is relaxed.

Provided the horse seems relaxed, swing your leg over his back (don't catch his hindquarters) and quietly sit up; have your assistant move the horse forwards a step. If all is well, progress to being led about, but if the horse is at all tense, just move a few steps at a time until he is happy.

For the first few days whilst your horse adjusts to having someone on his back again, have a leg-up to mount. That way you haven't got to

Fig. 11.2 Lie still and judge the horse's reaction to you being across his back before proceeding. If he is at all unsure, keep repeating the process until he is ok. (Photograph courtesy of Matthew Roberts Photography)

Fig. 11.3 Hold onto the off-side stirrup for added stability – not the reins. (Photograph courtesy of Matthew Roberts Photography)

tackle too much all in one go – such as asking the horse to stand beside a mounting block and accept weight in the stirrup.

Accustom your horse to the mounting block by letting him inspect the block, standing him by it, leading him around and also moving it around him.

Practise putting a little weight into the stirrup (just lean down on it) so the horse becomes used to how it feels; this can be done in the confines of a stable or arena rather than outside. Even using a mounting block a rider will still put weight into the nearside stirrup, which the ex-racehorse won't be used to.

Next, position the horse by the mounting block, and climb up and down it; you may need someone to hold the horse for you, as he is quite likely to try and walk off whilst you do this.

Once he will stand at the block and allow you to stand on it without trying to walk away, it's time to get on. Don't fuss about – make the decision to get on, and do so. Hopefully your horse will feel relaxed and won't try to walk away immediately – and provided your assistant remains in front of him, he shouldn't. However, let him if he wants to: this isn't the time to teach him to stand still, and your assistant is

Fig. 11.4 Have your helper hold the horse. Initially he/she should stand in front of him as this is what he is used to. The horse must not be allowed to move until you are safely in the saddle. (Photograph courtesy of Matthew Roberts Photography)

Fig. 11.5 At this stage don't be worried about taking up the reins as the less feel the horse senses on his mouth the better. Just gather them loosely in your hand; your assistant is there to control the horse. (Photograph courtesy of Matthew Roberts Photography)

there to keep control from the ground. Be pleased that you are safely on board and the horse wants to go forwards. You can practise standing still once you are actually in the saddle, doing it gradually.

Most mounting problems occur because:

● the horse isn't properly introduced to the mounting block

Fig. 11.6 Be sure not to catch your horse's back as you swing your leg over and lower yourself quickly but gently into the saddle. (Photograph courtesy of Matthew Roberts Photography)

● the rider fidgets too much, making the horse tense and apprehensive
● too tight a hold is taken on the reins causing tension; the reins should be loosely gathered
● the rider doesn't adopt the right position for mounting, so their toes dig into the horse's side; the side of the rider's foot should lay along the horse's belly, not be at right-angles to it
● the rider lumps down in the saddle – often the cause of horses jumping forwards
● once in the stand the rider expects the horse to stand still indefinitely and starts pulling on the reins in an endeavour to get the horse to stand.

Even with an assistant some horses become very agitated about standing still. Position your mounting block in a corner so that there is a 'restraining barrier' both in front and to the off side. This will stop your horse from walking forwards or going sideways as you put your foot in the stirrup. Should he then try to go backwards, place a few bales of shavings or

Fig. 11.7 Practice at standing still once the rider is actually in the saddle can be gradually introduced; keep your seat light and slightly inclined initially. Practise gathering up the reins a little too. (Photograph courtesy of Matthew Roberts Photography)

Fig. 11.8   As your horse becomes more accustomed and settled to being mounted from a block, you can dispense with your assistant and build on being able to mount unaided. (Photograph courtesy of Matthew Roberts Photography)

straw a few feet behind the block – in effect you will have created a three-sided box. Keep your seat light and slightly inclined initially. Practise gathering up the reins a little, too.

As your horse becomes more accustomed and settled to being mounted from a block you can ask your assistant to stand aside, and practise mounting without their assistance. Should your horse try to walk away as you mount, get him into a corner so he has nowhere to go.

TAKING CONTROL

Once on board, let your assistant lead you away. Don't be temped to take control – that is the task of your helper.

Initially be mindful not to press your legs against the horse's sides, and don't draw them back either; just let them hang down. Keep the reins loose and just relax! Your assistant shouldn't look at the horse.

When the horse appears relaxed and is walking calmly, very gently press one leg

against his side, then repeat with the other leg. Do this a few times to make the horse aware that your legs are there. If he reacts in any way, take your leg off for a few moments, then repeat the process. Racehorses do know about legs but they are not accustomed to how they are used for conventional riding; jockeys and work riders grip with their knees. If the horse jogs, just use your bodyweight to keep you balanced; your assistant is there for control.

Much as your instinct is to gather up the reins, don't be tempted take a firm hold of them as that is a cue to a racehorse to go faster! At this stage, until you are sure of the horse's reactions, it is better to have a slightly loose rein as your assistant has contact with the bit via the lunge rein. Also keep a light, slightly inclined seat so that the horse isn't taking your full weight on his back; and remember to breathe – long, slow, deep breaths.

Fig. 11.9   A picture of contentment: a relaxed horse ready to progress to the next stage of his training.

Fig. 11.10   *Don't take a firm hold of the reins. If you shorten them up, you have given the horse a clear indication to go faster. Let the horse begin to feel your legs against his sides. (Photograph courtesy of Matthew Roberts Photography)*

Fig. 11.11   *Be led around the school in large circles, loops, etc. as horses can react differently on the left and right reins. Gradually take a hold of the reins if the horse feels relaxed enough. (Photograph courtesy of Matthew Roberts Photography)*

How you now progress will depend entirely upon your horse – whether you need to repeat the above process over a few days, or whether you can move on.

The next step is to have your assistant let the line out a little so that you can quietly take a bit more control, and the logical progression is for them to keep letting the line out in conjunction with gradually adopting the lungeing position. Lungeing is something with which your horse is now very familiar, so the experience won't feel too different other than he is doing it with you on his back.

Initially walk, but move on to trot – even if you only feel confident enough to do a few strides or just half a circuit of the school – and don't forget to work on both reins.

Fig. 11.12   *As your assistant lets the line out, try not to make any sudden reactions such as tightening of your grip on the reins or clamping your legs onto the horse's side; nor should you try to influence the way in which your horse is walking by use of your seat.*

Fig. 11.13   *Most horses are absolutely fine when the lunge line is lengthened, but for the horse that is overly tense, perhaps because he has not had a rider on for a considerable time, take your time and build confidence on both sides.*

Fig. 11.14 Don't be afraid to relax and give your horse a reassuring pat every now and then! (Photograph courtesy of Matthew Roberts Photography)

When this exercise can be safely executed it's time to go it alone – well, almost. When you are first released from the lunge line, your assistant should remain walking at the horse's side for reassurance. Only when you feel the horse is relaxed should they gradually step further away from you, just as they would during lunge work. There is no need to set off round the whole school – stay in a smaller area, akin to a lunge circle, if you feel happier like that. This may seem unnecessary, but it is safer not to take anything for granted until a horse is established in his new routine.

MAKING CONTACT

Now you are on board and independent, basic training can begin.

Typically as you gather up the reins a little the horse will poke his nose out or even throw his head into the air, despite having lunged in a wonderful outline. It is important that you are sure there is no physical explanation for these reactions, hence the importance of a chiropractic assessment, dental attention and checks of the fit of saddle, bridle and bit.

Remember that the racehorse works or races by 'pulling' against the rider. They are ridden with a very loose rein in walk and trot, but the moment any kind of 'contact' is made – the mere weight of the rider's hand on the rein is enough – the horse feels a 'pull' on his mouth, which is the signal to go faster. When the reins are shortened and the rider inclines forwards as he stands in the stirrups this means 'break to canter'. Remember, if you pull against your horse, he will pull against you – he has been trained to do so; he has to be ridden into the contact, not pulled into it.

Fig. 11.15 Work riders and jockeys ride with bridged reins as this gives a very secure hold and the horse can lean against the hands. Any change on this hold is also an accelerant. (Photograph courtesy of Clive Cox Racing)

Fig. 11.16 While Rowena is just holding her legs off; ideally they could be slightly further forward, which would result in a lighter seat. (Photograph courtesy of Matthew Roberts Photography)

The term 'coming off the bridle' means the horse has stopped pulling, for some reason – so if your horse starts to go faster than you wish, *loosen* the grip on the reins and let them out, and sit down in the saddle.

Once mounted, continue to take things gradually. Initially just walk about the school on a long rein, but not a loose one: have enough feel on the rein so that the horse can feel the

Fig. 11.17 Pretty Officer reacts in typical fashion by throwing her head up as she breaks to a jog.

Fig. 11.18 Rowena sits quietly, doesn't react and makes no alteration to the hold on the reins. Pretty Officer soon realizes that walking around in a more sensible manner is much nicer than throwing herself about.

bit, but the bit action is not coming into play. Visualize the bit sitting on the gums – your task is to maintain its position.

If the horse jogs, don't be tempted to grab at the reins, because quite apart from having the opposite effect to the one you want, a sudden tightening of the reins may cause the horse to panic. It is important to keep the hands down and be supple through the arm joints so the horse feels no tension down the reins.

If the horse is suitably relaxed and you feel confident, have a trot about; keep a long rein, and don't try to organize or influence the horse. At this stage it is all about him being happy with you on his back, and you being able to move your body without causing him alarm. If he is a little too forwards, bring him on to an oval shape, rather than letting him speed up round the whole school.

It is important that the horse accepts the leg; this doesn't mean the application of any particular aids, or gripping with the legs, but just letting them gently rest against his sides. Remember that not every racehorse will be used to feeling a longer leg down his side. At suitable moments you can press gently but a little more firmly, though try and do this when you would apply a true leg aid, such as using the inside leg when going round a corner.

Move around quietly in the saddle so he can feel your weight shift, but be careful not to catch him in the mouth or bump his sides with your legs. It is important to be able to judge a horse and his reactions; what are his ears doing, has he suddenly shorted his stride, has his back tightened, has his neck shortened, has he dropped the contact (or whatever contact there was), is there an increased tension down the rein, etc? These are just some of the signs that a horse is about to spook, nap, whip round, buck, etc. A rider needs the ability to anticipate so that such reactions can be prevented.

If the horse appears calm and happy with what is going on you can move about in the saddle a little more – so quietly lean forwards a

Fig. 11.19   *As it had been a while since someone was on Oscar's back, we elected for his first non-led ride to be in confines of the Round Pen. If you don't have a suitably small area, then, as with lunge work, section off a corner of the school/paddock.*

Fig. 11.20   *When Rowena purposely moves her leg back, Oscar responds by lifting his head and shortening the neck slightly but otherwise he is fine. Oscar naturally carries his head high and did so whilst in training; he now needs to learn to lower that head.*

bit, and to the side. This will help him get used to how your weight moves when you are riding properly and jumping, or if he suddenly shies, or when you tighten the girth when mounted.

THE IMPORTANCE OF RIDER POSITION

The riding position is vitally important and influences a horse's whole way of going. Many 'issues' are actually because the rider isn't secure and balanced in the saddle, and so grips with the legs and hangs on with the reins. It is very helpful to have a friend watch what you are up to occasionally – or better still, take a video – then you can see what you need to address.

The better your position the more open the lines of communication, and the better your horse will be able to move. As a rider, if you are not sitting in a balanced manner, the horse has to counter your uneven weight distribution in order to remain balanced himself. This can lead to tensions in his body, which can be manifested in gait alteration.

Fig. 11.21   *This rider generally sat well, but had a habit of bringing her lower leg back a little too far, especially when the horse was unco-operative. By riding in symmetry straps for a while, she was able to learn where to keep her legs and strengthen her leg muscles at the same time.*

Fig. 11.22   Here Rowena demonstrates the rider that leans back coupled with a drawn back lower leg, turned out toes and slouching! Poor Hero Worship just doesn't know what to do. By sitting in this way, a rider is totally unable to impart a positive influence on the horse. If the aids are inaccurately or ineffectively applied, a horse cannot be expected to respond correctly. Thus the seemingly unresponsive, unco-operative horse is usually one that is not being ridden properly.

One of the biggest faults of riders is that they ride with their stirrups too short. This tips them forwards, bringing the lower leg too far back,

and means they are not in balance, which affects the horse.

It takes a while to adjust to riding with longer stirrups, and in the meantime the lower leg is weak, resulting in the rider being unable to keep their weight down in the stirrup and turning the toes out; try thinking pigeon-toed when you are in the saddle and this will help you train yourself to keep your feet parallel with the horse's side.

In Fig. 11.22, Rowena demonstrates the rider that leans back, coupled with a drawn back lower leg, turned out toes and slouching. Like this, the rider is totally unable to impart a positive influence on the horse, which doesn't know what to do.

To demonstrate the positive influence a better position has on the horse's way of going, compare Figs 11.23 and 11.24 showing Abi on Nic. Sitting as she was, Abi was not being effective in terms of getting responses from Nic when schooling him; she knew to keep her legs forwards, but she actually had them too far forwards, and this, coupled with her riding too short and with her heels pushed too far down, was causing her to sit too far back on the cantle of the saddle.

Figs 11.23 and 11.24   The influence of the correction is clearly evident by the improvement in Nic's way of going.

Fig. 11.25 Rowena demonstrates riding with a collapsed left hip and is clearly crooked in the saddle; if the horse was not being led he would most likely drift to the left as the rider's weight is more in the left stirrup. (Photograph courtesy of Matthew Roberts Photography)

Abi worked hard at riding with longer stirrups, and was able to be more influential over Nic's way of going (*see* Figs 11.23 and 11.24).

When a rider is sitting crookedly they genuinely can't feel this; likewise it is very easy to think that you are sitting up when in fact you are leaning forwards or slouching, especially when trying hard to teach or improve a movement – shoulder-in regularly causes tipped shoulders and strange twists of the rider's body.

Sitted crookedly doesn't just affect the side on which the rider is collapsing: invariably the other side of the rider's body is also affected because the leg comes back, and sometimes the toe turns out too.

However, when the rider can feel he is crooked because he can feel more weight in one stirrup, the lower leg feeling as if the belly is pushed against it, this is an indication that the horse may well be the culprit. From behind the horse will most likely be seen to walk in a slightly crabbed way, the hind legs not truly following the path of the forelegs. This is usually because the horse is stronger in one rein than the other so he twists into it.

Having had a physical explanation ruled out (saddle fit and chiropractic check), you can counteract this and straighten up the horse by consciously putting more of your weight in the stirrup on the offending side – so if the horse is pushing on your left leg, put more weight into your right stirrup (in all three gaits), softening your contact on the right rein at the same time – the horse must let go of the rein.

You should be able to feel through your seat, thighs and legs how the horse moves in his back and ribcage. Similarly the rider's hands follow the mouth – but how many riders have stiff wrists and locked elbows? Such restriction doesn't allow the horse to take up a soft, elastic contact with his rider.

In all three gaits the rider should be able to feel which leg is where: by knowing the footfalls the rider can achieve, for example, a flying change because when to apply the aids is dependent upon what the hind legs are doing. There is no point giving an aid, say, for

Fig. 11.26 The crooked rider – collapsed to the left causing the right leg to come too far back; uneven rein contact – causing the bit to be pulled through the mouth. Both result in a horse tense in the neck and through the back. (Photograph courtesy of Matthew Roberts Photography)

impulsion, when the activating leg is in the air – it must be on the ground so that the horse can 'push' into the movement.

A correctly timed aid obviously doesn't have to be reapplied, thus keeping communication clear and concise; it is also softer and virtually invisible to the observer.

Rider Exercise

To help you be more effective as a rider, try this exercise to improve co-ordination and positive application of the aids: put some blocks evenly spaced down the centre of the school, then ride in and out of them – as bending poles – using your legs rather than your hands: use your bodyweight and look where you are going, and imagine you haven't any reins to guide you!

Promoting Relaxation

Every horse reacts differently, but promoting relaxation is of paramount importance, even if it takes a couple of weeks. There is no benefit in trying to progress unless you can at least have a relaxed walk, because you need to establish a point of comfort for your horse that you can always come back to should he get upset, tense or confused.

It is very easy to gather up the reins at the first sign of tension in case the horse tries to race off, but you must resist the temptation to do so. Learn to sit still and do nothing, and don't react in any way apart from giving the rein – the racehorse is used to relaxing on a loose rein. Breathe deeply and slowly as this also influences the horse.

BASIC WORK

In all the following movements and exercises, remember that you are retraining an ex-

COMMUNICATING WITH THE VOICE

So many riders are silent, but talking to your horse as you ride is one of the best ways to communicate with him. With your voice you can convey praise and encouragement as well as let your horse know when he is not listening or trying hard enough! Think of the verbal communication we have with dogs: the horse is no different.

racehorse, not teaching a youngster from scratch, so you may not always ride in classic text-book style until the horse has learnt. Then you can begin to refine your aids.

Lowering the Head

Although you shouldn't be overly worried about seeking an outline in the early stages of riding, obviously achieving an outline is the goal, and it is important that work starts towards this as soon as is feasible – but a horse can't work in an outline until he lowers his head.

Fig. 11.27 The lowered head is achievable in walk, trot and also in canter.

Fig. 11.28 Once a horse has mastered 'forwards and down', you have one of the most useful tools in your kit bag that you will ever need. It is OK to incline yourself forward to encourage the horse to do likewise. Let the horse keep taking the rein forward, but without allowing him to fall onto his forehand. Do this by keeping the legs on. As the horse is allowed more rein, his stride will lengthen.

With the ex-racehorse it is essential to take things very slowly and not to ask or expect too much, too soon. It takes many months to build muscle, and training to higher levels is an on-going exercise throughout a horse's life.

The first requirement is to ask the horse to lower his head and stretch it forwards with the poll below the withers and the nose a bit forwards but not poking. From his lungeing and/or long-reining work, your horse will quite quickly understand the requirement to drop his head under saddle, in walk at least, as the feel of the reins will equate to what he has learnt during ground training.

There will have been no point to your groundwork if once in the saddle you are going to let the horse walk around the school with his head all over the place; that just undoes your work to date and has a negative effect on the muscle that has started to build. Even when walking around on a loose rein at the beginning of a training session you will eventually be able to exert enough influence over your horse that he walks with his head stretched forwards and down.

From walk, encourage the horse to lower his head by opening your hands quite wide, holding them away from the sides of the neck, and opening your fingers a little so you don't have a firm grip on the reins. This doesn't mean seeing daylight between the fingers, but just a less firm grip so that the horse feels no tension down the rein.

Be sure to use your voice to help convey your instructions; voice commands are something he learnt during ground training.

Shortening the reins will have the opposite effect of what you are trying to achieve, so at this stage if your horse won't comply just keep riding him forwards. If he is at all reactive to your legs on his side, put more weight into your stirrups as this minimizes leg contact.

Keep your elbows bent – straight, tense elbows transmit to the horse's mouth. Bent elbows also allow your hands to follow the horse's movement. It is important to be elastic

Fig. 11.29 Abi has her hands nicely open (wide and low), but she needs to feel down the reins a little more and push Hero forward into a more lowered outline. As can be seen from how loose it is, the Harbridge is exerting no influence in lowering Hero Worship's head.

in the contact even though at this stage the horse doesn't really understand what you mean by contact. If he feels heavy in your hand let the reins out a bit and push him forwards. If you experience head-tossing, again ease the hands and ride forwards into a giving hand.

It is perfectly acceptable to incline yourself a little forwards as well as lowering the hands; the hands can go towards the knees.

If the horse is walking too fast he won't respond; slow the walk right down, but use the seat to achieve this. There is a difference between a forward (active) walk and one that is hurried.

Some horses respond better if the rider gently moves the reins as if sending waves down them. This is not a sudden, hearty shake of the reins but a subtle movement that results in a slight movement reaching the bit.

As the horse relaxes and begins to stretch down you will feel the stride lengthen and a rhythm develop, and your body should move in

harmony. Be careful not to drive downwards with your seat – think gliding, like a swan on water. Hold this in your mind so that you know what you are always aiming for.

From here, most horses will naturally begin to round a little in response to you giving a gentle 'on-off' squeeze down the rein. 'Off' doesn't mean letting go of the rein or releasing the fingers, but just a gentle movement of the little and fourth fingers against the rein, or a very slight wrist movement (with thumbs uppermost, move the wrist gently so that the knuckles turn inwards a little).

For the horse that doesn't want to respond positively, walk on a smallish circle – 15m or even 10m – as he will then have to lower his head in order to find his balance. Don't worry if the circles are an odd shape: this exercise is for getting the horse's attention and lowering his head, which leads to a softening of the inside neck muscles, not about accuracy of school figures.

Encourage him to lower his head by opening the inside rein away from the neck and gently squeezing 'on off' with the little finger and third finger on the rein and/or giving a slight flexion of the wrist. Some horses achieve this almost immediately, others will take a few days.

Now the horse can be asked to start developing an outline.

Using a Training Aid

Some horses can be more difficult to work with if they are excitable, easily distracted or stubborn. In these situations, in order that positive and meaningful progress can be made, using a Harbridge can be very helpful. It is far better to have a positive training session than one that ends up with a frustrated rider and a horse that has learnt nothing.

The Harbridge is easy to use and allows the horse to work out for himself what he is being asked. The Equi-ami also works well, although if a horse does not readily accept the lower leg (to

Fig. 11.30   Hero Worship in a correctly fitted Harbridge. A Harbridge is not a quick-fix gadget as it does not force an outline; its use allows the rider to work at achieving this for himself/herself, but without the horse being overly evasive.

come on to a large circle, as once again the horse must lower his head in order to balance – and provided you are sitting correctly, he can do this. As he lowers his head and finds his balance his stride will lengthen and become more rhythmic.

Fig. 11.31   With the horse's head up and Rowena again illustrating a poor rider position, leaning forward (and the lower leg coming back), we have a horse that is propping himself up. This illustrates the importance from the word go of the rider being in the correct position.

maintain forwardness), he can try and hollow against it. Once a horse lowers his head, the Equi-ami can greatly assist in working towards outline.

Working in Trot

When you first ask for trot don't be dismayed if the horse's head comes up: this is a typical reaction to your weight being somewhere different on his back.

Even if he sets off at full speed, be sure to keep the legs closed around him – don't hold them off his sides. He must learn to accept the leg both as an aid for moving forwards and for slowing down – the horse that is excitable actually needs more leg, not less.

If your horse takes a while to respond, don't worry: be sure your position and the aids are correct, and keep the pressure on until he does – don't give in and let him have his own way.

There is no point in trotting endlessly around the perimeter of the school: it is far better to

Fig. 11.32   If your horse goes off with his head in the air, don't grab the reins; if you keep at the horse's mouth he will just put his head higher and possibly poke his nose at the same time. This is another instance where the rider uses their seat and legs to convey slowing down.

As regards the tempo of the trot, some say that a more active trot – not to be confused with a trot where the horse is running – will encourage the horse to step under; others maintain that by slowing the trot right down – to the point where the horse is nearly breaking to walk – he has more time to think and respond. In fact you should do what works best for the individual, so try one way and then the other as there are no hard and fast rules.

Using a Training Aid

Figs 11.35 and 11.36 illustrate how using a training aid can psychologically help the rider with trot work. Like many riders, Lyn lacked confidence in herself, and her mare Bobbie had been in a field for four years since leaving the training environment. The Harbridge was the ideal aid to help them both: with the Harbridge fitted Lyn could practise getting Bobbie to listen to her aids, whilst she herself could get a sense of what she should feel from the mare; when it was removed Lyn was still able to lower Bobbie's head.

Fig. 11.33   Hero Worship wants to rush off but by keeping the legs closed around him and holding the reins (not pulling back, nor giving to him), he has to steady himself; he is not too happy initially as evidenced by the open mouth.

Fig. 11.34   By keeping the legs on and not responding to his attempted evasion, Rowena has persuaded Hero to accept the forward aids and lower his head; indeed he has adopted an altogether nicer way of going in a matter of a few minutes.

Fig. 11.35   Lyn practises getting Bobbie to listen to her aids while she herself gets a sense of what she should feel from the mare.

Fig. 11.36 With the Harbridge removed, Lyn is still able to lower Bobbie's head, even if the mare has gone on to her forehand; this is actually caused by Lyn tipping forward as a result of her own apprehension.

Fig. 11.37 Downward transitions are tricky for every young horse, not just ex-racehorses, as they need to rebalance as they learn to take their weight back – sit.

Slowing Down

Pulling on the reins is not the way to stop a horse out of training, since pull means 'go faster'. Ease the pace by using your body, so in trot, slow your own rising; the reins are not there to be pulled against. Sit tall and put weight into the stirrup, and concentrate on riding forwards into the transition and achieving the 'slow down'.

Downward transitions are particularly difficult for the horse out of training because he must learn to use his back in a completely different way. Don't be too concerned about head-tossing or the horse drawing his head in against the chest.

Halting

Racehorses never have to stand still so the concept is not in their vocabulary: it has to be taught.

Use your lungeing command of whoa (or whatever you used), and sit tall and deep, closing the legs very gently, and closing the hand. If the horse doesn't halt, give the rein and ask again – don't keep a steady pull on the reins otherwise he will probably pull against you and stick his nose out.

He may open his mouth even though the rein is not too short/tight, so on the next halt the rider needs to ride with a little more impulsion (forwardness) into the halt by keeping the lower leg more closed around him.

Once he has halted he may try to step backwards, but kick him back to the spot where you were: he must learn he can't evade by moving backwards (an important lesson in preparation for hacking out).

Opening the hands encourages him to drop his head so he is more comfortable through the neck and back and therefore less inclined to fidget. Be careful not to pull backwards on the reins as you do this.

Teach your horse to stand still for a slightly longer period by opening the reins away from the neck.

Fig. 11.38 The horse has opened his mouth even though the rein is not too short/tight; so on the next halt the rider needs to ride with a little more impulsion (forwardness) into the halt by keeping the lower leg more closed around the horse. In this instance the toes have turned out so lower leg contact is lost.

Fig. 11.39 Help teach your horse to stand still for slightly longer period by opening the reins away from the neck.

If he should keep walking backwards, release all the aids as no further amount of kicking him forwards is going to achieve a good end result. Let him stand for a minute or two to gather himself, flex him and ask him to walk on; try the exercise again.

The horse will soon learn that when you sit deeper and taller, that is the cue to slow down – another valuable lesson.

The Half Halt

The half halt is the most valuable aid to any rider, yet it is the most misunderstood and seemingly elusive. Even at this stage of training teaching the half halt is very useful as it helps with acceptance of the contact – and once you have that, you are well on your way to retraining your racehorse.

So what is a half halt and what is its purpose? It is what it says it is, namely 'half of a halt': you instruct the horse to stop, but just as he is about to do so you send him on again. Basically you are stopping the front end and allowing the back end to catch up, so *just for a moment* it should feel as if your horse has been squashed together. The half halt gains the horse's attention, and is a corrective and re-balancing mechanism: he steps underneath that little bit more and comes back to your hand; upon moving forwards again he is more focused and better balanced.

The aids are similar to those for the halt: sit tall with the hips square, head up, stretching up through the back and increasing the tension of your stomach and lower back – brace, pushing the stomach forwards. Keep the elbows soft.

Close the legs – all the leg: the thighs and knees 'lift' the horse, whilst the lower leg instructs the horse to step under with his hind legs – drives him on.

Keep the seat light, close the lower leg as this instructs the horse to step under more with his hind legs and drives him forward, close the

Fig. 11.40   Hero finds working in the larger school very exciting as there are lots of distractions; he has to learn to listen and the half-halt helps with this.

Fig. 11.41   Light the Fuse (Bombie) responding well with Rowena to the half-halt aids at a more advanced stage of training to collect the canter.

fingers on the rein (but don't pull back) and give a couple of squeezes on the outside rein and then release – it is a momentary action; timing is important as the leg aid must be given before the hind leg you wish to influence hits the ground.

This is a *very* simplistic description of half-halt on the outside rein to steady and balance the horse - get him listening but there are variations of the half-halt and the applicable aids depending on exactly what the rider is wishing to achieve and the level of training.

Hero Worship is typical of many horses, in that getting him to concentrate is one of the most difficult things at this early stage of re-training. Half halts get him to really step under with his hind legs, which helps to control the trot and will also encourage him to lower his head. The inside hand has been lowered and the rein slightly opened to help direct his head into the desired position.

As soon as you feel a reaction from your horse, soften the rein by easing the hand ever so slightly forwards: don't lose the contact. The rider's aids must be co-ordinated and

immediate, as the half halt when correctly executed happens within the scope of a single stride so that a horse is set up for the next movement.

When trying to create an outline, or when slowing a horse down, or when a rider thinks that the horse is too forward-going, be careful not to over-do the use of half halts as a horse can be shortened in the neck too much at a time when he needs to be stretching it forwards and down in order to develop balance and swing through the back.

The half halt must not be used as an alternative to using the seat and legs for slowing down.

The 'Almost Transition'

If the half halt is something you are not familiar with, use of the 'almost transition' is very beneficial as it still helps the horse to brings his hind legs more underneath him in the downward transitions, helps to steady him, and makes him listen to his rider as well as suppling the back. This is a simpler version of the half halt: in the 'almost transition' the horse very nearly breaks to walk (from trot) or to trot (from canter), but before he actually does, the rider pushes him forwards again, causing him to 'push' with the hindleg, but without letting him run.

The 'almost transition' is achieved by giving the aids as if you were intending to ride a downward transition, slowing the pace so the horse is still moving forwards, but slowly (think

Fig. 11.42 Here is a classic example of rider error. Rowena demonstrates not giving Hero enough rein – and what are the elbows doing? They should have more bend in them!

Fig. 11.43 With a little more rein, Hero can have a more open frame and that improves the walk. With bend in the elbow the outline is soft and the contact elastic.

slow motion). It is the same principle as for slowing down.

Working in Walk

Much can be achieved in walk, although you should regularly make the horse trot forwards to keep him thinking forwards. Even if you are struggling with work in trot – your horse is carrying his head too high, he is tense – don't worry, because by working in walk you give yourselves much more time to work things out and get co-ordinated. For the horse that is recovering from a leg injury, a few walk exercises will also help tone the all-important back muscles.

Much can be achieved with a purposeful walk; the outline should be low and slightly rounded. You can practise lengthening the stride without speeding up the pace: remember, when working with a longer stride your hands should move very slightly forwards, and your seat should make larger sweeps across the saddle.

Every exercise that is carried out in trot can be done in walk:

- Circles
- Leg yielding on the straight and on the circle
- Loops, tear drops and serpentines
- Shoulder-fore and shoulder-in
- Turn on the forehand.

In Fig. 11.43 Hero has a more engaged way of going and is capable of carrying out the above exercise with ease; practise the exercises with a more lowered head-carriage too.

Circles

In order to execute a circle and have bend in his body, the horse has to have a degree of flexion – flexion being at the poll; while you can have flexion without bend (i.e. when the horse is working on a straight line), you can't have bend without flexion at the poll. If your horse has not yet started to work in an outline when you ask him to turn left or right, or to go on a circle, he will not bend throughout his body – he may well turn his head in the correct direction, but his neck will be stiff. Racehorses are notoriously stiff on a circle. Carrying a rider's weight and circling is a balancing exercise in itself, so keep circles in trot very large to start with.

The aids for a circle so that the horse bends around the inside leg are as follows:

- Inside leg at the girth
- Inside rein asks for flexion
- Outside leg is positioned just behind the girth to stop the haunches going out
- Hips and body are turned to the inside
- Look in the direction you are travelling.

The horse's neck should only be bent as much as the rest of his body, so you should just be able to see the corner of his eye. To encourage a horse to have some bend to the inside, the outside rein is held against the withers and the inside hand opened slightly away from the neck; the hand can be moved more towards the knee if required. A horse can be prevented from correctly negotiating a circle if the rider does not allow with the outside rein in order to accommodate the inside bend.

Two exercises to help achieve lateral bend are neck reining, and following the rein.

TOP: Fig. 11.44 Rowena demonstrates that incorrect riding can prevent a horse from correctly negotiating a circle by not allowing the outside rein to accommodate the inside bend. Hence Hero Worship has no option but to shorten his frame and fall out through the left shoulder.

BELOW: Fig. 11.45 To achieve the lateral flexion, keep the inside leg on the girth to give the horse something to bend around. And remember you are re-training a horse, so as well as opening the inside rein, help him further by lowering the inside hand towards the knee – he will follow the rein.

Fig. 11.46 *Having been broken at the poll many years ago, Mr Bojangles will invert rather than flex (laterally) correctly if allowed to on the right rein as he is naturally stiffer when on this rein. Occasional neck reining keeps his mind on the job.*

Neck Reining

If a horse doesn't respond to an open inside rein, then neck reining can help him achieve lateral flexion. Neck reining is not acceptable in classical dressage training, but in this case you are retraining a horse trained to do another job, so initially, within reason, it is all right to try it.

Whilst your legs maintain the positioning as for a circle, move the inside hand close to the withers – not on top of, and most definitely not across – and slightly open the outside rein away from the neck. This takes the horse off the inside shoulder (which is what is basically blocking him from flexing) so he can be encouraged to bend around the leg rather than be guided by the rein aid. As he softens, then you can reintroduce the correct aid (*see* Fig. 11.46).

Be careful, as neck reining can easily become a habit, and it is not acceptable in dressage competition.

Figs 11.47 and 11.48 *Following the rein: in halt, gently ask the horse to bring his head round towards your leg. Do this by slowly moving your hand towards your hip or to begin with out towards your knee. Don't pull sharply or tug.*

Following the Rein

When a horse is reluctant to bend to the inside, it is usually because he is tight through the neck on the other side, which prevents the muscles stretching and thereby allowing the bend to the inside. The following exercise stretches the outside neck muscles, allowing the horse more freedom to bend to the inside. Be sure to do the exercise on both reins.

Slowly bring the inside hand back to the thigh, keeping the hand low so the horse can follow the rein. Note how soft Rowena is keeping the rein in the Fig. 11.49. Or slowly bring the inside hand to just in front of the stomach; the horse's neck can gradually be bent to the inside in an exaggerated manner. Abi demonstrates this beautifully on Hero in Fig. 11.50.

Figs 11.49 and 11.50   Two ways of achieving the same thing.

Rounding the Outline

An outline cannot be achieved until a horse is reaching forwards and downwards to the bit in both walk and trot. Some horses will do this naturally or will readily do so with a little encouragement, but if a horse is particularly tight or weak through the back he will find it hard, in which case ridden work should continue to be interspersed with ground work on the lunge with a Chambon or Equi-ami to help build the all-important abdominal and back muscles.

Riders have a tendency to fight and fidget in their quest for 'submission' and 'outline', but this comes from still hands coupled with a forward leg aid, not pulling and yanking at the mouth.

When asked to round, some horses will overreact and overbend – an evasion technique to avoid using the back – which results in the

Fig. 11.51   While we would like to see Hero at little lower in his head carriage, he is nonetheless ready to 'round up' a little. As he is a horse more prone to raising his head to evade, Rowena has slowed the trot to give him chance to respond. The reins are at a length to provide support but without pulling the head in.

opposite of what is wanted: a tight, shortened neck instead of a lengthened, rounded one.

An outline is not achieved by pulling the head in: the half halt and transitions are the key to helping achieve this, as both ask the horse to step under with his hind legs; this brings the pelvis under him and lifts the back, the lift through the back resulting in the arching of the neck into the bit, with the poll being the highest point.

An outline is easier to produce on the circle because the inside hind leg moves further forwards under the horse's body; so if you are not ready for half halts and/or your transitions need a bit more work, then circles are the answer.

Fig. 11.54   Rowena with Light the Fuse – a lovely working outline for softening and suppling. Note the stepping under with the inside hindleg. (Photograph courtesy of Matthew Roberts Photography)

Establishing Rhythm

'Fast' and 'forward' are not the same thing. Most people trot too fast so the horse can't get into a steady rhythm and loses balance; the rider then uses their hands, which results in the horse lifting his neck to evade the contact. Fiddling with the reins may work temporarily but doesn't solve the basic problem – that the horse is not moving in a rhythmical and balanced way.

Figs 11.52 and 11.53   If the horse (top) had his nose just in front of the vertical instead of behind it, that would be fine. By applying more leg in conjunction with an easing of the rein (lengthening slightly) the horse (bottom) is in a more open frame but it still rounded and so his back and topline muscles are really benefitting.

Fig. 11.55   Rowena with Tricky, working in a good rhythm.

You must be bold enough to give your horse the freedom to find his own balance otherwise he will lean and use you as his support; so give him the rein. This doesn't mean riding with the reins in loops, but with a length of rein. Try not to pull the head/neck in, as the horse will invariably fight against it; as he finds his balance he will start to work with an even rhythm, and from here you can work on suppleness.

You can help your horse by breathing slowly and deeply. You can dictate the speed in rising trot by controlling the speed of your own rising: with controlled, steady and rhythmical rising from yourself you will influence your horse's speed, and as he steadies you will feel his stride lengthen instead of feeling as if you are going up and down on the spot.

Transitions

The horse must react instantly to an upward transition – if he doesn't respond straightaway, he needs to be more forward and off the leg. It doesn't matter if the reaction to a downward transition is little slower, as to begin with the horse won't be balanced enough, and have his hind legs stepping under enough, to go from, say, trot to walk without slowing the trot. Far better that he maintains a soft outline, than have him hollow and then fall into the walk.

The rider must remember that even in a downward transition the horse should be ridden forwards in order to keep the hind legs stepping under. Keep the hands closed and don't give with the reins, but don't pull on them otherwise the horse will undoubtedly hollow.

Give a long outward breath (like a big sigh) as you ask for a downward transition, as this will help you sit more deeply, and guard against you tensing up.

If the horse drops the contact as a means of avoiding stepping under for the downward transition, push him forwards again into a

Fig. 11.56 Hero Worship has decided that he will drop the contact as a means of avoiding stepping under for the downward transition, hence the suddenly very loose rein.

rhythmical trot and try again, but keep more leg on next time.

Introducing Canter

Everyone wants to get cantering sooner rather than later, but it is far better only to progress to canter once you have control of the legs in walk and trot and on large circles. How long it takes to get to this stage varies considerably depending on the horse's suppleness and his rider's ability.

Be aware that the horse won't suddenly understand the canter aids. However correct your aids he won't necessarily break to canter straightaway, or if he does, he may not achieve the correct strike-off. But don't worry, this is perfectly normal.

To achieve the correct strike-off it helps to understand the footfalls in canter. Canter is a three-beat movement: that is, three footfalls with a moment of suspension when all four legs are in the air. The outside hind leg strikes off first (the three other legs being in the air), the inside hindleg and outside foreleg hit the

Fig. 11.57   Hero strikes to canter beautifully. He has lost his outline but the raising of the head is a natural response to something new. Note the easy inside rein which indicates that Hero is bending his neck, albeit not quite enough, to the inside.

Fig. 11.58   The two-point canter takes weight off the horse's back, allowing the horse to lift it to achieve canter strike-off.

ground next at the same time, followed by the inside foreleg (the 'correct' leg) – at this point the outside hind leg is off the floor, with the inside hind leg and outside foreleg being lifted as the inside foreleg hits the ground. Then comes the moment of suspension, after which the cycle begins again with the outside hind leg hitting the ground first.

Applying the canter aids at the right moment to achieve the correct lead is very important. Sit up straight with a light seat and flex the horse slightly to the inside; sit for a couple of strides of trot so that you can feel the movement of the hindlegs, put a little weight onto the inside seat bone, but don't lean in as this blocks the hindleg, throwing the horse onto his outside shoulder; then push your inside seat bone forwards, apply the inside leg at the girth (to ask for 'forward') and swing the outside leg back a little as you feel the outside hindleg come up (this tells the horse which foreleg to strike off with). As soon as you achieve strike off, keep the canter by activating the inside leg at the girth.

Problems often arise because the rider doesn't apply the aids correctly, hangs on to the inside rein too much, which closes the shoulder so the horse cannot lift and move forwards into the transition, or drives downwards with the seat blocking the lift of the back.

An alternative is to flex the horse slightly to the outside which, takes the weight off the inside shoulder. If you also turn your head as if to look over your outside shoulder this brings your inside seat bone forward and puts a little more weight into the inside stirrup, but doesn't allow you to lean inwards.

If you experience difficulties when first introducing canter, sometimes it is easier to achieve canter from rising trot, i.e. so that you are out of the saddle as the horse strikes off. Again this isn't classical dressage, but things must be kept as easy as possible for the horse at this stage.

When the horse does strike off, the canter may seem fast – though to your ex-racehorse he'll be hardly out of trot! Once in canter you can try sitting in the saddle for just a couple of strides at a time. However when you do sit, be ready for the horse to break into trot, because in racing the moment the work rider sits after a canter the racehorse takes this as the cue to trot and then walk.

The seat needs tucking a little more under

The inside rein needs to soften a little

Fig. 11.59   Rider position is important to help a young or lesser-trained horse in canter.

Maintaining the Canter

If the horse keeps breaking from canter into trot, make sure you are not holding the inside rein too tightly: it needs to be soft to allow him to step forwards. Using too much inside rein also causes a horse to go haunches out (and to fall in through the inside shoulder); correct this by softening the inside rein contact, which allows the hind leg to reach forwards properly.

Your hips should move with the horse so that you don't keep bumping on the saddle; don't push with the seat too much as this blocks the back, which in turn blocks the hind legs from coming through so the horse has to come back to trot.

Learn to maintain the canter with the seat and legs where necessary; many riders bounce or are not secure in the saddle, and this can cause a horse to break into trot.

Giving Away the Reins

This exercise tests whether the horse is leaning on the rider's hands, and relying on them to prop his head in position, or whether he is

carrying himself by pushing with his quarters. When you give away the reins – push your hands forwards – the horse should maintain his outline.

In Fig. 11.60, Mr Bojangles is very advanced in his work and his head and neck position doesn't change when given the rein. Hero Worship (Fig. 11.61) is just being introduced to this exercise in canter, and his first attempt is very good, telling us that his schooling to date has been correct.

Occasionally giving just one rein away for a stride lets you test if the horse is hanging on to one rein more than the other; if he drifts when you do this, or drops his outline, then he is not balanced and is also one-sided. In the

Figs 11.60 and 11.61   Giving away the reins: it doesn't matter whether the outline is an advanced one or still a very 'baby' one as long as the same outline is maintained when you ease the rein.

Figs 11.62 and 11.63   When given the rein (left) Light the Fuse (Bombie) slightly loses his self-carriage and hollows a little – loses balance. Having retaken the rein, Rowena gave a little nudge with the inside leg and a 'squeeze' on the outside rein to ask for a little more roundness; when given the rein again Bombie maintains a lovely outline (right). (Photograph courtesy of Matthew Roberts Photography)

photographs, when given the rein Light the Fuse slightly loses his self-carriage and hollows a little (Fig. 11.62). Having retaken the rein, Rowena gave him a nudge with the inside leg and a 'squeeze' on the outside rein to ask for

Fig. 11.64   The horse that is supple has a ease of movement, a rhythmical stride with true stepping under and suppleness over the back. The neck is soft and the contact with the bit light; that is what trainers strive to achieve. So while the ex-racehorse may not be capable of the wonderful movement of his non-raced counterpart, with time, patience and correct schooling, a re-trained racehorse is quite capable of achieving far more than he is often given credit for.

more roundness, and when given the rein again he maintains a lovely outline (Fig. 11.63).

SUPPLING EXERCISES

As your horse progresses in his training you can introduce more exercises to help him with suppleness, balance and co-ordination as you aim to get him on the bit. Suppling exercises are the best way to relax a tense horse and gain the attention of a distracted one.

Riding Shoulder-fore

Young or unbalanced horses, very often the ex-racehorse, fall in on corners and tend to run a bit free in canter as they haven't the muscle strength to support themselves as well as a rider correctly. Riding shoulder-fore helps them with this. It also helps to straighten the horse that tends to go quarters in, particularly in the canter, to teach the horse to accept the inside leg and bend round it, and to get him working into the outside rein and leg aids.

The aids for shoulder-fore are as follows:

- Inside leg at the girth (then used to keep the horse moving)
- Outside leg behind the girth (to prevent the quarters swinging out)
- Outside rein close to the withers to keep the neck straight
- With the inside rein, very slightly flex the horse to the inside so that you can just see his eye.

Keep your weight evenly centred over the horse, and test to see if he is balanced by easing the inside rein: he should not alter his way of going, and if he does, nudge him up with the inside leg – he must learn to accept the outside rein.

Leg Yielding

This is the first step towards teaching lateral work under saddle. If you have done some in-hand training your horse will at least have the concept of being able to move sideways either with just his back legs, front legs or both.

Horses naturally find one direction easier than the other, but they can also be influenced by rider crookedness and non co-ordination of the aids.

Work in walk to start with, and then progress to trot.

There are several ways to leg yield: from the quarter line, on the same rein; from the quarter line, changing the rein; along the arena side; and on a circle.

From the Quarter Line, on the Same Rein

This is the easiest way to teach leg yielding, as the horse naturally wants to return to the arena side. The movement is performed as follows:

- On the right rein, turn up the quarter line *after* 'A' or 'C'

Fig. 11.65   How not to ride shoulder-fore. By pulling on the inside rein, the neck has been shortened (equating to tension), the rider is tipping forward and is carrying in the inside leg too far back. The horse is not happy.

Fig. 11.66   How to ride shoulder-fore. With more rein, the rider sitting up and the lower leg in a better position, the picture is a much nicer one as the Light the Fuse is able to perform what is being asked of him.

- Flex the neck slightly to the right
- Draw your right leg back and turn your shoulders very slightly to the right as well (the rider's shoulders should always be parallel to those of the horse)
- Slightly open the right rein
- With an 'on-off' aid of the right leg, push the horse sideways
- The left leg should remain at the girth to stop the quarters overtaking the shoulders.

The horse is always flexed away from the direction of movement, travelling forwards and slightly sideways at the same time.

Practise on both reins in walk until the horse clearly understands you; then you can ask for a few steps in trot.

If your horse doesn't understand what you want, it may be that your aids are not clear. Have an assistant walk beside you and gently press the horse's side just behind your leg to reinforce the 'moving over' aid.

From the Quarter Line, Changing the Rein

The movement is performed as follows:

Fig. 11.67 *Leg yielding can be done along the side of the arena, not just from the centre or quarter lines back to the track.*

- On the right rein turn up the quarter line *before* 'A' or 'C'
- Flex the horse slightly to the left
- Draw the left leg back and push the horse back to the track (so you have changed the rein)
- The right leg remains at the girth to stop the quarters leading.

In both the instances the bend/flexion in the neck should be very slight, with the body remaining parallel to the side of the arena.

A typical fault in leg yielding is that the horse slows down and his quarters lead. This often occurs when the rider's leg is too far back and the rein contact is too strong.

Along the Arena Side

Traditionally leg yielding along the arena side is done with the horse's head towards the arena side – but why not place his head to the inside? As it is a different form of leg yielding, you can vary the angle of the horse's body to the wall (as long as he is straight through the body with only a very slight bend in the neck).

Take care not to create too much inside flexion otherwise the horse will fall out through the shoulder and not be able to work the hind legs and the back properly, which is the object of the exercise.

Leg yielding is of benefit in walk, trot and canter.

Leg Yielding on a Circle

This exercise can be done in walk and trot as well as canter when the horse is suitably controllable in his canter.

Spiralling in and then leg yielding out on the circle with the neck slightly more bent to the inside than would normally be the case is a wonderful suppling exercise because it works the intercostal muscles (which have to be supple for lateral work), also both hind legs

Fig. 11.68 *Leg yielding in canter from the quarter line to the arena side is a useful exercise to aid suppling. To be correct, Rowena's right hand should be slightly away from the neck but as Bo is stiffer on the right she is purposely bending him more through the neck to achieve maximum benefit from the exercise. (Please ignore the turned-out elbow – this is lack of flexibility due to Rowena's arm being in plaster at the time.)*

Fig. 11.69 *Light the Fuse is tense because he is somewhere strange to him, so leg yielding on a circle is a good exercise to help him focus and to soften the tense muscles. By getting the back working he will soften through the neck.*

thereby improving engagement, and helps to give a more consistent contact. It is important to work evenly on both reins.

This is a very useful exercise for the horse that is fresh or inattentive, as it makes him work through his back and accept the leg.

Don't worry if your horse can't do a 20m circle: just put him on the size of circle he is comfortable with. This exercise will help to supple him so that he can cope with smaller circles.

Establish an even rhythm and don't go too fast. Spiral in by pushing with the outside leg – don't pull the horse in with the inside rein. Push him out with the inside leg – don't pull him out with the outside rein, nor should you open the outside rein, as his neck must remain flexed to the inside.

Leg yielding when riding corners is a good way to achieve better lateral bend and to ride deep into a corner rather than cutting across it. Ride round the arena a couple of feet off the outside track; this allows you to ask for several strides of leg yield as you ride the corner.

Be careful not to drop the inside hand, otherwise the bit also drops in the mouth, which then doesn't apply the right action, and don't neck rein when leg yielding. Also be careful that your outside hip doesn't drop. Your shoulder must remain in line with the horse's shoulder.

As the horse becomes more supple, the circles can be made smaller to suit his increased agility.

LEG YIELDING

Leg yielding exercises are very useful exercises for the horse that is fresh, inattentive or setting himself against the rider, as it gets them working through the back and accepting of the leg.

Fig. 11.70   Leg yielding when riding corners is a good way to achieve better lateral bend and enable you to get a horse into a corner. Ride around the arena a couple of feet off the outside track. This allows you to ask for several strides of leg yield as the corner is ridden. (Photograph courtesy of Matthew Roberts Photography)

Serpentines

Serpentines are excellent for keeping the horse attentive and 'on the aids'. When changing direction be sure to straighten him over a couple of strides as you cross the centre line, and then change the bend as this helps to keep him balanced.

Use those two strides to prepare yourself, as well as your horse, for the change of aids.

Leg Yielding on a Serpentine

This is another wonderful exercise to get a horse listening. However, only progress to this exercise when the horse understands leg yielding as above.

Commence a serpentine on the left rein from 'C.' Turn at 'S', or between 'H' and 'E' in a short arena, and as you come out of the turn, leg yield (to the right) for three to four strides, straightening as you cross the centre line.

Having done the loop at 'B', as you come out of the turn, leg yield again (this time to the left), straightening up as you cross the centre line. Complete the serpentine at 'A' as normal.

Shoulder-in

Shoulder-in really gets the inside leg stepping under and so teaches a horse to take more weight behind.

Fig. 11.71   A common rider fault with shoulder-in is creating too much inside bend, which blocks the shoulder. The inside leg is also too far back.

Fig. 11.72   Faults in the rider position are usually the problem behind a poor understanding and execution of shoulder-in by the horse.

If the horse has difficulty understanding the exercise, or blocks through the neck, open the inside rein slightly away from the neck (this will also correct any head tilt) and make sure the inside leg is down the girth, and not drawn back.

Be sure to turn your body so that your shoulders are in line with the horse's.

Medium Trot

Don't be tempted to try medium trot until your horse has a balanced, rhythmical working trot.

Fig. 11.73   Medium trot is a trot with a lengthened stride, not a faster pace!

For medium trot, shown in Fig. 11.73, the horse has to take more weight behind in order to push the shoulders away. The forehand needs to be light, and the horse should be allowed to lengthen his frame. Ideally Hero Worship could be more open in his frame; the shortening of the neck is typical of the horse learning medium trot. More impulsion from the lower leg is required, and the rider could sit up a little more!

Counter Canter

Don't attempt counter canter until your horse is properly balanced in true canter, and you are able to flex his head both to the inside and outside as he canters.

The aids for counter canter on the left rein are as follows:

- The horse should be very slightly bent towards the leading (left) leg
- The rider should keep their left leg at the girth with the right leg drawn back to stop the quarters swinging and to prevent the horse from changing to a right foreleg lead
- The rider's weight should be more into the left stirrup.

A good exercise to practise counter canter is to ride a shallow loop down the long side of the arena, a few feet in from the arena fence; the loop can be made gradually deeper.

Another is to canter a tear-drop shape to change the rein, returning to the track and riding a few strides in counter canter, returning to trot for the corner.

When working round the entire school, keep turns as wide as possible; the horse will need to be very balanced and supple before he can work properly on the outside track. If you don't have a sound basis on which to build the counter canter, all manner of faults will arise. The rider is often the cause of problems with this exercise.

Improving Circles

Circles are one of the best ways to help supple a horse evenly on both reins.

First make sure your position is correct, with your inside hip slightly forwards and shoulder slightly back; if you look in the direction of travel the hips automatically move enough to assert a positive influence.

A horse may try and swing his quarters out as an evasion, as working on the bend is harder for him; so draw your leg back on that side to push the quarters back on track.

If he leans into his shoulder, then apply the inside leg (with a slight kick if necessary) and be sure to keep your hand closed on the rein on the side he is leaning.

The half halt is helpful to rebalance the horse; you can also ride in shoulder-fore.

Ride with the inside leg a little further back that would normally be the case, as if preparing to leg yield; this will help keep the inside hind leg actively stepping under.

Figs 11.72 and 11.73 illustrate really well what subtle differences the rider can make to their position and it has such a huge influence on their horse. In Fig. 11.74 Abi has her inside leg too far forward, blocking Nic's movement; the position of her leg has caused Abi to adopt an almost bracing posture – her lower back has gone stiff. Abi's left hand is 'locked' instead of being soft and the right elbow is turned out,

bringing the right rein away from the neck; Nic is unable to take up the outside rein and flex properly to the inside. Abi's upper body is not positioned for a circle. However, in Fig. 11.75 Abi's lower leg is in perfect position, her back is soft, her right elbow is back under control and she is focused on her direction of movement.

In Fig. 11.76, the horse's head is turned in, as a result of which he has fallen out on the left shoulder and the inside hind is completely hindered – he can't step under and there is no bend throughout the body. Rowena is leaning in, rather than just the weight going onto the inside seat bone and into the right stirrup

In Fig. 11.77 the horse is uniformly bent from nose to tail and his inside hind is stepping accurately with the weight being taken behind. The criticism would be that Rowena has tilted her head and her right foot has turned out.

Figs 11.74 and 11.75 In the first picture, Nic is basically going through the motions; he is going forwards, and he isn't hollow, but he looks stiff. In the second picture Nic looks completely different; he is really stepping with all four legs and his outline is soft and supple.

Note the muscle that is now working in Nic's neck

LEFT: *Fig. 11.76 Rowena shows how not to ride a turn/circle.*

RIGHT: *Fig. 11.77 This is a much nicer picture of horse and rider in harmony.*

Although Mr Bojangles competed at Advanced Medium level, Figs 11.76 and 11.77 illustrate that even a highly-trained horse will only go as well as he is ridden. This applies to jumping also. Getting turns correct is of particular importance if you are aiming for the dressage arena; turning up the centre line is where so many marks are lost as riders overshoot the marker. This is not the horse's fault, but that of his rider; he can only turn when and where he is told to.

Using Poles to Improve Flatwork

Poles can be laid out in many patterns to help with every aspect of improving a horse's flatwork, as well as adding interest to schooling sessions.

Tram lines: Riding between tram lines helps improve straightness in all paces; you can also practise halt and rein back.

Quarter-line poles: Lay a few poles end-to-end down the quarter line. Depending on which side of the poles you ride they can help you correct a horse that canters quarters-in or quarters-out.

Diagonal poles: Lay down a row of four, five or six poles, but instead of riding down the centre, ride diagonally down the line – so cross the first pole at its left edge and the last pole at its right edge. The aim is to give lift and energy to the horse's stride, and to improve his lightness in the hand.

Zig-zags: Lay poles in a giant zig-zag down the long side of the school, and ride down them in a straight line in both trot and canter.

10m circles: Lay three poles down the centre line approximately 12m apart. Trot over the first one, ride a right-handed 10m circle between the poles. Straighten up, trot over the next pole, ride a 10m circle to the left; straighten up for the third, ride a 10m circle to the right; immediately ride a tear-drop to the left to bring you back in front of the poles, but from the opposite direction. Repeat the exercise.

Altering stride length: Lay out a row of poles out at your horse's normal stride length, then gradually widen the space between them to help him learn to lengthen, or gradually shorten the distance to encourage him to snap his legs up more quickly. This exercise is good for suppling the joints of the fetlocks and hocks.

Alternatively you could lay out a fan of poles, and according to whether you work closer to the outside or inside edge of the fan, the horse will have to lengthen or shorten his stride; this can be done in both trot and canter.

Accepting the Contact/On the Bit

The horse is accepting of the contact when he is still in his mouth and seeks to follow the rein. Contact is the soft communication between the horse's mouth and the rider's hand; this communication should not change between gaits (in transitions) otherwise the horse will hollow, invert or overbend. Contact is achieved by the leg, not the hand – a horse must be ridden forwards into a contact, he can't be pulled into it.

Achieving contact is a fine balance: if the reins are held too tightly or too short, the horse will lock up or hollow; too loose, and he does what he likes, invariably running on the forehand. If you alternate between putting more weight in one rein than the other in an attempt to 'see-saw' the head down, then you get a swaying head.

Be aware that a horse may create the impression to his rider that he is responding when all he has done is slightly tip his poll down, creating the illusion that he is soft and round – far from it! This is illustrated in Figs 11.78 and 11.79.

Figs 11.78 and 11.79   Indie is not rounding accurately; he is stiff, but so is the rider (left). With a bit more work (trotting forwards plus more impulsion from the rider's leg into a hand that doesn't keep giving to the head), the picture soon changes. Indie looks a different horse (right).

The hands should follow the horse's movement, hence the importance of being flexible through the wrists, elbows and shoulders. The reins should feel even – the horse should not feel stronger/heavier on one side as compared to the other.

To help resolve resistance to the rein and hence improve contact, ride on a 20m circle and do a series of walk-halt-walk transitions. If the head comes up as you ask for halt, ride forwards a few steps and ask again. Keep repeating the exercise until you get some improvement, however slight.

Make sure the reins feel even in your hands so that the bit remains central in the mouth; if it moves from side to side the horse is less likely to soften, but more likely to sway his head. Don't use the reins for stopping: use your seat and body and also your mind – visualize what you are wanting to achieve.

When you have halted, just squeeze on the reins to encourage the neck to round up, and try and maintain that as you walk away. In walk before the next halt transition practise squeezing the rein and release, squeeze and release until he rounds up.

The poll can also be softened by gently

moving the bit in the mouth with a very gentle tweak down the rein.

Whatever the stage of your horse's training, the above exercise will help increase suppleness and improve the communication between you. Working with a rounded outline should be incorporated at intervals throughout a working period, particularly during early training.

In Fig. 11.80 Rowena is asking Light the Fuse to soften in preparation for lowering his head further so as to soften and lift the back muscles.

Fig. 11.80   Light the Fuse (Bombie) needs to soften further and relax through the back, which will open his frame.

Figs 11.81, 11.82 and 11.83 Rowena demonstrates with Tricky subtle changes in head carriage. Suppling exercises include moving the head position, the rider being able to place the horse's head wherever they wish. But beware of the horse going above the contact (Fig. 11.81) or behind the vertical (Fig. 11.82). Fig. 11.83 demonstrates perfect carriage for Tricky's level of training.

The rein can be slowly let out so that he can stretch down.

One of the biggest faults when riding is that in an attempt to lower the head and round a horse up, the rider is too busy with the hand. Resist the temptation to fiddle and instead fix your hands at the front of the saddle and just ride forwards – the horse will give to you eventually.

Additional Suppling for the Tense Horse

A horse may be working beautifully at home, but get him to a competition or in company and his excitement causes him to tense up – this is not so critical for showing or jumping, but the presence of tension if you want to do some dressage will bring the marks right down.

Encouraging a horse to work (in trot and canter) in a much deeper outline can really loosen the back muscles. Provided he doesn't lean (which can be tested by giving the reins

Fig. 11.84 Helping to relax a tense horse. Rowena has inclined slightly forwards to lighten the seat and encourage the stretch, although this is not so necessary in a more established horse. (Photograph courtesy of Matthew Roberts Photography)

Fig. 11.85   Relaxing the horse in walk.

away) and he is moving actively forwards, then these exercises can be really helpful. Shoulder-fore, leg yielding and shoulder-in can also be ridden whilst in the deeper outline.

In Fig. 11.84 the horse is moving forwards freely – his outline is soft and he is not on the forehand. Rowena has asked for a slightly exaggerated bend to the inside to really stretch the outside muscles, and although the inside rein has been given away, he has maintained his outline.

Walk the horse around the school on a long rein; promote relaxation, and a lowering and a rounding of the outline by taking the inside hand back to the thigh. Don't pull back on the rein but just have enough 'pressure' on it so as to gently encourage the horse to flex laterally slightly to the inside. This exercise can also be practised when exercising a horse in a field.

Schooling out of the Arena

In a Field

In the early stages of retraining, working in an enclosed space is recommended, in the interests

of safety for horse and handler. However, schooling in a field is perfectly acceptable as long as the going is good – neither too hard nor too slippery. Schooling is not just about riding endless circles, it is about changes of rein, shapes and figures, transitions, changes of pace, obedience and so on, all of which can be executed in a field. Portable arena letters can be set out so that you can still work accurately to markers if you want. The added advantage is that you are not confined to a specific working area, so a schooling session can actually be more interesting for both of you.

Working a horse on grass is also a good test of how well he is listening to you, as there are more distractions in the great outdoors than in an arena. Remember to use lateral work to regain your horse's attention if necessary.

Schooling out Hacking

Some horses just won't work in an arena,

BACK TO BASICS

There will be times when your feel that your horse has lost his softness, is not so supple, and is resistant in the mouth. This is normal: not every schooling session will be perfect. This also occurs when you become more demanding or introduce new exercises, or when a horse is excited/distracted.

In such situations take the horse 'back to basics' to ensure you get something out of your schooling session – work him in a lowered, rounded outline, re-establishing rhythm and balance.

It is going to take some horse and rider combinations much longer to achieve the desired results, so don't get despondent or frustrated, and if necessary seek professional assistance.

Fig. 11.86   Becky and Beetle demonstrate that it is perfectly possible to work outside on grass.

presumably because they find it too monotonous, and a horse can't be forced into being enthusiastic about schooling work, in the same way that a person can't be forced to be academic.

Hacking out provides a good opportunity to do everything you can do in the school or in a field – however, be sensible and only practise exercises if and when conditions permit.

PROBLEM SOLVING

Generally the young horse will be introduced to work on a circle (or at least an oval) very early on; he will learn about looking where he is going, and to use his body both with and without the weight of a rider.

The horse in training doesn't have to learn about the importance of looking in the direction of travel, he doesn't need lateral bend, and he doesn't have to canter on a given leg lead. With these factors uppermost in your mind, you will appreciate just what a huge learning curve your horse is on and be less

prone to getting frustrated and disappointed when progress is slow.

In the following pages we cover some of the typical problems that people encounter; this should help you realize that you are not experiencing anything different from anyone else, that there is nothing wrong with your horse, and that it is possible to improve any situation.

Problem: My horse is on the forehand/leans
Racehorses are on the forehand because they really only propel themselves from behind when in fast work. The horse on the forehand is not using his back, therefore he needs continuing work with a lowered, but slightly rounded outline to build the topline muscles. Equally the ex-racehorse needs plenty of time to develop the necessary strength and balance to gradually take weight behind.

Be sure that any physical causes are ruled out: a horse may be on the forehand because his teeth need attention, the saddle is pinching his withers, the rider is tipping forwards or the bit is unsuitable.

A horse will trot fast in order to evade, so don't let him go tearing around the arena. Equally, be sure to keep the forward movement: too fast or too slow and the horse will fall on the forehand.

Make sure you are not riding too short otherwise your aids won't be so effective or your legs supportive.

There are plenty of exercises that will make the horse step with his hind legs more under his body, thus lightening the forehand.

Beneficial exercises include:

- Leg yielding
- Leg yielding on a circle
- Spiralling in and out on a circle
- Shoulder-in
- Upward and downward transitions, and transitions within the pace
- Uphill work.

Fig. 11.87 Although Nic is stepping under well, he is not truly soft through his back, so Abi works him on circles to improve his self-carriage. She could ask for a little more inside bend and also counter-flexion to help engage the hind leg more.

Include more groundwork in your training – use a Harbridge or Equi-ami if necessary to help strengthen the back muscles.

For horses that are very weak through the back and really do bear down on the rider's hands, then a change of bit can be helpful. It is not a case of switching to something harsher, just more appropriate for the task in hand. The Waterford is a good bit to use in this situation.

A horse is sometimes described as being strong when in fact he is leaning, usually due to weakness.

Problem: My horse is stiff on one rein
All horses are naturally stiffer on one side than the other, but training will correct this. Stiffness is demonstrated by a lack of lateral bend through turns and corners, and when on the straight, the horse will slightly turn his head away from his stiffer side; he will also hang on to the rein on that side as this helps him to balance.

To remedy this problem, first check your rider position, and make sure you are sitting square/straight. If the contact is stronger on one rein, more bit is likely to be showing outside the mouth on that side.

Check that the horse is not uncomfortable somewhere: a tight saddle, an unsuitable bit or sharp teeth may be causing this problem. It may be that as a result of a racing injury, muscles are tighter on one side than the other, which is why it is important to establish as much of your horse's history as possible so you are aware of these things, enabling you to take the right approach when trying to resolve a situation.

If no physical or rider-related reason can be found, then resistance on a particular rein is because he will not accept the outside rein contact, or the opposite rein. In this situation don't try and force the bend, otherwise the horse will just resist even more: he needs more suppling work.

Asking for shoulder-fore is a gentle way of suppling to create more bend. Ride in circles, spiralling in and out, and leg yield on the circle. To help him, flex the inside hand, and hold it in a slightly raised position – but don't pull back

Fig. 11.88 Rider position can cause horses to be on the forehand. (Photograph courtesy of Matthew Roberts Photography)

Fig. 11.89 When learning about counter-flexion, a horse may well feel a bit stiff, lose his outline and the ability to walk in a straight line!

on it. Walk in large circles, bending the horse's head round to your knee.

Ride transitions on the circle from one pace to another, and within the pace, as this helps to bring the hind legs underneath him. Keep giving the rein away on his stiffer side, as this encourages him to find his own balance.

Practise counter-flexion in walk to begin with, and progress to trot and then canter as the horse learns to cope with this very useful suppling exercise. Don't worry if initially your horse seems resistant – this is only because you are asking him to do something new, and also because of the stiffness you are trying to correct.

Problem: My horse is not tracking up
Bear in mind that the horse's confirmation will affect his ability to track up: thus the horse that is longer in the back may appear as if he isn't, whilst a horse with a straighter hind leg can't. There may, of course, be another physical reason restricting movement of one or both hind legs.

To improve the hind leg, lunge rather than ride initially so the horse is not hindered by rider weight. Round the outline and keep the forward movement. An Equi-ami is good for this.

When riding, once the horse is rounded up, use your legs to activate his hind legs. If he is not responsive to the aids, reinforce them by use of a schooling whip (a sharp tap just behind the leg) or use impulse spurs.

A horse may also not track up because he is 'bridle lame': whilst not physically lame, he can give the appearance of being so by moving in a crooked or unbalanced way, and not moving with a free, flowing stride. This might be caused by an ill-fitting saddle, an unsuitable bit and/or noseband, sharp teeth, the rider's lack of balance, or tension on his own part and/or that of his rider.

Problem: My horse is crooked on a circle
Crookedness is often caused by the inside hind leg crossing too far under the horse (see Fig. 11.90), and is usually connected to weakness in the back and/or a sacroiliac joint injury. If it happens on just one rein, this indicates that probably one hind leg is weaker than the other, and may be the horse's way of compensating for an old injury.

Shoulder-in is one of the best exercises for helping to strengthen hind-limb or back weakness, as the horse has to bring the inside leg under the midline, not across it. He will instinctively try to swing his quarters out, so don't make the angle too steep – a very common fault with shoulder-in.

Problem: My horse is lazy
The thoroughbred is not lazy by nature. Laziness, or being slow off the leg – your legs ask him to do something, but he doesn't, or the response is somewhat delayed – is the result of incorrect schooling, inappropriate bitting or a lack of communication. Furthermore a lazy horse should not be confused with one that is finding his workload difficult.

There are several reasons why this situation might occur: the horse is not fit or strong enough; his tack is not fitting comfortably, or the bit is not suitable; he is not being fed

Figs 11.90 and 11.91 Bobbie brings her left hind far too far across under her body causing crookedness (regardless of her lack of outline) and her right hind leg extends too far out behind; her way of locomotion is not as it should be. Following chiropractic treatment and a few weeks of suppling exercises, there is significant improvement in Bobbie's way of going.

appropriately for his workload – he is under- or overweight; the rider is sitting incorrectly, or is not giving him clear instructions

It is often thought that because a horse has been in training, he must be physically strong because he is fit to race. However, this is not strength in the same way that the riding horse is strong: for example, he hasn't had to carry weight down on his back (and remember that we sit on the weakest part of the horse), nor has he ever had to carry his head in a particular place or move his body in a particular way. Furthermore a significant number of horses come out of training when they are just three and four years of age, and whilst they are fit to run fast, their overall structure may still be lacking strength simply due to their immaturity.

Continually kicking a horse that doesn't respond achieves nothing, and until the horse is physically stronger, there are other ways you can help him to understand about going forwards from the leg – for instance, use a sensible lead horse to help your horse understand about going forwards.

If one sharp kick doesn't do the trick, then give him a flick just behind the leg with a schooling whip; he must be taught to respond instantly to your aids. He may well kick out at

the schooling whip initially but as long as he then moves on, don't worry. Only if he doesn't respond should you flick him again. Have an assistant on the ground to help move him forwards by encouraging him with a lunge whip directed towards his quarters.

Alternate between work on the ground and work under saddle, and don't necessarily ride him every day. You might adopt a more forward

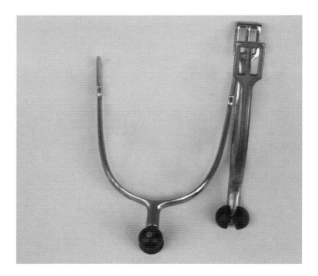

Fig. 11.92 You will see that impulse spurs are used in many of the photographs in this section.

seat for any canter work – don't sit in to the saddle but stay more on your knees.

Try wearing spurs so that your leg aid is sharper. If your lower leg is not stable, then use symmetry straps to be sure your leg doesn't move too far backwards. Impulse spurs are best for the thoroughbred initially as they are not too sharp against more sensitive skin.

Problem: My horse tosses his head

Head tossing is often tantamount to bit evasion, and basically relates to contact, or rather lack of it.

First check for any external contributory cause: saddle fit (including the girth), teeth, feet (a sore-footed horse is not going to work well), and most significantly in this case, the bit: ensure that the tongue has enough room, that the bit is not too high or too low in the mouth, and that the bit arms are not too long, which will cause a lozenge to sit too low. The horse may find the curve of the bit too severe so that when the reins are taken up it 'closes' too much; it may find the mouthpiece too thick or too thin.

If you have elected to use a drop or flash noseband it must be fastened quite tightly to be effective, which some horses object to; although you may have good reason for fitting one – to prevent the tongue coming over the bit or being poked out – you could be making the situation worse. If you are using it to help keep the bit up and still in the mouth, for early retraining, use a grakle or, better still, a Mexican noseband, as the latter in particular doesn't have to be fitted too tightly.

If you are still experiencing problems, then the solution is down to correct and effective riding, namely making the horse accept the contact by riding forwards whilst keeping a hold on the reins – not pulling back, but not letting the horse pull against you either.

It is often better to go back to groundwork and carry out some lunge work using side reins three to four times a week for a few weeks.

If you find that the problem arises again when you get back in the saddle, this would clearly indicate that the horse indeed has either a saddle problem or a back issue, as it is clearly weight on his back which is causing the evasion.

Problem: My horse falls out through the shoulder

This can be the result of the rider having too strong a contact on the inside rein and creating too much bend in the neck; even on a circle, a horse's neck should be basically straight (only enough bend so as to see the corner of the eye) unless you are specifically asking him to bend. Take more contact with the outside rein, keeping the inside leg on and slightly opening the inside rein away from the neck to encourage the horse to take up the outside rein.

Also, riding in counter flexion helps to bring the shoulder back in line and riding as small as your horse can cope encourages him to accept the outside contact, thus shifting his weight to the outside, as does leg yielding on a spiral, but be sure to soften the inside hand as you do so.

Fig. 11.93 As the inside rein is opened and slightly softened, more contact is taken with the outside rein which brings a horse off the outside shoulder.

Problem: My horse is stiff in shoulder-in

Stiffness in shoulder-in is so often the result of the rider sitting crooked and actually tipping their weight to the outside, so concentrate on putting more weight into your inside stirrup. Make sure you have slightly turned your shoulders; you can't expect your horse to turn his if you have not turned yours! Work on building the horse's hindquarters by using lots of transitions, both on the straight and on circles. Direct transitions (e.g. halt to trot, trot to halt, walk to canter, canter to walk) help to activate the hindlegs.

Problem: My horse is unbalanced in counter canter

Most horses are initially unbalanced in counter canter because they are not balanced in true canter, so improve the canter first. However, faults generally lie with the rider – over-riding, resulting in a lengthened outline and a loss of balance; pulling on the rein in an attempt to keep the bend, which results in too much bend, leading to a blocking of the hindlegs; reins held too tightly so the horse stiffens through the back and the canter breaks, the contact is lost so the horse goes onto the forehand; leaning forwards, putting their weight over the horse's shoulders leading to loss of balance.

Problem: My horse canters quarters-in

This is very common in horses. Generally it is acceptable for the rider to bring the inside leg back a little to help push the quarters back into line. Flexing the head/neck slightly to the inside (shoulder fore) also helps to straighten the horse. To practise straightness, lay some poles end to end down the quarter line and centre line, and canter between them.

Problem: My horse won't stop when out hacking

It is not unusual to find that whilst you have perfect control in the school, in the open it is your horse that sets the pace! This is because in the school environment he is doing something new and is contained, so he is prepared to listen to you; but he associates being out in the open with canter work up the gallops.

Safe hacking out depends on established schooling work, so that your horse is responsive and well mannered.

In the early days of ownership, if there is any indication that the horse is likely to rush off, then take certain precautions when you hack out: for example, keep to walking and trotting, and avoid riding in a group for a while; when riding with another horse, alternate between your horse taking the lead and going behind, as well as walking and trotting next to his friend.

Avoid riding across open land, but stay close to hedges and fences; and when you have a canter, choose an enclosed field and again remain close to the hedge – and head towards something solid, rather than across a large open space. If you are with others, be sure to go in front and ask your friend(s) to stay a good distance behind you, and to one side; if they come up behind your horse he will probably think of his racing days and pick up speed – and don't be tempted to canter side by side until you have good control!

Using a harsher bit can sometimes make the situation worse because the horse will just fight against you; it is better to use a bit that by its action backs him off. A combination bit affords control without compromising a sensitive mouth, and ported bits are also good; a grakle or a Mexican noseband can also help with control.

Problem: My horse is too forward in the school

When a horse drops its head down and keeps going despite being asked to stop, a different bit is sometimes the answer – but ultimately flatwork is the key to achieving long-term success with a horse that is too on-going.

Slow the trot right down almost to the point where the horse feels lazy and is dragging his feet. Keep hold of the reins (not to be confused with pulling on them – pulling on the reins is not an effective speed control method); it may feel that the horse is pulling against you (don't confuse this with thinking he is being strong/leaning), but if you don't keep a contact then he won't learn. Keep your rising really slow.

A good exercise to practise is to walk for five strides, then canter for five strides, then come back to walk for five strides; canter on again and back to walk (it is fine to go through a few trot strides on both the upward and downward transitions). Keep practising this exercise (on both reins) until your horse becomes more responsive. This won't happen in one session, but it is something to work on. It can also be done whilst out hacking as a good exercise to keep you in control.

Forwardness is not all bad even if it feels as if you are not in control! Forward is something that the ex-racehorse is good at, although usually on his terms; but once schooling work becomes more established you may well find that his sharpness goes as he learns about moving off the leg.

Problem: My horse keeps tripping

Firstly it is important to discuss this problem with both your farrier and vet, as there may be a problem with shoeing and/or general locomotion. Alternatively it could be that the horse is just weak. Also some horses do find schooling on certain surfaces hard work, especially if the surface is deep.

Tripping can of course be due to the rider not riding the horse properly, and having the reins too slack, in which case they should shorten up the reins and push the horse into the contact. It may be necessary to keep asking with the leg to maintain forward impulsion.

If the horse is not working from behind, then more schooling exercises are required.

Problem: My horse bolts in the school

A horse doesn't take off across the school for no reason: either something has frightened it on that particular day, or it has a past association of a fright, or of something that has caused it pain. Horses have great memories, and once a horse has spooked he will invariably tense up as he approaches the same spot next time round. Then the rider begins to tense up too, to the point where the horse's overriding instinct is to flee.

To resolve this problem you must focus yourself and ride positively forwards, otherwise your horse will continue to spook at the same spot. Distract him by asking for some leg yield, or turn a circle just before he begins to tense up. If possible give him a few minutes on the

Figs 11.94 and 11.95   If possible, give the horse a few minutes on the lunge line to rid him of excess energy or under saddle give him a canter round the school a few times before expecting him to settle into his work.

lunge line to rid him of excess energy, or if he is under saddle give him a canter round the school a few times before expecting him to settle to his work.

Most instances of the horse suddenly taking off are pain-related, whether from a one-off occurrence such as a sting, or because something is pinching – the girth or saddle. Or maybe a heart flutter or a bubble of air moving through the alimentary canal caused temporary discomfort. A horse can sometimes get his tongue over the bit without the rider being aware of this until a rein aid is made which hurts, so the horse reacts – but often by the time the rider has stopped him he has managed to get it back into the right position.

Because the ex-racehorse is on such a steep learning curve he is automatically on 'alert', so if the rider accidentally kicks too hard or bumps down on the saddle, he might react quite violently. If he does, perhaps by rearing right up or giving a huge buck, it is advisable to have a vet check him over as there could be some more serious underlying trigger, such as back pain.

Such behaviour is disconcerting, but it is important to block it out of your mind otherwise it will affect your riding and potentially cause more problems.

Bucking, bolting and spooking can also be the result of a lively horse that is feeling well, so check that you are not feeding him too much.

Problem: My horse keeps bucking
Horses that don't want to go forwards often buck – it is a resistance to the forward aids when the rider puts the leg on, and is an indication that they have not been taught to respect the leg aids and respond appropriately when asked.

First and foremost any physical explanation must be ruled out, such as the saddle being too tight. However, such horses tend to be generally evasive, and even at walk are reluctant to take the contact. Disciplining them by means of a sharp kick or even a slap with a stick often results in more bucking. Unfortunately many

riders can't anticipate a buck – though in the school environment the horse will swing his haunches, and this is your warning.

The way to resolve this problem is to sit quietly (sit up) with a secure lower leg and *ride forwards*: the horse that is moving forwards can't buck because in order to do so he has to slow down a bit.

Keep the legs on: an instant response by riders when the horse bucks is to take the leg off when actually it should be kept as that is what he is objecting to. If you take the leg off each time he bucks, he has got what he wants. He is training you!

Keep an even contact with the legs on, and ride him into the bridle. As many riders actually lean forwards when they ride they are easily dislodged when a horse bucks because their lower leg is too far back – they are not secure in the saddle.

Half halts will prevent the horse from running through the contact, and ride him on small figures of eight – this keeps him more forward-thinking and attentive than when ridden on a circle.

Problem: My horse is spooky and shies a lot
Spooking is often a result of the rider being nervous, and of inadequate training: the horse is not on the aids, is tense or distracted, or simply isn't 'way wise'.

In this situation it is important to ride more positively, and to convey forwardness and confidence to the horse. The rider should remain attentive to the horse's body language and so be able to anticipate most spooks.

Long-reining is a good way of getting your horse out and about, but you must be experienced at this and know exactly what to do if he attempts to spin round. Therefore it is sometimes better to lead out in hand.

To begin with, keep outings short, and avoid routes where you know there are many potential scary things. Give your horse a chance to accept things gradually.

As herd animals, horses usually feel safer in company although some will spook and shy regardless. Generally though, riding out with another is a good option but the companion must be quiet and dependable. Be sure to ask your horse to take the lead sometimes.

Schooling is the most important factor, as this makes the horse more responsive to the aids as well as building his confidence, giving you much more control when he starts to think twice.

Some horses are spooky through genuine fear or phobia. The traditional way of dealing with this was to force a horse with whip, spurs and rough handling to face the object that was frightening him; these days, however, it is accepted that this is actually not the way to go about curing his fear, as the scary object will then be associated with punishment and so further distress. Rather, it is better to let the horse view the scary object from a distance and be gradually encouraged to go nearer, step by step. Let him keep looking if he so wishes, but don't pressure him – reassurance is required.

Fig. 11.96 *Hero Worship can't be classed as nappy but if he saw or heard something he would typically start the stilted/propped walk of a horse that is about to stop (and possibly spin around).*

Problem: My horse is nappy

A nappy horse refuses to move, spins around, rears up or does any combination of these evasions. Nappiness can be a progression from spooking.

Once a horse starts to react negatively in a given situation, the rider begins to anticipate trouble, which often leads to tension and nervousness on their part, which in turn is transmitted to the horse, thereby making the situation worse. Nevertheless, if a horse suddenly starts napping there has to be a reason.

The most common scenario out hacking is when a horse sees something he doesn't like or isn't sure about, and stops and plants himself, or spins round and tries to run off in the opposite direction. Some horses hack out to a certain point and then turn for home. In this latter case, before the horse actually stops himself, *you* stop him and head for home – the

Fig. 11.97 *The way to correct this and nip any such possibility in the bud is to ride forwards. Everything about riding a horse is 'think forwards' even when slowing down!*

idea being that it is your decision and not his. Don't feed him as soon as you get back, otherwise that is an excuse for him to get back home quickly.

It is wrongly assumed (or advised) that nappiness is *always* because the horse is naughty or lazy, when often napping stems from fear of something. Being overly forceful by using a stick can make the situation worse, because a nappy horse usually doesn't have confidence in his rider – so what to do?

The horse needs to see you as a confident leader, a safe person to be with, so use ground-training exercises to re-establish confidence. Progress to having short in-hand walks, then go out under saddle for a short hack – just for a matter of minutes initially.

The first part of overcoming nappiness is to teach the horse to stand rather than trying to turn tail. By getting him to stand you have more control over his feet, and therefore of the horse. If you are trying to pass a static object, let the horse take a good long look, asking him to move forwards a step a time and praising each positive movement.

The nappy horse will generally either spin round or plant himself. Block the spin by opening the opposite hand wide and pull firmly on the rein, pulling his nose round towards your leg; put your weight into the stirrup on the same side as the open rein.

With very firm legs, alternate between kicking with the leg on the same side as the open rein to push his quarters round, and kicking with the leg on the opposite side (with this leg at the girth) to push him off the shoulder.

Continue to spin him round into a full circle – this is actually quite easy to do as he is already on the turn.

Then kick him on in your desired direction of travel.

If he repeats his spin, you repeat yours – but next time he may plant himself.

Planting is often the horse's tactic when you have worked on the spinning, and the best way to resolve it is to get him off balance by turning his head round to his girth and kicking his quarters over.

Whilst a lead from another horse is sometimes all that is required, the determined planter won't respond to this either, so shock tactics are required. If you are close to home, ask an assistant on the ground to chase him up with a lunge whip in conjunction with your own aids. Alternatively you could ride with a companion and ask them to give your horse a tap on the backside (though be careful he doesn't kick out).

Some horses do take advantage of the less effective and/or less confident rider, so you may need to ask a more experienced rider to help work your horse through this phase. It may be that he does need one sharp 'smack', but you will need to be able to sit out any possible consequences of doing so!

If the horse plants himself quite soon after leaving the yard, and usually at the same place, then lead him out in hand to begin with. When he stops, just put pressure on the lead rope. Don't pull, as he will pull back harder, and may even rear up. Just maintain an even pull, and wait until he gets fed up and gives in. The moment you feel him beginning to concede, give a short sharp tug. You may need to repeat this two or three times, but be patient.

Problem: My horse rears

Rearing often follows on from reversing/planting; seen as a means for a horse to get his own way, it is actually his way to say you are not listening to him. Horses rear for a reason; with physical reasons (ill-fitting tack, teeth, pain, etc.) ruled out, it may be that he has lost his confidence in you or has become confused. Check your riding and application of the aids.

A horse has to be stopped still or moving only slowly in order to go up – he can't rear up in any pace other than walk – so one way to resolve the problem is to keep him on the move, if possible. The more experienced rider will be able to feel when the horse is about to rear as he will suddenly go light in front, so they can ride him forwards immediately. If the horse rears up without the rider being able to anticipate it, as soon as his feet hit the floor again, make him go forwards, with a great big kick or a sharp smack with a whip.

It is a case of being really positive and forceful, as rearing is the one way a horse can get the better of his rider if this behaviour is not dealt with as soon as possible.

When a horse rears up the rider must be careful not to pull on the reins, as this can pull the horse over backwards.

As rearing is so dangerous, it is better to seek professional assistance should your horse persist with such behaviour.

IN SUMMARY

Working on a horse's flatwork is an on-going exercise as there is always something to work on, something to improve. And you should always remind yourself that what you have taken on is the bigger and more satisfying challenge of changing a horse's lifestyle and career.

Comparing Fig. 11.94 with earlier ones of Hero Worship points up just how much a horse changes in his physique with the correct training. Training does present its challenges, but then it does with any horse.

Fig. 11.98 Keep a photographic record as it is very easy to become disillusioned about how your horse is performing, especially when everyone else around you suddenly seems to be coming home with an array of red rosettes. This horse will change significantly if correct training continues.

12 Basic Jump Training

Jumping tests the horse and rider relationship. Lack of confidence by the young or inexperienced horse in his rider will lead to him running out and/or refusing. If a rider is at all nervous then they should be riding a horse that is already very familiar with jumping and can help the rider out.

Very few horses have no jumping ability whatsoever; most are readily able to tackle up to 2ft 6in without any real difficulty; thereafter a horse needs to show a certain aptitude. Although 2ft 6in isn't very high, once fillers and width are added, a fence looks much bigger, particularly if it is solid.

Retraining the ex-racehorse as a show jumper or an event horse can be quite a challenge, because their style of jumping is completely different. The hurdler especially is taught to get from one side of the hurdle to the other as quickly as possible; he mustn't

lose his race in the air, thus he jumps fast and flat. The chaser obviously needs to get a bit higher, but he can readily brush through the top of a fence in the interests of speed. However, this jumping technique is no good for the horse that has to leave poles in cups or jump solid timber.

The horse off the flat may never have actually been tried over a jump of any description, so you can work with his natural ability and inclination; the National Hunt horse, already familiar with jumping, has to be taught to jump in a different manner and at a much slower speed. Seeing coloured poles for the first few times can have the effect of backing a horse off, but more often than not, it is a case of getting to and over the jump as fast as possible. Whilst often put down to enthusiasm – indeed some horses are very keen – sometimes what appears to be enthusiasm is tension and that is why

Figs 12.1 and 12.2   The racehorse jumps in a different way to the event or show jumping horse. (Photographs: left courtesy of Jon Fullegar, Sandown Racecourse; right courtesy of John Pike, Racing Images)

such horses often make an awkward jump because they are not really concentrating on the fence itself.

On a general level, jumping tests the horse and rider relationship: if the horse doesn't have confidence in his rider he will run out or refuse, and if a rider is nervous they should not be training an inexperienced horse. Most horses will tackle fences up to 2ft 6in (75cm) without any real difficulty, but thereafter they need to show a certain aptitude. Although 2ft 6in isn't very high, once fillers and width are added, a fence looks much bigger, particularly if it is solid.

Before starting jumping training, work should commence over poles so that you can develop control and help the horse understand that there is no need to tackle everything at full speed.

POLEWORK

Polework is the best way to introduce the horse to jumping, whether from on the ground or under saddle. It is beneficial to both horse and rider, even if there is no desire to jump. It improves his balance, engagement and

Figs 12.3 and 12.4   Hero Worship at first is not sure about a pole on the ground and his reaction to seeing one is typical. He basically reached the pole, stopped, had a look and hesitated, but with gentle persuasion (a giving hand, legs on and an inclined body to portray moving forward), decided to step over it.

Fig. 12.5   Having repeated this a few times, then approaching in trot and adding a second pole, it is not too long before Hero is happy to negotiate three poles with confidence.

athleticism, it creates elevation to the stride, especially when he is worked over raised poles, and it teaches him to lengthen.

Riding over a row of poles demands accuracy and concentration – it isn't just a case of just trotting over them: you need to keep straight, the horse must maintain a balanced, rhythmical trot, and whilst he must learn not to rush, he must also maintain impulsion. The rider must remain in balance with the horse, as well as controlling him.

For riders who are unfamiliar with polework, it is better to work with a horse that is used to the exercise before trying to teach your ex-racehorse.

> Always use protective boots or bandages on the horse.

Getting Started

Ideally for polework it is helpful to have an assistant who can adjust the poles as required. Firstly you need to know how your horse will react to a pole on the ground. Put down a single pole and let him walk and trot over it, off both reins. Then put down a second pole about 4ft 6in (approx 1.40m) – the average stride length – from the first, and repeat the exercise so that you can ascertain your horse's length of stride.

Whilst polework can be used to help both lengthen and shorten the strides, it is important to work with the individual horse's natural stride length initially, until he is negotiating a row of four, six or even eight poles in balance without getting anxious. Then you can begin experimenting with different stride lengths.

Some horses take to polework very quickly, others take more time. Don't be influenced by other people, who may try and tell you what you should or shouldn't be doing, or compare your horse to others: each one is different, so it is important to manage the individual horse and the particular situation.

In Figs 12.6–12.9 it can be seen that Bobbie has a Harbridge fitted. This illustrates that the Harbridge is fine to use for ridden work over poles and small jumps. At no time is it pulling Bobbie's head down or forcing an outline. Lyn (Bobbie's owner) was apprehensive about working over poles as she wasn't sure how Bobbie was going to react.

Figs 12.6 and 12.7   Bobbie was fine but Lyn tensed up as evidenced by her stiff elbows and rigid spine. However, after a bit of practice, Bobbie just kept improving and Lyn relaxed, becaming more a part of her horse.

Figs 12.8 and 12.9   The raised poles don't present a problem for Lyn and Bobbie. Lyn has elected to remain in sitting trot as this helped her maintain balance and stay in rhythm with Bobbie.

A few more poles were introduced, and once again this had an effect on Lyn but after a little more practice she found her composure. Bobbie is working nicely, although ideally Lyn could have been slightly inclined forward to take weight off the mare's back.

Raised Poles

Exercises over raised poles increase the need for accuracy from both horse and rider, and promote athleticism and suppleness, as well as presenting a new challenge. The poles don't have to be raised very high in order to achieve this objective. Alternately raised poles are very beneficial for horses that have had pelvic

troubles, and often form part of their required rehabilitation work following chiropractic treatment.

Working over raised poles is strenuous for a horse, so don't expect too much, too soon, and keep the training sessions short. If your horse has had treatment from a vet or chiropractor, check with them first before embarking on this type of exercise.

If after working over raised poles you feel any deterioration in your horse's way of going, don't do any more until he has been checked by a vet and/or a chiropractor in case he has pulled a muscle or strained something.

Some trainers like the rider to use rising trot for raised trotting poles, whilst others prefer that they are out of the saddle all the time. As the object of the exercise is to increase the horse's flexibility and suppleness, particularly through the back, then it is better to remain out of the saddle allowing the horse the freedom to lift his back. However, a rider needs good balance to do this: it is easy to lose impulsion, and this can result in them using the reins to maintain their balance, which is definitely not

Fig. 12.10 By working Nic around and occasionally over the poles, Abi will be able to break what really has become a habit rather than an issue.

Figs 12.11 and 12.12 Note how even with this simple exercise Abi is so focused; she is looking where she is heading whilst negotiating the pole. This is already setting Nic up for the turn – good riding.

helpful to the horse. So ride according to your ability, so as to keep in balance with the horse.

PROBLEM SOLVING

Problem: My horse rushes over the poles

Some horses get tense or excited at the sight of poles. Lay single poles randomly around the school and occasionally walk or trot over them as part of your routine flatwork; the horse will then learn that they are nothing to get excited about. From there, build up to two and three poles placed in a row or a fan.

As can be seen in Figs 12.10–12.12, Nic finds poles very exciting indeed and as soon as he sees one, tenses up and forgets his otherwise generally good manners. However, by working him around and occasionally over the poles, Abi should be able to teach him to go more steadily.

Another way to prevent the horse rushing is to stay in walk until you get closer to the poles, so he doesn't have the opportunity to pick up speed; push into trot just two or three strides away.

You could try removing every second pole from your line so that the horse takes a non-pole stride between each pole; and place the poles on a circle rather than on a straight line.

Problem: My horse keeps raising his head when trotting over poles

This problem is very common, as it is easier for the horse to do this than work his back properly: he is basically evading. To resolve it, first try plenty of practice in walk, because it is easier to maintain the outline in walk. As above, just push into trot a few strides from the poles – in fact, see if you can get within a couple of strides and then push into trot.

Make sure that your seat is light and that you are not blocking the movement; that your hands are not too high; and that your wrists, elbows and shoulders are soft (the elbows should be bent).

Place the poles away from the arena edge so that you have plenty of room around them; this allows you to trot around the poles on a circle, which helps in rounding the horse's outline. Edge closer and closer to the poles, but don't go over them until the horse is working well on the circle.

Alternatively, lay the poles in a fan shape rather than a straight line. If your horse is raising his head more because he is getting excited and trying to rush, then go back to walking in your approach.

Make sure that you are not allowing the horse's head to come up by dropping the contact as the poles are negotiated. This can cause him to lose confidence.

Problem: My horse is on his forehand when going over poles

Falling on the forehand is primarily caused by lack of balance on the part of the horse as well as lack of strength behind the saddle. This will improve as the horse's muscle structure and suppleness improve. Make sure that you aren't contributing to this problem by inclining too far forwards.

Fig. 12.13   Hero is not using his back, as evidenced by the lack of joint flexion and that he is on the foreground, although the situation is not helped by the fact he is busy looking at the green block that has fallen on the ground just in front of him!

Fig. 12.14   Lyn has done the typical rider tense-up, producing the 'water-skiing arms'; however, she is still riding Bobbie forwards; the little mare is clearly focused on the job in hand with her ears pricked and her head lowered.

Fig. 12.15   A lovely first jump from Lyn and Bobbie; note Lyn's low and soft hand, allowing Bobbie the freedom of her head.

BASIC JUMP SCHOOLING

Jumping is a natural progression from polework and can be readily introduced by placing a small jump at the end of a row of poles. This allows the horse to do something that it has become used to, whilst also tackling something new.

To introduce the first jump, put down a row of trotting poles, then remove the second to last pole in the row, and replace the last pole with a small cross-pole fence. The poles will help horse and rider maintain their rhythm, and

they also help to establish the correct take-off point, which will give the horse confidence.

If you've been using a few poles in front of the fence to help you maintain rhythm and balance, now use just one to help achieve the correct take-off point. As confidence and ability grow, then you can dispense with the pole, but initially keep things as easy as possible: the aim is to encourage, not discourage, the horse. Using a place pole encourages a horse to round, as well as helping with the take-off.

Always start with a cross-pole, just to get the horse off the floor. Once he has happily

THE RIDER'S JUMPING POSITION

The balance and stability of the rider in the saddle is very important, and if it isn't very good, then the success of teaching a horse to jump correctly may be compromised.

Fig. 12.16   Practise achieving a good jumping position on an established horse before attempting to teach a young or novice horse.

The rider should have a secure lower leg which doesn't swing but remains at the girth; the weight should be in the heels, and they should not grip with the knees: this actually makes the rider more insecure. Be sure not to tip the head down and/or to the side as this causes the body to collapse, resulting in the lower leg going back, which affects the centre of balance and hence security in the saddle.

On the approach the rider should sit up tall with the shoulders back. Don't push the horse into a longer, flatter stride otherwise he will be flat over the fence and so more likely to knock it down. Keep the impulsion – a shorter, bouncy stride – but don't chase him: the horse should be in front of the leg and taking you to the fence. Be quiet in your position, and control the speed with your seat, not your hands.

Be sure that the horse is not receiving conflicting signals from legs and hands – your legs saying 'go' and your hands saying 'perhaps not'.

Another common fault when jumping is that riders move around too much and often appear to be throwing themselves at the fence so they end up with their upper body up the horse's neck. This makes it harder for the horse to bring his front legs up.

The rider's position when landing is also important, and especially so when riding an ex-racehorse, as these horses gain so much speed in the air: the balance must still be there so that they are able to get back into the saddle in order to steady and control the horse, ready to set him up for the next jump.

If you haven't jumped for a while it's worth having a lesson or two before attempting to start training your own horse.

Fig. 12.17   The rider's position when landing is also important; the balance must still be there so that they are back in the saddle and ready to set the horse up for the next jump.

Fig. 12.18   Hero Worship tackles his first jump. Although it is small, to Hero it is a new experience – one he coped with very well.

negotiated this off both reins you can be a bit more adventurous by making little uprights or spreads and introducing fillers. Keep the jumps small: you are not testing how high your horse can jump, and a smaller, well-constructed fence encourages a better bascule than a larger fence.

Initially just be pleased that your horse has had the confidence to negotiate a coloured jump – encourage him and praise him, because

until he will go to a jump happily and steadily, however small, you can't set about improving his technique.

Adjusting the Stride

If you are planning a jumping career for your ex-racehorse, rather than just popping over the occasional log or hedge when out hacking, then it is important to be able to adjust your horse's stride. Many riders struggle with this, perhaps because their horses take on the fences so enthusiastically, or they can't 'see a stride', and either 'fire' the horse at a fence or hold him back too much.

Being able to adjust the stride at will in order to achieve a correct take-off will make the difference between leaving a fence standing or knocking it down. Whilst this is not so important for a small jump, as the height goes up, accuracy is everything.

First, lay out some canter poles (about four walking strides apart, but canter normally over them to check). A little later you can adjust the distance between the poles so that you can practise lengthening and shortening the canter stride, either by opening them all up a little, or making them closer.

Figs 12.19 and 12. 20   Rowena is approaching the jump with a defensive seat in that she is making sure that Indie doesn't stop – a good policy when jumping a horse for the first time. After a couple of jumps, Rowena and Indie are in perfect harmony. Using a place pole doesn't just help with the take-off, it also encourages a horse to round.

Fig. 12.21   It soon becomes evident that Indie loves jumping and is generally much happier, and indeed confident, with a good shape over a slightly larger jump.

Doubles and Combinations

When you build two fences together, always start with at least two non-jumping strides between them so the horse has enough time to see the second fence and you have the opportunity to help him, either by encouraging him forwards or checking him back slightly. If you wish, you can continue to use a place pole in front of the first jump to help maintain the correct take-off point.

As with the single fence, start off with low cross-poles to find out what the horse will do. He will most likely canter between the jumps – so let him, and don't try and bring him back to trot otherwise you will encourage a refusal. Once a horse is confident with two fences, you can then begin to correct the pace.

HOW A HORSE JUMPS

Typically the show jumper makes a shape termed a 'bascule' when he jumps. He pushes off from his hocks and rounds his back; as he lifts his shoulders to clear the fence his neck stretches down and forwards, and his forelegs are drawn up and folded. Whilst many horses can tackle lower heights successfully without the best of techniques, once the fences start going up, poor or incorrect technique results in knock-downs.

In general terms the take-off point for a jump is approximately 6ft (2m) away, but the horse will come in closer to tackle a wider fence, and take off a little further away for an upright. Ultimately though, much depends on the size and type of the fence, and the ground conditions and gradient must also be taken into account.

The way in which fences are built can remedy poor jumping style; however, correcting faults is the preserve of an experienced trainer, so if your horse's technique needs improvement it is best to seek practical help from someone with the requisite knowledge.

Fig. 12.22   Neither of these hurdlers has jumped as a show jumping horse would with properly tucked forelegs; they have jumped in typical hurdler style by bringing the forelegs forward and not folding the knees. (Photograph courtesy of John Pike, Racing Images)

*Figs 12.23 and 12.24
Rowena gently coaxes
Light the Fuse through a
very small double.*

It is not usual to have a spread fence as the first fence, nor to have it higher than the second, as in Fig. 12.24; however, in this instance we are still working on encouraging Light the Fuse to have the confidence to go to a second jump: by keeping it small we are hoping not to put him off.

When you feel the horse is ready to move on to a combination, lower the fences again: just because he has happily negotiated two jumps doesn't mean that he will do so over three. Don't take anything for granted, but be sure to build up his confidence.

Likewise, when you elect to make a two-stride double a single stride, lower the height of the jumps.

You should only move on to a bounce when your horse is really confident, when you can control his approach, and are secure in the saddle. Some horses may be tempted to tackle a bounce as one fence, which is why it is important to keep the jumps small, and to be able to control the speed – the faster your approach, the more likely that the horse may take it on as a single jump instead of two.

Fig. 12.25 Mr Bojangles is a very confident jumper – doubles and bounces hold no fears for him. This shot shows a lovely straight, central approach to the second element.

Jumping Grids

Gridwork teaches a horse to adjust his stride, it develops and improves his technique, and helps to build up his confidence. The rider can also work on their own style. Gridwork is also very good for the rider as they too can work on their style and correct errors such as one-sidedness and uncontrolled hands and legs. However, for resolving rider errors it's better to work with an experienced horse not a horse that is learning.

Grids involve jumping three or more fences, using both single and non-jumping strides. If you have a long enough arena, using four or

Figs 12.26 and 12.27 Initially start grids with cross-poles, or straight poles if you prefer, to get the horse underway.

Figs 12.28 and 12.29   When riding down a grid it is important to keep the horse straight and keep both his and your own focus right until the last jump however small the jumps may be; it's not a case of jumping the first fence and the rest will take care of itself.

five jumps really allows you to play around with stride variations. However, what you build – whether single fences, oxers, true parallels, reversed oxers – will depend on what exactly you are trying to achieve, and you will need an experienced trainer to identify the aspects of technique in your horse that might be improved with gridwork, and to advise on how a grid should be built to achieve that end.

The keen, more established jumping horse will negotiate a grid without much influence from the rider; however, always be alert to the feel of your horse, and don't get complacent otherwise you could find yourself on the receiving end of a very quick stop!

Using 'V' Poles

Placing two poles on the top pole of a jump to form a 'V' has several purposes: it keeps a horse straight; it trains the rider to ride to the middle of a fence; it teaches a horse to pick his feet up; it encourages lift from the shoulder, and helps to teach a horse to take weight on the hindquarters. 'V' poles are usually placed on a single fence or on the first part of a double, though they can be used on both elements of a

double for maximum effect.

To begin with, make the 'V' quite wide by placing the ends resting on the top pole of the jump quite close to each wing. As the horse gets the idea, the ends on the top pole can be moved closer together to make more of a true 'V' shape. The closer together they are, the more difficult it is for the horse, so if he becomes anxious or is clearly not managing to tackle the jump, widen the pole ends again until confidence is restored.

Using 'V' poles is difficult for a horse especially as the poles get closer, so don't overwork him and risk fences being knocked down because he is tired. 'V' poles can be used on any height of fence.

Preparing to Jump a Course

Once your horse is happily negotiating single jumps, doubles and combinations, it's time to think about placing fences randomly around the school so that you can commence your preparation for jumping a course by incorporating turns and jumping on an angle.

There are many books and DVDs with all manner of exercises and tips to help you

Fig. 12.30 Rowena and Mr Bojangles are nicely centred for take-off.

Figs 12.31 and 12.32   Closing the 'V' has the effect of making Bo jump with more lift from the shoulder rather than just folding his knees. Rowena's elbows should be closer to the body (left) and Bo could have been given slightly more rein (right).

progress from here. Any difficulties that you encounter from this point on will not really be anything to do with the fact that you are on an ex-racehorse, but because you are not communicating clearly or there are still confidence issues – in which case you need to take one or two steps back.`

CROSS-COUNTRY JUMPING

There is no greater thrill than to jump across open country, especially on a horse that is as keen as you are. However, in the open with no arena fence to contain you, there is plenty of opportunity for a horse to run out. 'V'-pole practice will help you to keep your horse straight and to the middle of the fence, which is

Fig. 12.33 Whether or not you are actually a horse-racing fan, it is quite a sight to see several horses coming over a chase fence. (Photograph courtesy of John Pike, Racing Images)

Fig. 12.34 This photograph shows how differently the racehorse jumps compared to his non-racing counterparts. (Photograph courtesy of Jon Fullegar, Sandown Racecourse)

just as important when jumping in the open as it is when in an arena – unless of course you purposely want to jump on an angle.

Introducing a horse to solid fences is really no different to coloured fences, but may seem more daunting because possibly you have other issues to deal with, such as excitement or speed control. It may be an idea to consider changing the bit (to one with a different action, as opposed to a stronger one) so that you do have enough control, both on approach and landing.

Introduce the idea of solid fences by using jump fillers in the safety of a more enclosed space. Also, rather than suddenly making a fence appear more solid with a filler, do this in stages, first by pulling the fillers to each side of the jump leaving the centre of it open, then pulling the fillers in gradually. If possible use brush or timber fillers rather than coloured ones initially, so the horse gets used to jumping something more natural looking and less spooky.

In the early stages of cross-country schooling approach the cross-country fence in the same way that you would a show jump; until you and your horse are working as a team there is no need to go fast – speed can come later. Let the

Figs 12.35 and 12.36 Leosaid (Georgie) loved solid timber and proved to be bold across country whereas he disliked coloured fences. George (bottom picture with Fred) was happy doing both.

LEFT: Fig. 12.37 Leosaid (Georgie) happily continued to jump chase fences whether quietly (as here with Fred) or at speed if he was acting as lead horse for young NH horses or point-to-point horses. Given his buzzy temperament, it was quite a feat of achievement to readily switch him off like this.

BELOW: Fig. 12.38 The only way to get a horse used to cross country jumping is practice, so hire a course and go and have some fun. Tackle as many different types of fence as possible. The height doesn't matter; it is the variety that is important, so introduce your horse to as many different types of fence as possible.

horse see what he is jumping so as to give him the confidence to jump – but be ready for him to jump big over relatively small jumps because a small, solid fence seems much bigger than a more flimsy show jump.

For your first few outings keep to the more straightforward fences; when you and your horse are jumping these confidently you will be happier about tackling a variety of more difficult fences and combinations, such as drop fences, skinnies, coffins and sunken roads. Some horses are naturally bold; others need more encouragement. Of course there are those that are just not confident above a certain height, but hunter trial and team chase courses offer courses to suit all levels.

If your horse lacks confidence, where possible let him follow a lead from a reliable companion,

Fig. 12.39   Narrow fences pose no problem for Clare Stringer and Kitty Way. (Photograph courtesy of Michael Rogers, MDR Photo)

Fig. 12.40   Lucius Lockett has put his racing career well behind him and has been a reliable mount for several members of the Saunders family. (Photograph courtesy of Tik Saunders)

particularly when asking him to jump a ditch or go into water for the first time.

Approach jumps from a trot if you prefer, especially if you are worried about getting the take-off right – but you must always ride very positively forwards, with your legs firmly round the horse. Jumping solid fences isn't for the faint-hearted: if you are not committed then you can't expect the untrained horse to take you – you are the one responsible for imparting confidence.

Your position for negotiating cross country fences is equally important as for tackling show jumps, if not more so, as often horses jump higher than necessary or can readily leave a leg, causing them to stumble on landing. So you need to be doubly secure in the saddle to ensure you don't go over his head.

By the time you are confidently popping over logs, hedges and small ditches, your progress to more difficult fences will be like that of any other horse, and the fact that you are riding an

ex-racehorse will be irrelevant, because there is nothing peculiar to the ex-racehorse that isn't true of any other horse by this stage of his retraining.

PROBLEM SOLVING

Many jumping issues, though seemingly the fault of the horse, have in fact developed as a result of rider error, so whilst they are not necessarily specific to the horse out of training, they do appear regularly as 'problem' issues.

Problem: My horse refuses

If a horse has been jumping without problem but then suddenly starts to refuse at fences, take a look at anything which you have changed, and which may be affecting his confidence: for example, are you using a different saddle and/or numnah, a different bit and/or noseband, or new jumping boots – they may be too tight.

If nothing is new, then check the fit of his current saddle, have his teeth checked, make sure he isn't sore somewhere. He may have problems with his shoes or pain in his feet – a horse can be put off jumping because he is frightened to land. Many jumping issues have been found to be foot-related, especially if there is a problem involving the pedal bone.

Perhaps he has simply gained weight, so doesn't feel like being too athletic.

Refusals can also be caused by the rider: if you keep putting the horse wrong at a fence he will lose confidence; and he will be confused if you give him mixed signals because you are not confident yourself – for example, if you take too firm a hold on the reins when at the same time you are driving him with the leg.

He may be refusing because he is frightened – perhaps he had a nasty fall when racing which has made him wary of the whole jumping experience. Maybe he is not sure what is expected of him: remember he is learning, so are you making everything simple and clear to him? Be sure you are not bustling him along: let him take his time.

There are several ways you can try to resolve the problem of your horse refusing.

If he seems reluctant to jump over poles, make the fence appear more solid by using a couple of jumping blocks or similar. Poles do worry some horses even if they have not had a bad experience with them.

Loose jumping is the best way to introduce a horse to jumping as he can work things out without a rider getting in the way!

Don't expect too much, too soon: he needs time to work out what to do with his legs. Take a few steps back, and set out some trotting poles with a small jump at the end. The trotting poles will restore confidence, and gradually the end jump can be raised, made wider, or incorporate a filler. The horse that doesn't jump with confidence is a horse that is ultimately going to put in a stop at some point.

If the problem persists, ask someone to come and take a look at what is going on, as you may be unintentionally doing something that is exacerbating the problem; this is very easily done, so don't be afraid to ask for advice.

Problem: My horse rushes
Many people believe that a horse rushes into his fences because he is excited and enthusiastic, but this may not be the case, and it may be that he is nervous because he doesn't really know how to jump properly, and is actually afraid of falling. A racehorse must gallop fast into his fences and so he jumps flat and often trails a leg, or he may make a mistake on take-off and dive over the fence.

Retraining the horse off the flat will involve teaching him to jump right from the beginning. Retraining the ex-hurdler will also involve starting his jump training virtually from the beginning, because all he knows is to get from one side of the fence to the other very quickly; he seems to gain speed in the air, and often the next fence is upon you before you feel you've landed over the first.

These horses must be taught to wait and listen so that they can learn to jump in a more controlled manner. Schooling (flatwork) is obviously of great importance to teach them to listen and respond – but often when the ex-racehorse sees a jump, he forgets all about control and tries to go flat out.

There are several ways that might help you resolve the problem. For instance, a double of fences generally backs a horse off – though while your horse is still learning about jumping make this a two-stride double, as a single-stride double may be too much for him to cope with.

Build a couple of jumps on a very large circle, and ride on the circle until you can keep him more controlled.

Don't approach fences from too far away, as the horse can then very readily pick up speed;

Fig. 12.41   The National Hunt horse seems to gain a lot of speed in the air and it is very easy for the rider to be caught unawares – as Rowena demonstrates.

build your fences quite close to a corner so you have only three or four strides before each one.

Keep the horse on an even, bouncy canter rather than letting him run, and to begin with, jump from trot.

Practise pulling up as soon as you have reached the landing side, rather than racing off around the arena.

Having jumped a couple of fences, go back to doing some flatwork for a few minutes to refocus his mind.

Some horses throw their heads up when asked to slow down: counter this by lifting your hands up into the air a little, rather than pulling back against the horse.

An exercise that can help to steady a horse, especially between fences, is to place a ground pole between the two elements of a double. This will often effectively slow the horse (and actually help him to make a round shape) as he looks at the pole on the ground. If you are

working over a two-stride double try putting a ground pole approximately 10ft (3m) from the first jump, and another one the same distance in front of the second jump.

Some horses will still try and race on, however, and the pole on the ground only causes them to make an awkward leap. So if the pole is not having the desired effect after a couple of tries, remove it.

Problem: My horse charges off when he lands

Rushing off after landing from a fence can go hand in hand with rushing into it, in which case the problem should be addressed in the same way. Remember, the racehorse always jumped at speed, so it was always natural for him to land and accelerate away from the fence, so this is a mindset that has to be broken.

There are several reasons why a horse might rush off on landing: this habit often starts because he received a kick in the ribs from a rider wearing spurs, when their insecure lower leg has swung back; or the rider might have landed heavily on his back following a bad/awkward jump.

He might have a pain-related issue. As in every situation when something seems to be not happening as it should: check all physical explanations.

You can try to correct this problem first of all by keeping the horse straight when he lands as you have a better chance of controlling him. Use a tramline of poles on the landing side to help with straightness.

Initially just trot into the fences so he can't gain too much speed in the air; and jump towards the perimeter fence rather than towards the open arena.

Fig. 12.42   *As Bo takes the next stride he will move to his right and jump the next element closer to the right wing because Rowena's weight has gone to the right.*

Problem: My horse jumps to the side

This problem can be caused because the horse is in pain, or the rider is one-sided, or is not keeping the horse straight. It is really important that the rider is square in the saddle, with the weight even in both stirrups, and with an even contact in both hands. Jumping to the side might also be habit, in that a racehorse will often move rapidly to one side of a fence to give himself more room if the stride is wrong, rather than shorten up.

You can correct this problem by placing a tramline of poles on the ground to keep the horse straight on the approach, or by using 'V' poles in the centre of the fence so that the horse has to jump in the middle.

You should also check your riding position: if the horse veers off to the side on landing, the rider invariably has too much weight to one side. However, by placing a tramline on the landing side of the fence, the horse will get used to keeping straight.

Problem: My horse jumps flat

Jumping flat is linked to the problem of approaching a fence too fast, because when jumping at speed a horse can't bascule, and usually also trails a leg. Jumping flat is typical of the racehorse, but if it continues it is an indication that the training is not correct, or that something could be physically wrong.

To resolve this problem, do plenty of flatwork to round up the outline generally. Flatwork will also improve the horse's balance, so he will become more controllable.

Work over doubles, trebles and down grids will improve the shape a horse makes.

Be aware that a horse will tend to jump flatter over a very small fence, so although you have to start off small, the jumps should not be too low and simple: he has to have something to jump.

Problem: My horse goes sideways into his fences

This behaviour is generally interpreted as the horse being keen and excitable, but in fact it is more often because the rider takes too firm a hold on the reins, or a one-sided contact, or uses one leg more firmly than the other.

Try to correct the horse's approach by riding more from the leg whilst just holding the horse together with the reins, rather than actually pulling on them.

It can also be a consequence of using a bit that is too harsh, and the horse is actually fighting it; so take a look at your bitting arrangements. Whilst you may consider you need a harsher bit, this is not always the answer, and instead it might be advisable to look at bits that use a different action.

Problem: My horse has a very unathletic jump

This problem is linked to jumping flat. It is of paramount importance that any causes of pain are ruled out, whether from the tack used, an injury (or any other veterinary reason) or a shoeing problem.

The rider must also look to themselves to be sure they are not blocking the horse's movement in some way, such as holding the reins too short and too tightly.

It may be simply that the horse is overweight (although this is not very likely in the case of a thoroughbred) – or on the contrary, underfed and he hasn't enough energy to jump!

Athleticism can be improved by making sure first of all that the horse is fit enough, and adjusting his diet if necessary. Similarly, if a horse doesn't have good musculature then he won't find jumping easy, so make sure his groundwork is well established.

A horse's jump technique can be improved in several ways. Try slowing him right down on the approach, so that he can see what he is doing and organize his legs; use place poles or trotting poles in front of a fence to help slow him down and make him look. Walk over the poles and squeeze him into trot at the last moment.

Gridwork is always useful in improving athleticism. If necessary seek professional assistance, as it is important to know what type of grid to build, the distances to use, and the type of jump.

Do some loose jumping so the horse can sort himself out without the weight of a rider.

Problem: My horse lacks confidence

The horse should grow in confidence as time goes by, but an apparent lack of confidence may be due to shortcomings in the rider, or because the horse is experiencing discomfort. These are all issues that have to be ruled out.

Use hacking time to pop over any small logs that you come across; like this, jumping becomes less of an issue, and the horse is more relaxed about it altogether.

If you can ride out with a friend, then their horse can give you a lead if necessary.

However, if you are in the early stages of retraining your ex-racehorse, take care that this doesn't lead to overexcitement and an attempt to relive the Champion Hurdle!

IN SUMMARY

Jumping can throw up a whole new set of challenges, as it tests the confidence of horse and rider as a partnership. Whilst a schoolmaster horse can help a rider learn, the untrained horse can't help his rider: he needs the rider to help him. Of course many horses out of training do prove to have a very bold, athletic jump, and training work consists mainly of teaching them to jump more slowly and being sensible on the landing side.

Others just take a bit of time to get started, so if initially you think you are not making any headway, don't give up. Sometimes it is a case of doing a little bit of jump training and then leaving it completely for a while – several weeks – to give the horse time to digest everything. Or you can pop over an unexpected log whilst out hacking: the element of surprise can work wonders!

The following pictures are proof that many ex-racehorses have a very good jump in them; there is plenty of talent out there.

LEFT: *Fig. 12.43 Leosaid (Georgie) had the potential to be an event horse, but he didn't settle enough in dressage. This didn't stop us from having tremendous fun cross-country schooling.*

BELOW: *Fig. 12.44 With hindsight, the owners of Mr Bojangles probably would have sent him eventing, but at the time of his retirement from racing, dressage beckoned.*

ABOVE: **Fig. 12.45 Clare Stringer has successfully shown Kitty Way, but is now concentrating on eventing. Last year saw Kitty Way fly through BE80 and BE90; BE100 now beckons. (Photo courtesy of Michael Rogers, MDR Photo)**

BELOW: **Fig. 12.46 Lucius Locket has proved to be a bold horse, always willing to tackle a fence even if it hasn't always been in the best of styles. On the first occasion we took him cross-country schooling he would jump from an almost stand-still rather than say 'no'. (Photograph courtesy of Tik Saunders)**

13 In Conclusion

It is a great accomplishment to retrain a racehorse, whether or not the horse then becomes a star in his new career, and of course it is truly wonderful that increasing numbers of ex-racehorses are doing so well in such a variety of equine sports. Nevertheless quite a number of horses, although making an easy transition to a new life, don't have enough talent or the temperament to attain red rosettes in competition. Fortunately there are plenty of people willing to provide homes for them as they still have a tremendous amount to offer in terms of fun and fulfilment for many riders.

Of the countless horses that have passed through our hands, very few owners have elected to call it a day – and certainly no more in number than owners of non-racing types; this speaks volumes for the ex-racehorse. Unfortunately when difficulties are encountered it is mostly a case of handler/rider error, or problems with the environment in which the horse is kept.

Fig. 13.1   Polo has always been a sport at which the ex-racehorse has excelled; thus many polo teams have former racehorses in their strings. (Photograph courtesy of Hurlingham Polo Assocation)

Fig. 13.2 Leosaid (Georgie) had a very challenging temperament and at times we did question whether we were being sensible in carrying on with him. However, he became the most wonderful horse to have around.

The thoroughbred is a very intelligent breed but one that has been developed for racing. Nevertheless, once the memories of racing have receded, or at least put on the back boiler for most of the time, there is nothing to stop the horse out of training becoming a riding horse. If you are looking for a serious competition horse then of course you have to look at an individual in a more critical way, just as you would any horse you went to view with the thought of purchase. But for some reason there still remains an element of doubt, simply because it's an ex-racehorse. What do people mean when they say this – that the horse is wholly incapable of doing anything but gallop?

Several thousand horses leave the training environment each season, so retraining them isn't a new concept. However, in recent years awareness has grown, and their appeal has widened to a larger proportion of the equestrian fraternity. Nevertheless the behaviour of the ex-racehorse is constantly under scrutiny – but why? The club isn't exclusive to these horses: any breed can join!

No one is saying that the re-training process is all straightforward – but nor is the training path of any horse. Forums and magazines are full of discussion about how to 'work through this', 'improve that', 'resolve an issue'. That you have a horse that has raced doesn't make any difference to the training required, just that a little more time and patience is required because the horse must put his past behind him and learn a whole new set of rules and regulations. Inevitably this takes time – a considerable length of time in some cases – but it is time well invested, well spent, and with tremendous satisfaction to be gained. If things do go slightly amiss every now and again, then see it as a way of learning more and improving your skills, not as a problem with your horse: rise to the challenge!

Whilst there are plenty of well-meaning people who do genuinely want to help you, our one criticism of the equestrian world is that equally there are plenty of people who will sit on the fence and tell you what you should, or should not, be doing – yet none of them will actually come into the school and physically show you what to do, or get on the horse and feel for themselves what the horse is trying to say.

Understandably, this is when owners become very confused, because they just don't know who to listen to, especially when those doing the telling appear to have years more experience of riding and horse ownership. 'I've been riding since I was four years old' is a typical statement, as is 'in all my years of riding', but just because they have been on the back of a horse doesn't necessarily make them a good rider! In a livery yard environment it seems that either you are bombarded with 'knowledge', or no one offers any suggestions at all, leaving you and your horse to career at full speed merrily round the school!

It is always best to get independent advice from someone who not only has true knowledge and experience of horses, their training and behaviour in general, but who also has practical experience of working with, and retraining, the racehorse. They will have a much broader knowledge, and will have experienced at first hand anything that you will have done; nothing you say about your horse will cause raised eyebrows, a dreaded silence or lots of head-shaking. Such a person won't pre-judge your horse on what they have seen him do or not do, or form preconceptions as to what he should or should not be doing.

Fig. 13.3 *Brave Inca is reunited with jockey A.P. McCoy at Sandown in 2010, following the RoR Parade. (Photograph courtesy of Sandra Dillon and Kirsteen Reid)*

Fig. 13.4 Horseball is rapidly gaining popularity and many ex-racehorses are proving their capability in this sport. In fact there are already teams compromising wholly of horses out of training. (Photograph courtesy of the Horseball Association)

WHAT THE FUTURE COULD HOLD

We have worked with many, many horses out of training over the years, and each one has something to offer in its own right, whether simply as a pleasure hack, an affiliated competition horse, or something in between. Just because a horse has not been successful on the track doesn't mean that he is not capable of doing something else; there are many that go on to enjoy, and indeed do well in, another activity. On paper he may be bred to win the Derby or the Gold Cup, but breeding doesn't take account of whether the horse actually enjoys racing and the environment that goes with it. Put into different surroundings and asked different questions, many horses are finding their forte lies somewhere else.

Given that the majority of riders don't compete beyond, for example, Medium dressage, Grade C show jumping or Novice eventing, the ex-racehorse can aptly fit any of these categories – although this doesn't mean that he isn't capable of going further, and indeed he may have untapped talent beyond the capability of his rider! In short, the retrained racehorse is athletic, has stamina and enthusiasm, and is extraordinarily able.

Whatever your level of riding ability, there are competitions and clubs to suit, or if you are not of a competitive nature, then there is a variety of fun and sponsored rides. The main thing to be aware of is that whatever you elect to do, there is plenty of help available so that you can enjoy your horse and school him according to your individual requirements.

Brave Inca (Fig. 13.3) won the inaugural Racehorse to Riding Class at Dublin Horse Show in 2009. Trained by Colm Murphy, Brave Inca had numerous successes, but he is most renowned for winning the Champion Hurdle.

The RoR showing classes are now very well established, with qualifiers held around the country; likewise there is the RoR Challenge which incorporates jumping and so is basically the equivalent to working hunter classes. The showing classes have become extremely competitive, requiring a well moving, well mannered, blemish-free horse. For horses that have a lump and bump here and there, the Ex-Racers Club and TARRA have classes which allow for this.

The RoR also runs performance awards for eventing, dressage, show jumping and endurance, whereby horses compete on an even footing with their non-raced counterparts, and win points that they accumulate over the season: the horse that attains the most points in a given discipline receives the award. Ex-racehorses competing in horseball, polo, le trec and Trailblazers are also recognized by the RoR, with prizes given at various competitions and championships and at selected team chases, as well as through the Ex-Racers Club.

Whether you partake in RoR classes dedicated to the ex-racehorse, or take on the rest of the equestrian community, you must register your horse with the RoR and he must have raced in the UK, not just have been in training (correct at the time of publication). TARRA and the Ex-Racers Club have less strict criteria, and allow for unraced horses, and also accept blemishes; however the latter requests that a horse is registered with the club. Both organizations run their own classes, culminating in championship shows.

So if you are of a competitive inclination there is plenty out there for you to do. If you are not, then the RoR runs clinics and training days regardless of whether you are aiming to compete with your horse or not. The RoR also has a helpline which you can email or telephone; you can be put in touch with someone who can provide practical help if required, or a training establishment should your horse need a more intensive period of retraining. Help is out there.

PORTRAIT GALLERY

Many horses off the track are proving to be wonderful all-round horses for owners wanting to take part in various sports at whatever level, affiliated or unaffiliated. It is clearly evident from all the people we encounter just what great fun they are having with their horses, which is exactly what we want to hear.

Here are a few more photographs that hopefully will inspire you to take up ex-racehorse ownership.

Light the Fuse (Bombie), also owned both in and out of training by Dee and Tony Lousada, had the potential to go far in dressage; however, he is an example of the ex-racehorse who doesn't relax enough to give of his best under competition conditions – if only the judges could come and judge training clinics instead!

Bombie has also been an inspiration to us, proving that age is no barrier providing the mind is willing: the body needs to be able, but with the right training a horse can overcome so much. This little horse incurred a raft of injuries in his racing days, but he has not lost any of his *joie de vivre*; he was in the yard of several trainers, including Kim Bailey, Henrietta Knight, Brendan Powell and Simon Dow, and had the reputation of being a live-wire – and he still is every inch of that today at nineteen years of age. Perhaps he has understood what his name means (especially given that his dam was called Celtic Bombshell and his sire Electric!).

It is also interesting to compare early photographs of Indie, Hero and Bobbie with later ones in this book. Such comparisons are to give you inspiration: take a look at your own horse and think 'Yes, we can do that!'

ABOVE: *Fig. 13.5 Rowena and Bombie training at Paul Hayler's.*

ABOVE & RIGHT: *Figs 13.6 and 13.7 Look how Bombie developed physically over the course of six months of dressage training.*

Fig. 13.8 Quite what our own challenge Leosaid could have done competitively we shall never know as, although we owned him for twenty-one years, he only competed at hunter trials.

Fig. 13.9 We have high hopes of Call Oscar who, at the time of writing this book, is being retrained.

Fig. 13.10 Hero Worship, from Darley Rehoming, changed so much in the nine weeks he was with us. Comparing the photographs when he was first being lunged to this one taken a few days before he left us shows how, in a short space of time, a horse can physically change and develop with the correct training – provided, of course, that he is able and willing to learn.

Fig. 13.11 No-one other than those connected with the sport gets to hear about Monkey Boy, owned by Sue Henry (previously in training with Jack Berry), now excelling in Endurance and winner of the 2009 RoR/SEIB Elite Performance Award, something he also did in 2007. The pair came second in the 2010 Challenge. (Photograph courtesy of Endurance GB, Jan Clarke and Eric Jones)

Fig. 13.12 Island Sound ran a total of forty-four times on the flat, over hurdles and fences achieving seven wins, five seconds and six thirds. After retirement 'Issie' went in the show ring but then turned to dressage before pursuing show jumping. In 2007 he qualified for the British Notice Regional Finals, the Equissage Discovery Regional Finals, the Scope Festival and the Amateur Showjumping Regional Finals. In 2009 he qualified for the Equissage and Amateur Showjumping Regional Finals as well as the Scope Festival. (Photograph courtesy of Graham Loader, Blue Print Studios)

Fig. 13.13 Lucius Locket ran thirteen times on the flat when in training with Jack Berry gaining three seconds and a third. He is a truly versatile thoroughbred, taking part in numerous disciplines. (Photograph courtesy of Tik Saunders)

Fig. 13.14 Averlline ran in seventeen races as a two- and three-year-old, achieving a win, two seconds and three thirds on the flat. Taking part in show jumping, dressage, combined training, hunter trialling, hunting and team chasing, she provides tremendous pleasure for her owner. (Photograph courtesy of Hannah Drury)

Fig. 13.15 Mulligatawny, a Nick Gifford-trained horse, is a family fun horse as happy out hunting as he is in the show ring or hacking out with the children's ponies. (Photograph courtesy of Claire Bowers)

ABOVE: **Fig. 13.16   Rockcracker is owned and ridden by Sam Perks. The combination were second in the RoR/SEIB Elite Performance Dressage Award in 2009. This Ballad Rock gelding won and was placed several times on the flat.**

LEFT: **Fig. 13.17   Tina's Magic is by the late Primitive Rising, a prolific sire who has not only sired many racehorses, but was also a leading sire in the eventing world for many years. Tina and owner/rider Victoria Trafford are now competing at Novice level eventing, and aiming for their first three-day-event this year. Tina and Victoria also compete in pure show jumping and dressage competitions. (Photograph courtesy of Mrs Trafford)**

ABOVE: Fig. 13.18   Bold Hunter ran ninety-two times (on the flat, hurdling and over fences, as well as point-to-point), not retiring until he was thirteen years of age, but this hasn't stopped him making a successful transition into the dressage arena. Bold Hunter with his owner Anne Bostock was the winner of the RoR/SEIB Elite Performance Dressage Award in 2009 and came second in the same event this year. (Photograph courtesy of John Tyrrel Photography)

RIGHT: Fig. 13.19   Mr Bojangles (Bo) proved to have such good movement that he easily attained Advanced Medium with Paul Hayler and finished in third place in the 2009 RoR/SEIB Elite Dressage Award.

ABOVE: Fig. 13.20 Unfortunately Tanner's Den did not show any form on the racecourse, either on the flat or over hurdles and fences; however, he has now found his forte and is enjoying life in the world of eventing. (Photograph courtesy of W. Parrott Photographic Service)

LEFT: Fig. 13.21 Light the Fuse (Bombie) raced for eight years, leaving the training environment having incurred many injuries. These he has all overcome. He finished eighth in the inaugural RoR/SEIB Elite Performance Award in 2009, despite very few outings that year.

Our final 'feature horse' is Janet Nevard's Gift Star (Toby). Purchased from Ascot sales, Toby is one of the most successful, if not *the* most successful, ex-racehorses on the dressage circuit. Having come over from America as a yearling, Toby found his way into the Newmarket yard of Chris Murray. Although in training for two years, he only ran once, in a bumper.

Toby's retraining progressed in leaps and bounds and he was competing in Novice dressage classes when he was five years old, Elementary classes towards the end of his sixth year, and a few Medium classes towards the end of his seventh year. He won the affiliated dressage section in the 'Racehorse to Riding Horse' competition run by SEIB in 2003 by a huge margin, and has now amassed 350 dressage points.

Janet describes Toby as a cheeky horse, 100 per cent honest, and a gentleman in the stable. Although not good in traffic he will pass heaps of rubbish or a dumped fridge as if it wasn't there! Toby has always been very reactive to noise and would definitely not suit a novice rider; although he seems laid back, at times he

Fig. 13.22 With scores of up to 68 per cent in Prix St Georges classes and 63 per cent in Intermediare, Toby has proved that all good things come to he who waits. (Photo courtesy of John Tyrell Photography)

would become very stressed if the person meant to be in charge wasn't in charge!

Janet goes on to say that she feels very privileged to have found such a lovely horse, and is absolutely delighted to have achieved so much with him, saying that what Toby lacks in talent he makes up with his honesty, trying so hard to do what is asked of him. She never dreamed Toby would progress beyond Elementary level, let alone get to Intermediare 1.

In summing up her approach to retraining ex-racehorses – Toby not being her first – Janet says that you need to appreciate just how different the way of going is for the horse whilst he is racing, to the way of going he is now asked for. You must therefore be tactful, and try to give your horse confidence in what you are trying to achieve, never asking for more than he is capable of giving at that moment. She tries to think outside the box to establish why a particular problem might have cropped up, and affirms that the old saying 'more haste, less speed' is very true. Finally she says to all of you out there: 'Keep trying, you will get there in the end, although some will take longer than others.'

JOURNEY'S END

Hopefully within these pages you will have found helpful and constructive advice to assist you with the retraining of your ex-racehorse. The horse out of training is still misunderstood, and sometimes unfairly labelled as being a source of hassle for owners, but this is a very biased opinion usually offered by those who have not given such a horse the chance to prove otherwise.

From our point of view we encourage anyone to join the growing numbers of ex-racehorse owners, but do so in the knowledge that there will be ups and downs. This is true, of course, for the training path of any horse – but view it as a journey, at the end of which you will have achieved so much, learnt so much, and given a beautiful horse a second chance in life.

Further Information

SOURCING A HORSE

The four RoR-funded centres have rehoming projects and spend a considerable amount of time in trying to achieve the best match of horse and new owner.

The Thoroughbred Rehabilitation Centre
www.thoroughbredrehabilitationcentre.co.uk

Greatwood Caring for Retired Racehorses
www.racehorsesgreatwood.org

Moorcroft Racehorse Welfare Centre
www.racehorsesgreatwood.org

HEROS
www.heroscharity.org

There is also a dedicated website purely for the buying, selling, loaning and rehoming of ex-racehorses.
www.sourceanexracehorse.co.uk

Although not connected with the RoR another re-homing project is established at Darley Rehoming
www.darleyrehoming.co.uk

There are other non-RoR charitable re-homing centres around the country, but we are not familiar with these so independent enquiries should be made.

Horses out of training can be purchased from the following:

Doncaster Bloodstock Sales (DBS)
www.dbsauctions.com

Ascot Bloodstock Sales
www.brightwells.com

SEEKING HELP

The RoR has a very informative website (www.ror.org.uk) and helpline (asktheexperts@ror.org.uk, telephone 01780 740773).
Staff at any of the four RoR centres will also be pleased to provide help and advice.

The Ex-Racers Club is an extremely friendly and enthusiastic organisation with Regional Representatives who will always do their best to help and support ex-racehorse owners.
www.horse-directory.co.uk/exracers.htm

EQUESTRIAN SPORTS GOVERNING BODIES

There is a wide range of equestrian disciplines so there is something for everyone. Contact the relevant Governing Body for further information.

British Dressage
www.britishdressage.co.uk

British Showjumping
www.britishshowumping.co.uk

British Eventing
www.britisheventing.com

Showing – RoR Classes/Performance Awards
www.ror.org.uk
www.seib.co.uk

Hurlingham Polo Association
www.hpa-polo.co.uk

Endurance GB
www.endurancegb.co.uk

Polocrosse Association
www.polocrosse.org.uk

British HorseBall Association
www.british-horseball-association.btik.com/

TREC
www.bhs.org.uk

Trailblazers
www.trailblazerschampionships.com

Showing – Non RoR
www.britishshowhorse.org

EQUIPMENT AND FEED PRODUCTS

That a direct reference has not been made to any other products does not constitute an opinion, expressed or otherwise, that such other products are not as suitable as those we have referred to.

Equipment

Hilary Vernon – Bitting
www.informedbitting.com

Barnsby Saddlery
www.barnsby.com

Dr. Cook's Bitless Bridle
www.bitlessbridle.co.uk

Equi-Ami
www.equiami.com

Equissage
www.equissage.co.uk

Myler Bits
www.belstane.com

Neue Schule
www.neueschulebits.com

Polypads
www.polypads.co.uk

Prolite
www.prolitepads.com

Feeds/Supplements

Allen and Page
www.allenandpage.com

Baileys Horse Feeds
www.baileyshorsefeeds.co.uk

Cool, Calm and Collected
www.equifeast.com

Dengie Horse Feeds
www.dengie.com

Dodson and Horrell
www.dodsonandhorrell.com

Nupafeed
www.nupafeed.co.uk

Relax Me
www.horsefirst.net

Saracen Horse Feeds
www.saracen-horse-feeds.co.uk

Simple System
www.simplesystem.co.uk

Spillers Horse Feeds
www.spillers-feeds.com

Multi-worm Natural Horse Wormer
Contact Phil Gardner telephone 07771 932268

Verm-x
www.verm-x.com

MISCELLANEOUS

Emma Overend
www.equinetouchcourses.co.uk

TTOUCH
www.ttouchteam.com

**For further information about the authors
and their work, please visit
www.equinetraining.co.uk.**

Acknowledgements

A considerable number of people have played their part in the production of this book and we are most grateful for their kind co-operation.

SPECIAL THANKS

Hilary Vernon, bitting Specialist
(www.informedbitting.co.uk)

Craig Millard, formerly of the
National Saddle Centre
(www.nationalsaddlecentre.co.uk)
now Craig Millard Saddlery

Katie Williams and Tracey Hammond,
Dengie Horse Feeds
(www.dengie.com)

Tom Phillips, equine dental technician
(Tel: 01529 241522/07710 742719)

Heather Hyde, Neue Schule Bits
(www.neueschulebits.com)

Georgina Sim, McTimoney animal chiropractor
(Tel: 07718 158515)

RACEHORSE TRAINERS

These trainers have kindly given either their time or supplied photographs:

Clive Cox
(www.clivecox.com)

David Arbuthnot
(www.uplandsstables.com)

Bryan and Vicky Smart
(www.bryansmart-racing.com)

Marcus Tregoning
(www.marcustregoningracing.co.uk)

Alan King
(www.alankingracing.co.uk)

PHOTOGRAPHS

Matthew Roberts, assorted photographs
of the authors
(www.matthewrobertsphotographer.co.uk)

Cecil Swan, Natural Balance Shoeing
photographs
(www.gasforges.co.uk)

Fellowes Farm Equine Clinic,
skeletal photographs
(www.fellowesfarm.com)

John Tyrrell Photography, photographs of
Louis Feraud, Bold Hunter, Gold Star and
Mr Bojangles competing
(www.bigtimemedia.co.uk)

John Pike Racing Images, assorted racing
photographs
(www.racing-images.co.uk)

Jon Fullegar, Petra Gough, racing photographs
from Sandown Park
(www.sandown.co.uk)

Tim Kent and Trevor Jones, photographs
from Doncaster Bloodstock Sales
(www.dbsauctions.com)

James Zwetsloot, photographs of Louis Feraud
working at home
(www.zwets.co.uk)

Michael David Rogers, MDR Photo,
photographs of Kitty Way
(www.mdr-photo.co.uk

Graham Loader, Blue Print Studios,
photograph of Island Sound
(www.thefotografer.co.uk)

Hurlington Polo Association, polo photographs
(www.hpa-polo.co.uk)

Horseball Association, horseball photographs
(www.british-horseball-association.btik.com)

Endurance GB, Sue Henry and Monkey Boy
(www.endurancegb.co.uk)

W. Parrott Photographic Services,
photograph of Tanner's Den

Dr Cook, Bitless Bridle™
(www.bitlessbridle.com)

OWNERS

The owners of the horses featured in
this book:

Light the Fuse, Dee and Tony Lousada

Mr. Bojangles, Dee and Tony Lousada

Vin Verdi (Vinnie), Dee and Tony Lousada

Hero Worship (Hero), Abi Drury

Bob's Return (Bobbie), Lyn Flanagan

Indie's Rock 'N' Roll (Indie), Su Morgan

Dr Sean (Nic), Abi Winterburn

Arctic Top (Dora), Dorothy and Tasha Lyth

Beetle, Becky Doyle

Louis, Laura Hirst

Pretty Officer (Wynnie), Nicky and David
Creasey

Lucius Lockett, Tik Saunders

Gift Star, Janet Nevard

Tricky, Victoria Spicer

Island Sound, Marion Meredith

Monkey Boy, Sue Henry

Tanner's Den, Penny Gilbert

Brave Inca, Kirsteen Reid

Mulligatawny, Claire Bowers

Averlline, Hannah Drury

Tina's Magic, Victoria Trafford

Kitty Way, Clare Stringer

Index